THE OFFICIAL
JOHN WAYNE
REFERENCE BOOK

The Wayne stance appears in this publicity pose from
THE MAN WHO SHOT LIBERTY VALANCE.
Wayne was 6'4" tall, 225-240 pounds, blue eyes,
brown hair.
When Wayne was born on May 26, 1907, he weighed
13 lbs.

THE OFFICIAL
JOHN WAYNE
REFERENCE BOOK

by Charles John Kieskalt

A CITADEL PRESS BOOK
PUBLISHED BY CAROL PUBLISHING GROUP

For Dad and Tom and the company they keep

Carol Publishing Group Edition - 1995

A Citadel Press Book
Published by Carol Publishing Group
Citadel Press is a registered trademark of Carol Communications, Inc.

Editorial Offices: 600 Madison Avenue, New York, NY 10022
Sales & Distribution Offices: 120 Enterprise Avenue, Secaucus, NJ 07094
In Canada: Canadian Manda Group, One Atlantic Avenue, Suite 105
Toronto, Ontario, M6K3E7
Queries regarding rights and permissions should be addressed to:
Carol Publishing Group, 600 Madison Avenue, New York, NY 10022

Manufactured in the United States of America
ISBN 0-8065-1443-4

12 11 10 9 8 7 6 5 4 3 2

Carol Publishing Group books are available at special discounts
for bulk purchases, sales promotions, fund raising, or
educational purposes. Special editions can also be created to
specifications. For details contact: Special Sales Department,
Carol Publishing Group, 120 Enterprise Ave., Secaucus, NJ 07094

Library of Congress Cataloging-in-Publication Data

Kieskalt, Charles John
        The official John Wayne reference book.
        Bibliography: p.
        1. Wayne, John, 1907-1979—Miscellanea. I. Title.
PN2287.W454K54   1985
791,43'028'0924   85-18985

CONTENTS

ACKNOWLEDGMENTS

I wish to express my gratitude to the following individuals and organizations that provided endless effort and sources. I will always be eternally grateful to the chosen few.

Academy of Motion Picture Arts and Sciences
Mike Appel
Tom Appel
Belleville Public Library
Alfred Brady—Planner with John Wayne Airport
    Administration
Robert Bridges
Harry Carey, Jr.
Don Clark
Laurie Cummings—Colt Firearms
Rich Dauer
Kelly Ekizian—John Wayne Cancer Clinic
Marjorie Hagenah
Hollywood Chamber of Commerce
Hollywood Reporter
Ben Johnson
Kieskalt Archives
John Kieskalt
Marvin's Camera
Jim Murray Jr. and Sr.—The Movie Poster Place,
    Pennsylvania
Robert Murphy

Tim Neeley
Betty Jane Reed—NBC
Roman Distilled Products Company, Martin B.
    Schrero, Director of Marketing
James Ruhl
St. Louis Downtown Public Library
David Strauss—Mr. Trivia
Neil Summers
United States Trivia Association, Ltd., and
    Trivia Unlimited Magazine
Ashley Ward
Toni La Cava and the Wayne Family

Photographs courtesy of:
ABC
CBS
MGM
National General Pictures
NBC
Paramount Pictures
Republic Pictures
RKO Radio Pictures
20th Century-Fox
United Artists
Universal Pictures
Warner Brothers Pictures

and special thanks to my wife, Ann, and to my family, Jennifer, Kim, and John Ethan.

FOREWORD

On Monday, June 11, 1979, John Wayne became a legend. My first memory of him was in the film *The Alamo* on June 11, 1961. Eighteen years later to the day, an era ended in motion picture history. Over the years, I have obtained books and magazines and saved clippings for numerous scrap books. I found many discrepancies due to inept research. This has always irritated me. To clarify the record, I decided to write this book. The facts have been checked and I have watched the Wayne films. I sincerely hope that as you turn the pages of this book, you will think of the man and the movies he made. His wish was to be remembered by a Spanish proverb: *"Feo fuerte y formal,"* meaning he was ugly, strong and had dignity.

Let it be known that this book is dedicated not only to the man, but his legacy.

Charles Kieskalt

Shortly after Laurence Harvey died in 1973, I sent Wayne a photo of Wayne and Harvey from *The Alamo* and a shot of Wayne and Director John Ford on the set of *The Cowboys.* Ford did not direct that film. I knew that Wayne was bothered about their passing. He sent me this photograph.

PART ONE

THE EARLY YEARS

Before he would be known to the world as John Wayne, Duke Morrison would graduate from Glendale High School in California, receiving an athletic scholarship to U.S.C. Football not only gave Morrison pleasure on the field but also brought him in contact with a teammate who would become a longtime friend, Ward Bond. Most of the time, Morrison was just a relief player. To earn extra money for his education, Morrison took a job at Fox Studios as an assistant prop man, moving scenery and sweeping the sets on various films in production. In 1929 he would leave U.S.C.

Morrison appeared in his first motion picture in 1926, MGM's *Brown of Harvard*. In it William Haines played Tom Brown of Harvard who has reregistered to play football. His competition is fellow player Francis X. Bushman, Jr. Both put aside their differences to help defeat Yale during the crucial game (with footage used from the previous year's Yale–Harvard meeting). Morrison would double Bushman in the football scenes. The following year, in *The Drop Kick* (First National), Richard Barthelmess was the star. This film too had a football setting, and young Morrison was selected as one of ten college players from various universities to appear, picked from a nationwide film test and seated in the bleachers.

While working property at Fox, Morrison was a goose herder for fowl that appeared in *Mother Machree* (1928). The film's director, John Ford, took notice of the six-foot-four prop man. Finding Mor-

rison a worthy adversary when practicing football positions, Ford saw the young man's curiosity about all facets of the film's production, studying Ford and watching how he handled the actors, always knowing exactly where the camera should be placed. Ford commanded top respect and the studios knew he was a master at story-telling. *Mother Machree*, which dealt with an Irish mother taking her son to a new life in America, was a training ground for Morrison.

Hangman's House (Fox, 1928) would be the first time that Morrison would clearly be seen—more than once. Hobart Bosworth is a hanging judge who has visions of the men he sentenced to death. In silhouette, Morrison is seen five minutes into the film standing on the gallows awaiting execution. Although the scene runs just a few seconds the victim's stature makes him clearly recognizable. Twenty-one minutes later, Morrison is seen in a head shot as another victim in the tortured judge's mind as he greets death. Clearly visible thirty-eight minutes into the film, young Morrison is seen in four quick shots that total ten seconds. In an exciting John Ford-filmed horse race, crucial to the storyline, Morrison portrays a waving spectator, becoming increasingly excited. A picket fence slowly falls apart as he starts pounding on it as his frenzy grows. The more he pounds on the boards, the more the fence crumbles. As the race ends, Morrison crashes through the fence as other spectators follow and then he disappears from the scene.

Again on a Ford film as a prop man, Morrison doesn't appear in *Four Sons* (Fox, 1928). Reportedly during filming, Morrison inadvertently appeared on the set sweeping leaves while the camera was shooting. Noticing the camera, Morrison yelped in shock and ran off of the sound-stage with Ford and the crew laughing.

He moved props on *The Black Watch* (Fox, 1929) but is not in the film, which starred Victor McLaglen. *Salute* (Fox, 1929) was the first sound film in which Morrison would appear. He performs triple duty by turning up in some football scenes as a freshman recruit and later as an upper class midshipman hazing new students. With him in the scenes was actor-friend Ward Bond. "D. Morrison" is stenciled on "Wayne's" uniform top. Stepin Fetchit, a popular black actor who appears in the film, was also an early acting coach for Morrison, helping him with the dialogue.

In *Words and Music* (Fox, 1929), Duke Morrison would be credited sixth in the billing. In competition for a $1,500 prize, he portrays Pete Donahue, a composer vying for the love interest.

Men Without Women (Fox, 1930) concerns itself with the rescue of sailors trapped inside a submarine. Director Jon Ford would use Morrison not only as a radio operator on the deck of one of the ships, but also as a diver who assists in the rescue.

Morrison had small roles in *Rough Romance* (Fox, 1930) as a lumberjack and *Cheer Up and Smile* (Fox, 1930, as a collegian manhandling Arthur Lake.

Fate was about to knock on Morrison's door. John Ford heard that fellow director Raoul Walsh was searching for a lead in an epic he was to begin, *The Big Trail* (Fox, 1930), and recommended candidate Morrison to him. Walsh liked Morrison's rugged look and walk. While being interviewed, Morrison thought he would have a small part in the film. The scout role Walsh wanted to fill was patterned for a leader whom wagon train members would follow without question. Walsh was sold on the young actor but an obstacle loomed: Morrison's name. Box-office appeal dictated a star name, so between the two, veteran director and tyro actor, a new one was born. John would be the first name and Wayne the last, a name Walsh likened from Revolutionary War hero "Mad" Anthony Wayne.

So, John Wayne it was and *The Big Trail* went into production for six grueling months, an epic in the making. The role of Breck Coleman would be an early career milestone for Wayne, leading the wagon train from St. Louis along the Oregon Trail. Coleman is bent on revenge but his prowess is proved during an Indian attack, the hunt for buffalo, and the treacherous fording of the river. The film would cost $2 million to produce, an exorbi-

tant amount for 1930, and would be photographed in Grandeur 55mm, an innovative wide-screen process with a multiple soundtrack.

The Big Trail was released in November 1930, capturing the epic quality of motion pictures. However, because of the Depression, the audiences were small. Fox was exhibiting the film in New York City and Los Angeles in the expensive Grandeur process, and costs of installing the equipment resulted in higher admission to the film, sealing its box-office fate. Sixty-three years later, in spring 1993, American Movie Classics showed *The Big Trail* in letter-boxed format on cable TV. This meant showing most of the image on the screen with dark bars at the top and bottom of the screen. The epic proportions and a struggling young actor still hold one's attention.

Wayne went on personal appearances to promote the film, and audiences decided he had star potential. Wayne had the looks but needed a dramatic edge that would later be perfected. The camera liked what it saw in Wayne but down the road "Poverty Row" studios would beckon.

Girls Demand Excitement (Fox, 1931) had Wayne as Peter Brooks on a coed campus, and taking second billing to Virginia Cherrill. An architect role awaited Wayne as Gordon Wales in *Three Girls Lost* (Fox, 1931), set in Chicago. Reviewers of the time would mention Wayne's voice and manner.

Men Are Like That (1931)—the original title was *Arizona*—took Wayne to Columbia Studios. He portrayed Lt. Bob Denton, a West Point graduate traveling to an Arizona army post. Laura LaPlante was the star; Wayne was second billed.

Dusty was Wayne's character name in *Maker of Men* (Columbia, 1931) as a football player who is the heavy. In *The Deceiver* (Columbia, 1931), Wayne played a stand-in for the corpse of Ian Keith who is murdered in the film's plot. Three westerns then brought Wayne back into the saddle. *Range Feud* (Columbia, 1931) features Wayne second billed to Buck Jones, one of his cowboy heroes. Playing Clint Turner, Wayne is a cowpoke set up for a murder that he didn't commit. Quick thinking by Sheriff Buck Jones saves him from the hangman's noose. Next came *Texas Cyclone* (Columbia, 1932), a starring vehicle for Tim McCoy. Wayne is third billed as Steve Pickett and first appears eighteen minutes into the film as a ranchhand assisting McCoy in setting things right. McCoy loses his ranch in *Two-Fisted Law* (Columbia, 1932) and attempts to expose the scheme which will lead to its return. Wayne, sixth in the credits, portrays loyal employee Duke. His total footage in the film is 5:37 and he is visible in four scenes. Wayne doesn't appear at all in the last twenty-three of the film's fifty-seven minutes running time.

A change of pace awaited Wayne as he ventured into a new area. He would appear in three twelve-chapter serials, all produced by Nat Levine.

The Shadow of the Eagle

Mascot, 1932

Chapter 1—The Carnival Mystery (27 minutes)
Chapter 2—Pinholes (19 minutes)
Chapter 3—The Eagle Strikes (12 minutes)
Chapter 4—The Man of a Million Voices
(17 minutes)
Chapter 5—The Telephone Cipher (18 minutes)
Chapter 6—The Code of the Carnival
(18 minutes)
Chapter 7—Eagle or Vulture? (18 minutes)
Chapter 8—On the Spot (18 minutes)
Chapter 9—When Thieves Fall Out (17 minutes)
Chapter 10—The Man Who Knew (16 minutes)
Chapter 11—The Eagle's Wings (16 minutes)
Chapter 12—The Shadow Unmasked (15
minutes)

Wayne is featured as Craig McCoy, a stunt flier who does circus sky-writing. The Eagle is a mysterious figure attempting to blackmail directors of an airplane factory. A secret invention is up for grabs as McCoy attempts to help the circus and expose the Eagle's true identity. Thrills and suspense were crammed into this three and a half hour serial released on March 1, 1932. During the filming, Wayne would encounter actor-stuntman Yakima Canutt and develop a lifelong friendship. The two men would develop fight innovations in future westerns.

The Hurricane Express

Mascot, 1932

Chapter 1—The Wrecker (28 minutes)
Chapter 2—Flying Pirates (16 minutes)
Chapter 3—The Masked Menace (17 minutes)
Chapter 4—Buried Alive (19 minutes)
Chapter 5—Danger Lights (17 minutes)
Chapter 6—The Airport Mystery (20 minutes)
Chapter 7—Sealed Lips (18 minutes)
Chapter 8—Outside the Law (19 minutes)
Chapter 9—The Invisible Enemy (18 minutes)
Chapter 10—The Wrecker's Secret (16 minutes)
Chapter 11—Wings of Death (17 minutes)
Chapter 12—Unmasked (17 minutes)

In this Levine serial, Wayne portrayed pilot Larry Baker whose father is killed in a train derailment caused by a mysterious figure known as "The Wrecker." The railroad has had several accidents of this type and Baker vows to unmask "The Wrecker," who has hijacked The Hurricane Express with its gold shipment. Complicating

Baker's search is that "The Wrecker" is a master of disguise and assumes several identities including that of Baker himself. This serial delivers the goods and is the best of the three Wayne would film. His natural physical abilities and prowess are at the heart of the action sequences. The serial was released on August 1, 1932, and ran three hours and forty-two minutes total.

The Three Musketeers

Mascot, 1933

Chapter 1—The Fiery Circle (27 minutes)
Chapter 2—One for All and All for One
(19 minutes)
Chapter 3—The Master Spy (18 minutes)
Chapter 4—Pirates of the Desert (17 minutes)
Chapter 5—Rebel Rifles (16 minutes)
Chapter 6—Death's Marathon (16 minutes)
Chapter 7—Naked Steel (16 minutes)
Chapter 8—The Master Strikes (16 minutes)
Chapter 9—The Fatal Cave (16 minutes)
Chapter 10—Trapped (17 minutes)
Chapter 11—The Measure of a Man (15 minutes)
Chapter 12—The Glory of Comrades (15
minutes)

Wayne's final serial has him portraying yet another pilot, Lt. Tom Wayne, saving the lives of the Three Musketeers from the clutches of the evil El Shaitan (The Devil), and becoming the "D'Artagnan" of the group. Someone is furnishing El Shaitan with weapons to instigate a revolution. Wayne helps the Foreign Legionnaires by revealing the hidden identity of the leader. The serial, with Wayne listed fourth in the credits, lasts three and a half hours and was released April 7, 1933.

George Bancroft is the star of *Lady and Gent* (Paramount, 1932), playing boxer Slag Bailey and preparing for a match with Buzz Kinney (Wayne). Wayne appears fifth in the credits and is seen ten minutes into the film, in a scene in the locker room before the fight. He doesn't have dialogue and is seen for 2:38. The second scene features Wayne for five seconds in a restaurant, and later he is seen through a two-minute sequence, involved in a fight at the same restaurant. Wayne is next seen seventy-one minutes into the film for about 1:05 having dinner with Slag. Wayne's total screen time is less than six minutes.

Wayne is playboy Dick Wallace in *His Private Secretary* (Screencraft/Showman's Pictures, 1933 with Evalyn Knapp; his presence was improving and star quality was beginning to show.

Warner Brothers signed Wayne to star in their "B" westerns and would utilize him in smaller roles of the studio's "A" films.

The first, *Ride Him, Cowboy* (1932), features

Wayne and Virginia Cherrill as they appear in *Girls Demand Excitement.*

Wayne leads the way to Oregon in *The Big Trail*.

Wayne fights with the mysterious "Eagle" (Edmund Burns) in *The Shadow of the Eagle* as Dorothy Gulliver watches.

The Wrecker's henchman (Glenn Strange) has his hands full as Wayne attempts to stop him in the serial *The Hurricane Express.*

Wayne as John Drury saving "Duke The Wonder Horse," charged with murdering a rancher. The two would team to become an unbeatable combination. Wayne appears six minutes into the film and is on the trail of the territorial bandit known as "The Hawk." *Variety* indicated Wayne could be a second Gary Cooper. Story lines would need to be improved. Action sequences such as Wayne fighting villain Bud Osborne in an ore bucket car halfway across a cableway are highlighted in *Haunted Gold* (1932). An interesting credit sequence with animated bats and a secret presence known as "The Phantom" give promise to this installment western with Wayne as John Mason and Sheila Terry as his leading lady.

Wayne portrays John Steele in *The Big Stampede* (1932). With his horse, Duke, Wayne as a deputy sheriff helps open the range to settlers. A rousing stampede adds thrills and suspense in the last reel.

Wayne as John Trent and Duke venture into *The Telegraph Trail* (1933). The first transcontinental wire line is in danger of not being completed because of warring Indians, and the supply train with equipment to help finish the job is attacked. Audiences thrilled to an exceptional climactic action sequence assisted by Ted McCord's top-notch cinematography. The Wayne hero image is beginning to show itself.

Central Airport (1933), a Richard Barthelmess-Sally Eilers film, features Wayne fifty-six minutes into the proceedings as an officer on a downed plane in the Gulf of Mexico. Wayne's screen time is a short thirty-two seconds as he helps passengers onto the plane's wing and drowns while attempting to save a passenger. Director William Wellman kept the pace exciting. In Warner's *Somewhere in Sonora* (1933), Wayne plays John Bishop on the trail of a missing person, shanghaied into a bandit gang.

The Life of Jimmy Dolan (1933), starring Douglas Fairbanks Jr. and Loretta Young, features Wayne tenth in the credits. Seen as Smith, Wayne appears fifty-five minutes into the film as a nervous fighter awaiting a match with boxer King Cobra. Wayne bites the canvas offscreen and appears in four scenes lasting less than four minutes.

Barbara Stanwyck uses Wayne (as Jimmy McCoy) as a notch on her ladder to success from barmaid to big time in *Baby Face* (1933). Eighth in the credits and seen nineteen minutes into the film, Wayne has two scenes totaling less than two minutes of screen time.

Production values improved in *The Man From Monterey* (1933) with Wayne as Capt. John Holmes astride Duke for a sixth and final time. Wayne fares better in standard military uniform than in Mexican outfits as Spanish land grants are at stake.

William Wellman's *College Coach* (1933), a Dick Powell film, features Wayne eleven minutes into the proceedings. Upon uttering, "Heard you broke the rules, Phil. Studied during vacation," Wayne disappears after a total of seven seconds.

A new phase was about to commence in Wayne's career. Monogram, a Poverty Row studio, signed the up-and-coming actor for sixteen "B" westerns. Each would have a $10,000 budget with Wayne earning $2,500 per film, shooting over a three- to-four day schedule. Wayne would become the number one star of these vehicles, showcased as a formula western hero.

Riders of Destiny (1933) was the first outing in the Lone Star/Monogram westerns for producer Paul Malvern. Wayne played an undercover agent "Singin' Sandy" Saunders assigned to aid farmers who are battling a rancher over water rights. Wayne, of course, proved stalwart in the action department but his character was a singing cowboy. There are two schools of thought as to who provided the singing voice of "Singin' Sandy." Some believe the dubbing was done by Bill Bradbury, son of western director Robert Bradbury (and brother of western star Bob Steele). Others say it was Glenn Strange, a "B" westerns veteran who would become known as Sam the Bartender in the television series *Gunsmoke*.

Originally Malvern wanted Wayne to sing a ballad as he gunned down the villains. Wayne opposed the idea. An unknown would later be hired to become a singing cowboy. Wayne naturally succeeds and becomes the hero. The action and stunts pleased the western aficionados as well as the matinee audiences. Better writing would improve the characters as Wayne enhanced his western image.

Fight scenes were also inventively staged between Wayne and stuntman Canutt, and realistic punches were added as the two would rehearse these sequences. Aided with clever camera angles, the punches appeared to connect with the opponent. Wayne would develop what he referred to as "the 'why me' look" when struck. This expression would be used throughout Wayne's career as would his killer haymakers. Canutt would double Wayne and others in the "B" westerns, and the two would give movie audiences rousing entertainment through Canutt's second-unit direction on Wayne's *Rio Lobo* (1970).

Sagebrush Trail (1933) has Wayne portraying John Brant, a fugitive from prison who joins an outlaw gang. Framed for murder, he seeks the real killer.

When he first sees Wayne in *The Lucky Texan* (1934), George "Gabby" Hayes utters; "Say,

Wayne as "Singin' Sandy" Saunders and Cecilia Parker live to tell the tale in *Riders of Destiny*.

Wayne has a short chat with Lane Chandler in *Sagebrush Trail*.

Wayne and Bud Osborne do battle in *Haunted Gold*.

Wayne as he appears in *The Telegraph Trail*.

You're a regular mountain, ain't ya." Wayne is Jerry Mason, who teams with Hayes, his late father's former partner, in search of gold. Hayes later appears to be murdered, but isn't; Wayne is accused of the "killing" and, of course, sets things right. Two pieces of action are most commendable in this production. During a pursuit of claim jumpers, Wayne enters a sluice while standing on a raftlike piece of wood with a pole to steer. Whisked along by the current, Wayne catches up with and captures the bad guy. At the film's conclusion, Wayne on horseback and Hayes in a car pursue villains Yakima Canutt and Lloyd Whitlock. The varmints commandeer a gasoline-powered railroad handcar and escape. Wayne, as usual, catches the two with the help of Hayes. Again, the fights look real and director Robert Bradbury added dialogue to the action. Hayes's character support is another contributing factor to the film's success.

Wayne plays Ted Hayden, returning to the scene of his youth and trailing the man who murdered his father, in *West of the Divide* (1934), while in *Blue Steel* (1934), George Hayes is after the Polka Dot Bandit. Guess who Hayes thinks is the bandit? Is he or is Wayne government marshal John Carruthers?

In *The Man From Utah* (1934), Wayne is Deputy John Weston, traveling to the Dalton Valley Rodeo. The bad guys, including Yakima Canutt, are cheating honest folks and need to be exposed, and Wayne rides in to solve the mystery with the assist of George Hayes.

An eerie start greets Wayne (as Randy Bowers) as he enters a saloon with bodies strewn about and a player piano still playing in *Randy Rides Alone* (1934). Outlaw Marvin Black is on the loose and it's up to Randy Bowers to foil his nefarious plans and bring him in. Wayne again would improve, perfecting the fights with Canutt.

Wayne as Marshal John Travers pursues outlaw leader "The Shadow" (George Hayes) in *The Star Packer* (1934). A hollow tree stump is part of the puzzle Wayne must solve with the assistance of Indian friend Canutt, while cleaning up Hayes's gang. *The Trail Beyond* (1934), meanwhile features Wayne as Rod Drew, hired to locate a friend's missing niece. Weapons and bullets are being stolen and a mountie wants to arrest Wayne in this standard "B" with a rousing climax.

A change of pace awaits Wayne, playing Chris Morrell, in *'Neath Arizona Skies* (1934), the guardian of a little Indian girl (Shirley Rickert) who stands to inherit oil lands. Villainous Sam Black (Canutt) wants the girl but his foolhardy attempts to capture the youngster by killing her father will fail. Wayne has an interesting relationship with the young girl and shows he can work

with a small child as a father figure.

The Lawless Frontier (1935) has Wayne as John Tobin on the trail of a criminal named Zanti, and in the course of events rides a piece of wood down a storm drain in pursuit of the villain.

Thinking he has killed his best friend in *Texas Terror* (1935), Wayne as John Higgins turns in his sheriff's badge and considers another career as a prospector. Stolen express money aids in leading him to the real killer.

Rainbow Valley (1935) features Wayne as government agent John Martin sent to prevent a gang from halting construction of a vital road. A routine western.

Wayne as John Mason sees only the polka-dot kerchief of the man who kills his father in *Dawn Rider* (1935), but later heads for the inevitable four o'clock gunfight, only to learn that the bad guy's accomplice has emptied the bullets from his gun. The suspenseful buildup is handled nicely as the gunfight begins.

As Wayne's Lone Star Westerns were drawing to an end, film audiences were forming a sharper heroic image of their new hero. Box-office receipts were acceptable, with short dialogue, simple scenes, and blazing guns to fan the action.

The Desert Trail (1935) features Wayne as rodeo performer John Scott who, with friend Kansas Charlie (Edward Chandler), is accused of robbing rodeo receipts. They attempt to clear themselves in another routine western.

The last Lone Star/Monogram western was *Paradise Canyon* (1935). Wayne is John Wyatt, on the trail of counterfeiters, joining a medicine show while working undercover. Wayne and Canutt participate in two screen fights. The Lone Star/Monogram westerns weren't always polished but action was aplenty. With America coming out of the Depression, Wayne was becoming a representative symbol to film audiences. A studio merger was about to occur benefiting not only audiences but also Wayne, as stardom was nearing.

"Republic. I like the sound of the word."
—*The Alamo* (1960)

Monogram and Mascot Pictures and other, smaller independent companies merged in the fall of 1935, forming Republic Pictures. Tycoon Herbert J. Yates, who helmed the studio located in the San Fernando Valley, decreed that its films would have budgets increased to $15,000 and two weeks would be allowed for shooting. More horses and nonstop action would be the order of business. Wayne would eventually become the studio's biggest star, and during the years 1935–52, he would appear in thirty-three motion pictures at the studio, entailing approximately 21 percent of his film career.

Westward Ho! (1935) was not only Wayne's

Wayne and Yakima Canutt duke it out in
The Man From Utah.

Wayne stops Noah Beery, Jr. from belting the mountie
in *The Trail Beyond*, who may be either a disguised
outlaw or the real mountie..

Wayne, Bert Dillard, and Gabby Hayes perfect a plan
in *Texas Terror*.

Gino Corrado as the Rurale captain (black scarf)
nabs Yakima Canutt as Marion Burns, Wayne, and
Earle Hodgins (right) watch in *Paradise Canyon*.

first Republic film but also the first film released by the studio. Wayne plays John Wyatt, on the trail of the man who killed his parents and kidnapped his brother (Frank McGlynn, Jr.). Wyatt vows vengeance against outlaws who are after gold strikes of honest folk. To secure justice, Wayne organizes a vigilante group known as "The Singin' Riders," dressed in black shirts and white scarfs and astride white horses. Wayne's search and the gold strikes lead him to the same man. By using the Sierra Mountains as backdrop, a better visual sense is perceived in the film and justice is served as well.

As John Dawson, Wayne pursues an outlaw leader in *The New Frontier* (1935). *Variety* quoted Wayne as having "a good voice" and "nice personality," but with stronger stories and better production values, Republic could increase its profits.

A greedy plan to turn a valley into a ghost town occurs in *Lawless Range* (1935). Wayne as John Middleton organizes a wagon caravan to ship needed food to the townsfolk, and ferrets out the villain as well.

Wyoming statehood is jeopardized by opposing outlaw gangs in *The Lawless Nineties* (1936). Undercover government agent John Tipton (Wayne) is assigned the mission of eliminating the gangs and helping keep the election pools open for statehood annexation. Action galore in the last reel keeps Wayne busy.

Wayne plays John Clayborn in *King of the Pecos* (1936). Clayborn's parents were killed ten years earlier by a man intent on obtaining water rights in the territory, and he's out to right things. The flexible camera work enhances the best of the locales.

The Oregon Trail (1936) features Wayne as Capt. John Delmont, trailing the men who killed his father, and falling for pretty Ann Rutherford along the way.

A mail contract is up for grabs as Wayne (portraying John Blair) tries to secure it in *Winds of the Wasteland* (1936), competing with a rival stagecoach line. Is there any doubt who will win?

Wayne would film his last production for Republic during this phase by appearing in *The Lonely Trail* (1936). He appears seven minutes into the proceedings as John Ashton, returning home after the Civil War. Carpetbaggers are overrunning the area with Wayne opposing their plan.

At this time, Universal Pictures signed Wayne to a six picture deal. *The Sea Spoilers* (1936) features Wayne as Boatswain Bob Randall aboard a Coast Guard cutter in pursuit of seal poachers. Not only that but they've also kidnapped his sweetheart played by Nan Grey. A comical interlude develops between Mabel the Seal and Wayne who talks to Mabel as he will to Baby years later

in *Blood Alley* (1955).

As crooked fighter Pat, Wayne sees the error of his ways in the roaring nineties lumber camps in *Conflict* (1936), based on Jack London's story "The Abysmal Brute," and in *California Straight Ahead* (1937) as Biff Smith, Wayne is in competition against a rival trucking company. A cross-country race adds suspense to the action.

Newsreel cameramen are having difficulty trying to photograph the ever elusive bandit chieftain Muffadhi in *I Cover the War* (1937). Wayne as Bob Adams succeeds where others have failed. In *Idol of the Crowds* (1937), Wayne is Johnny Hanson, an up-and-coming hockey player. Competition tries to sway him from his goal but he doesn't succumb. Wayne's image is improving but he hungers for more. In the midst of this uncertainty, director John Ford was planning a project that would eventually deliver Wayne from his career doldrums.

Adventure's End (1937) would end Wayne's six-picture deal with Universal, as pearl diver Duke Slade working on a whaler in this inferior film.

Paramount Pictures borrowed Wayne for one film, *Born to the West* (1937), later rereleased as *Hell Town*. Wayne as Dare Rudd lands a job as a cook on the ranch of his cousin, played by Johnny Mack Brown. Assigned to deliver a herd of cattle to the railroad, Wayne is later involved in a crooked card game and is subsequently rescued by Brown. The combination of Wayne, Brown, and a Zane Grey story proved to be a successful venture for Paramount.

Uncomfortable with the films given him by Universal, Wayne welcomed an offer to rejoin Republic Pictures. A series of "B" westerns was being updated with Wayne moving into the role of Stony Brooke that was recently vacated by Bob Livingston. The Three Mesquiteers was a popular series for Republic and with his winning personality, Wayne could easily work with the other two already established characters: Ray Corrigan as Tucson Smith and Max Terhune as Lullaby Joslin, facing exciting adventures for six fast-paced films directed by George Sherman. A fourth character would share screen time with them: Elmer, a dummy operated by Terhune.

First up for the trio was *Pals of the Saddle* (1938), dealing with an illegal ammunitions ring. Monium, a chemical used in making poison gas, is being smuggled into Mexico for sale to foreign powers. Blamed for the death of a secret service agent working on the case, Stony infiltrates the gang, clears himself, and captures the villains with the assistance of his two pals of the saddle. In an exciting sequence when the trio ambushes the bad guys by firing on them from a rock formation.

Russell Hicks (seated) and Wayne talk as Harry Worth (left) and Fuzzy Knight listen in *The Sea Spoilers*.

Wayne stops Eddie Borden from pushing Margaret Mann as Jean Rogers watches in *Conflict*.

Max Terhune, John Wayne, and Ray Corrigan are the Three Mesquiteers in *Three Texas Steers*.

Don "Red" Barry (behind bars) vows escape as Ray Corrigan, Raymond Hatton, and Wayne listen in *Wyoming Outlaw*.

Overland Stage Raiders (1938) has the Mesquiteers talking the local ranchers into investing in a plane for shipping gold. The bad guys attempt to prevent a cattle herd from reaching the market, so that the plane can't be purchased and the ranchers lose. The plane carrying the gold later disappears and a twenty-four hour deadline is set. An exciting highlight occurs when the three attempt to stop a train after the villains have taken over the engine. This action pleases the audiences as Wayne attempts to board the moving train and thwart the plan.

Wayne is jailed for the murder of an old friend in *Santa Fe Stampede* (1938), and his saddle pals try to unmask the real killer; suspense is at a peak when a vengeful crowd tries to lynch Wayne. Editing is rapid fire as the jail is set ablaze with Wayne trying to reach the keys that will free him.

The Mesquiteers attempt to solve the mystery of disappearing cattle in *Red River Range* (1938). Refrigerated trucks are a key to the puzzle as the trio succeeds against the rustlers. In *The Night Riders* (1939), a land grant scheme endangers ranchers' properties so the trio become masked Robin Hood figures to restore the land to the owners. Wayne has by now developed a sharp sense of dialogue that is even more prevalent in *Stagecoach*. In *The Night Riders*, Ray Corrigan says, "You know, there used to be a time when being an American meant something." Wayne responds, "It still does. It stands for freedom and fair play." When deciding on what has to be done, Wayne expounds, "All the more reason we gotta fight. The men who opened up this country didn't sit around cryin' for help. They did somethin.'" The scheme is thwarted.

A circus owner (Carole Landis) is in danger of losing her land as a horse race will determine the winner in *Three Texas Steers* (1939). Rajah the Wonder Horse turns in a winning performance in this entry that marks the final appearance of Terhune with Wayne and Corrigan.

Raymond Hatton signed on as Rusty Joslin in *Wyoming Outlaw* (1939). Don "Red" Barry plays a rancher's son who turns to a life of crime, with the Mesquiteers trying to prevent further criminal activities. This role would make Barry a box-office commodity.

New Frontier (1939), later retitled *Frontier Horizon* (to avoid confusion with 1935 *New Frontier*), has the trio assisting residents being conned out of their properties. The Mesquiteers discover that the new land deeds are fraudulent and the properties are in the way of a reservoir. As the flood gates open, the saddle pals go into action and save the day.

At this point, director John Ford made his move. Ford successfully convinced producer Walter Wanger that Wayne would be perfect for the role of the Ringo Kid in *Stagecoach* (1939). Wanger had wanted star Gary Cooper but this would have increased the film's modest budget. Filming was done on location in Monument Valley and other desert settings, and Ford was able to capture the performance he knew Wayne had inside him. This star-making role would be the big break for Wayne placing him in a top "A" film. The "B" westerns had their following but a whole new audience was viewing Wayne for the first time. This tall, slow-talking actor had something to say and people were taking note.

Regarding the progression of events that led Wayne to stardom, one Wayne faction believes that he filmed all eight Mesquiteer features before *Stagecoach*. The other believes that Wayne made the first four Mesquiteer films, did *Stagecoach*, and then returned to make the final "B" westerns. Possibly what happened was that when *Stagecoach* was released, Republic issued the last four films trying to latch onto the rapidly rising star. *Stagecoach* was released in March 1939 and the last four Mesquiteers were staggered so that Republic could milk Wayne's success. This frustrated Wayne who was trying to completely escape those projects.

At any rate, the stagecoach arrived at the perfect time. Wayne achieved the screen presence that would sustain him through his final acting performance in *The Shootist* (1976).

Of the many people who took an interest in Wayne during the early years, eight could be singled out as major forces who chiseled away at the granite. Veteran western actor Harry Carey would teach Wayne a way of talking and telegraphing his lines when using dialogue. Paul Fix helped Wayne with his physical presence by teaching him to walk pigeon-toed and developing a trademark swagger, like walking on a tightrope. Yakima Canutt assisted Wayne in perfecting screen fights. Wayne would always have a deep respect for stuntmen on all of his productions. Director Raoul Walsh gave the world an actor named John Wayne. Producer Nat Levine introduced Wayne to serial audiences. Producer Paul Malvern developed a new audience for Wayne in "B" westerns. Herbert J. Yates gave Wayne further credibility in the Republic westerns. Director John Ford remembered the struggling actor who was striving toward something. Wayne succeeded with romantic dialogue in *Stagecoach* and could easily handle the action scenes. The association between Wayne and Ford would please audiences and producers as well with lines at the box office.

With World War II looming, Wayne would detract audiences from its harsh realities. A stagecoach not only brought Wayne success but also gave the world a presence that would endear him to future generations of movie fans.

Wayne takes over the engine from Olin Francis to prevent the theft of the cattle in *Overland Stage Raiders*.

George Douglas (in cloak) waits impatiently as the Three Mesquiteers—Terhune, Wayne and Corrigan—are about to be shot in *The Night Riders*.

Wayne offers solace to Hal Neiman in *Idol of the Crowds*.

Wayne fights bad guys Yakima Canutt (left) and Olin Francis in *Pals of the Saddle*.

PART TWO

TRIVIA QUESTIONS ON JOHN WAYNE

The career of John Wayne in this book stretches from *Stagecoach* (1939) to *The Shootist* (1976). What I have done is research his films and derived questions from those films made during this period.

Your job, pilgrim, is to move out and answer the questions. If you are stumped, simply check the answers at the bottom of the page or at the end of the section.

It doesn't matter how you do. There are no points or charts to tabulate the answers. It's enough simply to remember the magic moments the "Big Duke" gave us on the movie screen.

John Wayne in *THE ALAMO:*
"Now that ain't a bad stab at putting it into words."

Without further ado, this book is now yours.

Wayne and Claire Trevor face a new future at the end of *Stagecoach*.

Wayne discovers Claire Trevor's disguise in *Allegheny Uprising*.

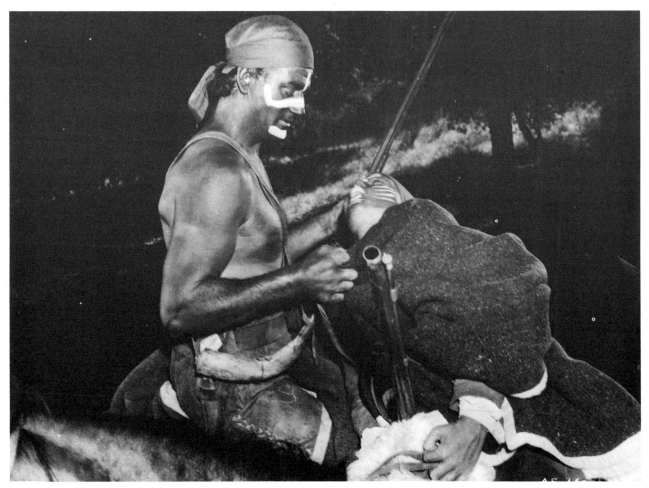

THE 1940's

Stagecoach (1939), UNITED ARTISTS

1. Name the actor who plays the stagecoach driver.
2. Name the actress who plays Dallas.
3. Name the actor who plays Doc Boone.
4. From what town does the stagecoach depart?
5. What town is the destination of the stagecoach?
6. What is Mr. Peacock's profession?
7. What Indian chief is on the rampage?
8. What is the name of the family that killed Wayne's father and brother?
9. What are the two items Wayne is carrying when he is first seen?
10. What had happened to Wayne's horse?
11. How did Wayne know of Indian trouble when the stagecoach arrives?
12. From what had Wayne escaped when he encounters the stagecoach?
13. Whose broken arm had Doc Boone fixed in the past?
14. Why does Wayne help sober up Doc Boone?
15. What happens when the stagecoach crosses the salt flat?
16. What passenger is killed during this sequence?
17. How many bullets does Wayne have left when the stagecoach enters town?
18. Name the actor who plays Luke Plummer?
19. What is Wayne seen doing before the gunfight commences?
20. What happens to Wayne after the gunfight?

AUTHOR'S NOTE: Wayne was actually the one who discovered Monument Valley, not John Ford. Ford liked the location and received the credit for its film discovery. This locale was used by Ford the first time in STAGECOACH.

AUTHOR'S NOTE: Wayne thought Lloyd Nolan should have played the role of Ringo, when asked by John Ford.

1. Andy Devine.
2. Claire Trevor.
3. Thomas Mitchell.
4. Tonto.
5. Lordsburg.
6. A whiskey salesman.
7. Geronimo.
8. Plummers.
9. A rifle and saddle.
10. Wayne's horse went lame.
11. Wayne tells Devine he saw a couple of ranches burning the night before.
12. Prison.
13. Wayne's brother.
14. So Doc Boone can help deliver a baby.
15. The Indians attack.
16. John Carradine as the gambler.
17. Three.
18. Tom Tyler.
19. Wayne is walking down the street and dives forward before the gunfight starts.
20. Wayne is freed and Trevor and he are sent away to face a new future.

Allegheny Uprising (1939), RKO

1. Who is given first billing in the film?
2. What is Wayne seen as in his first scene?
3. Name the actor who plays Trader Callendar?
4. What does he sell to the Indians?
5. Name the actor who plays the British officer, Captain Swanson.
6. Name the fort used to protect the settlers?
7. Name Wayne's female co-star who plays Janie McDougle.
8. What type of business does her father run?
9. How do Wayne and his men disguise themselves in order to destroy illegal goods?
10. Name the actor who plays M'Cammon?
11. Why doesn't Janie join Wayne's raid?
12. In what city does Wayne report about the illegal goods?
13. What historical governor wants proof of these activities?
14. What is Wayne's battle plan to capture the fort from the British?
15. How is Callendar punished?
16. What piece of clothing is used to clear Wayne during the trial?
17. Why is this used?
18. What two characters clear Wayne of the murder charges?
19. What happens to Captain Swanson?
20. Where is Wayne headed at the film's end?

AUTHOR'S NOTE: Wayne and Claire Trevor were to star in this film because of the popularity of *Stagecoach*, in which both stars appeared. RKO thought their combination would result in a hefty film gross. It didn't.

1. Claire Trevor.
2. Wayne is being held prisoner.
3. Brian Donlevy.
4. Guns and liquor.
5. George Sanders.
6. Fort Loudon.
7. Claire Trevor.
8. A tavern.
9. Indians.
10. Chill Wills.
11. Wayne's men remove their shirts and paint themselves black.
12. Philadelphia.
13. Penn.
14. To surround the fort with continuous rifle fire.
15. He is flogged.
16. A shirt.
17. To prove that a rifle was fired from some distance to kill the man Wayne was accused of killing.
18. Trevor and the local magistrate.
19. He is sent back to England.
20. Tennessee.

The Dark Command (1940), REPUBLIC

1. What do Wayne and the dentist have going at the film's start?
2. Who is the actor that plays the dentist, Doc Grunch?
3. Who is Wayne's female co-star, who plays Mary McCloud?
4. Who is the western star in the film, other than Wayne and Doc Grunch, who plays Fletch McCloud?
5. Who is the actor who plays Cantrell?
6. Which historical character is his role based on?
7. What deficiency in Wayne is discovered during the debate?
8. What is Wayne's comeback when his deficiency is mentioned?
9. What is Wayne's new job?
10. Who is the actress who plays Cantrell's mother?
11. Who does Mary McCloud marry first?
12. Why are the neighboring towns attacked instead of Wayne's town?
13. Who is the actor who is Cantrell's second in command?
14. What incident separates Wayne and Mary?
15. When does Mary realize she married the wrong man?
16. What town is the battleground in the fight against the raiders?
17. Who tries to kill Cantrell before Wayne arrives?
18. How does Wayne find where Cantrell is hiding?
19. How is Doc Grunch vindicated?
20. Who is the film's director?

AUTHOR'S NOTE: *The Dark Command* was Republic Pictures' most expensive film at that time, with a $700,000 budget.

1. A con game.
2. Gabby Hayes.
3. Claire Trevor.
4. Roy Rogers.
5. Walter Pidgeon.
6. Quantrill.
7. Wayne can't read or write.
8. "I'm better at smelling than spelling."
9. To be town marshal.
10. Marjorie Main.
11. Pidgeon.
12. Wayne's town is a hub in the wheel the other towns form around it.
13. Joe Sawyer.
14. Wayne is going to arrest Rogers.
15. Pidgeon's raids increase.
16. Lawrence, Kansas.
17. Main.
18. As Main dies, Wayne hears her and shoots Pidgeon, who is next to her.
19. He saves Rogers, who had been shot.
20. Raoul Walsh.

Three Faces West (1940), REPUBLIC

1. What is the name of the radio program broadcast at the film's start?
2. Name the actor who plays the Austrian doctor sent to Wayne's town.
3. Where is Wayne first seen in the film?
4. Name Wayne's female co-star.
5. In what area of the country is the film located?
6. What is the name of Wayne's community?
7. Name the actor who plays Wayne's uncle.
8. Where does Wayne offer to take the doctor and his daughter on the day after the storm passes?
9. What kind of car does Wayne tell the girl he drives?
10. Who is the gal Wayne says keeps kicking him in the teeth?
11. Who tells Wayne the land is doomed?
12. Wayne says, "Our law is written by _____"
13. Where does Wayne want to move the community?
14. How many miles will the trip be to Oregon?
15. What is Wayne assigned to keep for the passengers?
16. Name the actor who plans to divide the passengers for California.
17. What happens when Wayne and the girl make plans to marry?
18. What does she discover about him?
19. What is the name of the new settlement?
20. Where are Wayne and the girl married?

AUTHOR'S NOTE: This film also had another title, *The Refugee*. Director Bernard Vorhaus never attained true recognition as a director.

1. "We the People."
2. Charles Coburn.
3. Waiting in the train station.
4. Sigrid Gurie.
5. The Dust Bowl.
6. Asheville Forks, North Dakota.
7. Spencer Charters—his occupation is veterinarian.
8. To church.
9. A jalopy.
10. Mother Nature.
11. An agent with the Department of Agriculture.
12. "The wind and the dust."
13. Oregon.
14. 1500 miles.
15. The funds of the people.
16. Trevor Bardette.
17. The girl's ex-love arrives in the U.S. at San Francisco, looking for her to marry.
18. He is with the Third Reich.
19. Asheville Forks, Oregon.
20. Under a tree in Oregon.

The Long Voyage Home (1940), UNITED ARTISTS

1. Who wrote the story?
2. What is Wayne's native homeland in the film?
3. What was Wayne's native occupation?
4. What is the name of the ship Wayne and the company are on?
5. What type of vessel is it?
6. What is the cargo aboard the ship?
7. Name the actor who plays Donkeyman.
8. Name the actor killed on the ship during the storm.
9. Name the actor who plays Axel Swanson.
10. Where does he sew Wayne's wages before leaving the ship?
11. At what city do they land to visit the pubs?
12. What does Wayne get to drink in the bar?
13. Name the actress who plays Freda the prostitute.
14. What does Wayne call her?
15. What is her mission?
16. Name the character shanghaied in Wayne's place.
17. What is the name of the shanghai ship?
18. What is the newspaper headline at the film's end?
19. Who did the cinematography?
20. Who directed the film?

AUTHOR'S NOTE: Wayne appeared in the *Saturday Evening Post* of July 9, 1949, in an article entitled "My Favorite Role." According to the article, Wayne selected *The Long Voyage Home.* In each issue a film star was asked to select his or her favorite role.

1. Eugene O'Neill.
2. Sweden.
3. A farm.
4. *Glencairn.*
5. A tramp steamer.
6. Dynamite.
7. Arthur Shields.
8. Ward Bond.
9. John Qualen.
10. His suit.
11. London.
12. Ginger beer.
13. Mildred Natwick.
14. Miss Freda.
15. To drug Wayne so he can be shanghaied.
16. Drisc.
17. Amindra.
18. *"Amindra* Sunk"
19. Gregg Toland.
20. John Ford.

Seven Sinners (1940), UNIVERSAL

1. Name the actress who plays Bijou.
2. What type of performer is she?
3. Name the actor who plays Doctor Martin.
4. Name the actor who plays Finnegan.
5. Name the actor who plays Sasha.
6. Name the actor who plays the club proprietor.
7. What does Wayne help Bijou over when they meet?
8. What is the name of the club in which she sings?
9. Why does Wayne enter the club while she is singing?
10. What song is she singing when Wayne interrupts her?
11. In what is she clad at the time?
12. Name the actor who plays Antro.
13. What type of weapon does he use?
14. What game do the sailors play in the back room?
15. Name the actress who plays Dorothy Henderson.
16. What is the decision that Wayne must make?
17. What actor assists Wayne in the fight at the finale?
18. Where is Wayne at the finale?
19. Who is Bijou with at the film's end?
20. Name the film's director.

AUTHOR'S NOTE: Supposedly Wayne's role was originally written for Tyrone Power. Power's contract with 20th Century-Fox ended his plans for this film.

1. Marlene Dietrich.
2. A cafe singer.
3. Albert Dekker.
4. Broderick Crawford.
5. Mischa Auer.
6. Billy Gilbert.
7. A herd of sheep.
8. "7 Sinners' Club."
9. To reprimand the junior officers for leaving an official reception.
10. "The Man's in the Navy."
11. A naval uniform.
12. Oscar Homolka.
13. A knife.
14. Billiards.
15. Anna Lee.
16. To keep Dietrich or stay in the Navy.
17. Crawford.
18. Wayne is back in the Navy.
19. Dekker.
20. Tay Garnett.

A Man Betrayed (1941), REPUBLIC

1. How is Wayne's friend killed at the film's start?
2. What is Wayne's occupation?
3. Name the actor who plays Tom Cameron.
4. Name the actor who plays the news reporter Casey.
5. What is the name of the town in which Wayne arrives?
6. Why is Wayne in town?
7. What does Wayne do to the butler when Wayne is refused entrance?
8. Who is Wayne's female co-star, who plays Sabra Cameron?
9. What is Wayne looking at when she first meets him?
10. What is the name of the local night club?
11. How does Wayne enter the club?
12. What does the waiter (dressed as a devil) keep doing to Wayne?
13. On what type of carnival ride do Wayne and Sabra embrace?
14. Where do they stop on this ride?
15. How does Wayne pay the ride operator?
16. How does Wayne test his gunshot theory in the night club?
17. What does Wayne wrap Sabra in to escape the bad guys?
18. Who mistakenly gets shot in the street instead of Wayne?
19. Name the actor who did murder Wayne's friend.
20. What does the butler do to Wayne at the film's end?

AUTHOR'S NOTE: In the theatres, the film was released as *A Man Betrayed.* When the film appeared on television, the new title *Wheel of Fortune* appears. These two titles are one and the same film.

1. He is shot as lightning strikes the lightpost next to him.
2. A small town lawyer.
3. Edward Ellis.
4. Wallace Ford.
5. Temple City.
6. To investigate his friend's death.
7. Wayne gives him a black eye.
8. Frances Dee.
9. A model train board.
10. Club Inferno.
11. Wayne goes down a large slide.
12. His tail keeps hitting Wayne in the face when he turns around to leave.
13. A ferris wheel.
14. At the top.
15. Wayne throws the money down to him.
16. He fires the gun and the loud club noise muffles the shot.
17. A tablecloth.
18. The dead friend's mother.
19. Ward Bond.
20. The butler gives Wayne a black eye.

Wayne gets the drop on Walter Pidgeon as Roy Rogers watches in *The Dark Command*.

Wayne leads the way to the promised land in *Three Faces West*.

Ward Bond, Wayne, Joe Sawyer and John Qualen are all shipmates in *The Long Voyage Home*.

Wayne gives Marlene Dietrich a pointer in the billiard room from *Seven Sinners*.

Ward Bond gets the drop on Wayne in *A Man Betrayed*.

John
WAYNE
Frances
DEE

A MAN BETRAYED

A RE-RELEASE

WITH EDWARD ELLIS · WALLACE FORD · WARD BOND · HAROLD HUBER · ALEXANDER GRANACH

Screen Play by ISABEL DAWN · Original Story by JACK MOFFITT   Directed by JOHN H. AUER   A REPUBLIC PICTURE

Lady from Louisiana (1941), REPUBLIC

1. What is Wayne's occupation?
2. Name Wayne's female co-star, who plays Julie Mirbeau.
3. Where does Wayne meet her the first time?
4. What organization does Wayne belong to?
5. What does Julie's father run?
6. What city is used as the film's background?
7. What gala event is used as a backdrop?
8. How does Julie convince Wayne of her view that the lottery is harmless?
9. Name the actor who plays the governor's lieutenant.
10. Where does the governor think the lottery monies are going?
11. Name the actor who plays Cuffy.
12. What unfavorably changes Wayne's opinion of the lottery?
13. Who gets the blame for the governor's death?
14. What does Julie do that foils Blackie's plans?
15. How does Wayne succeed in exposing the lottery?
16. What happens during the trial?
17. What happens to the courthouse?
18. Where does Blackie leave Julie to die as Wayne pursues him?
19. How does Blackie meet his fate?
20. What is used to plug the breach in the dam?

AUTHOR'S NOTE: Wayne worked with Director Bernard Vorhaus a second time on this film.

1. A lawyer.
2. Ona Munson.
3. On a Mississippi riverboat.
4. The Anti-Lottery League.
5. A lottery.
6. New Orleans.
7. Mardi Gras.
8. She takes him to the Mardi Gras.
9. Ray Middleton.
10. To build hospitals, orphanages, civic improvements, etc.
11. Jack Pennick.
12. A lottery winner is murdered.
13. Wayne, of course.
14. She decides to run the lottery herself.
15. Wayne obtains the lottery records.
16. A storm causes the river to rise and the levee breaks.
17. The storm weakens the foundation.
18. On the levee as it is about to collapse.
19. He drowns after getting knocked off of the boat by Wayne.
20. A riverboat commandeered by Wayne plugs the breach.

The Shepherd of the Hills (1941), PARAMOUNT

1. Where is the film set?
2. What is Wayne's means of living?
3. What type of weapon does Wayne carry?
4. Why does Wayne hate his father?
5. Who is Wayne's female co-star, who plays Sammie?
6. Why doesn't she want to marry Wayne?
7. Who is the actor who plays Daniel Howitt?
8. What is the name of Wayne's home?
9. Who first spots the resemblance between Wayne and Howitt?
10. Who is the actress who plays Aunt Mollie?
11. Who is the actor who plays Pete the Mute?
12. What does Wayne bring Pete from town?
13. Who is the actor who plays Mr. Palestrom?
14. Who is the actress who is given her sight back?
15. Who is shot in the showdown?
16. What is the reason that Howitt didn't return home when Wayne was young?
17. What is Wayne's line when he regains consciousness?
18. What is the significance of this film in Wayne's career?
19. Who is the film's director?
20. What type of color was used the first time on a Wayne film?

AUTHOR'S NOTE: Olive Carey, wife of Harry Carey, Sr., gave Wayne a piece of advice that assured his success. Wayne told her early in his career that he didn't care for the way he walked or talked, and was discouraged. Olive Carey asked him if he thought Harry Carey, Sr., should change his mannerisms. Wayne said Carey's audience would be hurt if Carey changed his style. Olive Carey said the same applied to Wayne. Wayne remained the same and the rest is history.

1. The Ozarks.
2. A moonshiner.
3. A rifle.
4. Wayne's father had deserted his mother, and she died.
5. Betty Field.
6. Wayne had vowed to kill his father.
7. Harry Carey, Sr.
8. Moaning Meadow.
9. Betty Field.
10. Beulah Bondi.
11. Marc Lawrence.
12. Candy.
13. Fuzzy Knight.
14. Marjorie Main.
15. Wayne.
16. Carey was in prison for murder.
17. "I ain't lost from nobody no more."
18. This was Wayne's first film in color.
19. Henry Hathaway.
20. Technicolor.

Lady for a Night (1941), REPUBLIC

1. What is Wayne's means of making a living?
2. Name Wayne's female co-star, who plays Jenny Blake.
3. In what state does the film take place?
4. What is Jenny's ultimate goal?
5. What society does she want to join?
6. What does she own?
7. What title does she win?
8. Who has rigged the election so she can win?
9. Name the actor who plays Wayne's bodyguard, Boris.
10. Why does the society not want Jenny to win?
11. Name the actor who plays Jenny's new husband, Alan Alderson.
12. What is the deal Jenny has with Alderson?
13. What is the name of the plantation at which Jenny will live?
14. What happens to Wayne when Jenny achieves a place in society?
15. What is the name of the business that Wayne opens?
16. What is the name of the book Wayne gives Jenny?
17. Who drinks the poison meant for Jenny?
18. Who clears Jenny of the false murder charge?
19. What is the new name Jenny gives Wayne's club?
20. What is Wayne's response when Jenny asks him to marry her?

AUTHOR'S NOTE: Joan Blondell was billed first over Wayne in the film's original release.

1. A gambler and con man.
2. Joan Blondell.
3. Tennessee.
4. To achieve a place in society.
5. Memphis Society.
6. A gambling riverboat.
7. "The Queen Of The Mardi Gras."
8. Wayne, of course.
9. Leonid Kinskey.
10. Because of her gambling activities on the riverboat.
11. Ray Middleton.
12. She will cancel his gambling debts when he marries her, because he is a bad gambler.
13. "The Shadows."
14. She discards him.
15. "The King's Club."
16. "How to Be a Lady."
17. Middleton.
18. The good aunt.
19. "The Queen's Club."
20. "Sure I'll marry you if you promise to sew on my buttons and cook my meals and darn my socks."

Reap the Wild Wind (1942), PARAMOUNT

1. Wayne is captain of what shipping line?
2. What is the name of Wayne's ship?
3. In what geographic area does the film take place?
4. Name Wayne's female co-star, who plays Loxi Claiborne.
5. Name the actdor who plays lawyer Stephen Tolliver.
6. Name the actor who plays King Cutler.
7. Name the actor who plays his younger brother.
8. What is the fate of Wayne's ship?
9. Where are the sunken ship models placed in the inquiry room?
10. What will Wayne lose as a result of the sinking?
11. What does King Cutler arrange for the lawyer?
12. How many fathoms deep are Loxi's eyes?
13. Name the actress who plays Drusilla Alston?
14. Who is doomed in the hold of the sunken *Southern Cross?*
15. What is Wayne's resolution in the courtroom?
16. What does King Cutler tell Wayne about Tolliver as Wayne prepares for the dive?
17. What is found showing that the death occurred on the *Southern Cross?*
18. What is Wayne's dilemma?
19. How does Wayne meet his fate?
20. Name the film's director.

AUTHOR'S NOTE: In 1942, when the film was originally released, Ray Milland was billed over Wayne. However, in the 1954 re-release, Wayne had top billing over Milland. Milland's popularity had decreased at that time, and Wayne had more boxoffice punch.

1. Devereaux.
2. Jubilee.
3. The Florida Keys.
4. Paulette Goddard.
5. Ray Milland.
6. Raymond Massey.
7. Robert Preston.
8. The ship is forced onto the rocks and looted.
9. In the fireplace.
10. The command of the *Southern Cross.*
11. To be shanghaied.
12. Ten.
13. Susan Hayward.
14. Hayward.
15. To dive with Milland to prove that Hayward did die.
16. That only Wayne is to surface.
17. Hayward's shawl.
18. To kill Milland or to rescue him from danger, which will lead to Wayne's conviction.
19. A giant squid kills Wayne.
20. Cecil B. DeMille.

Wayne makes his escape in *The Shepherd of the Hills*.

Wayne fights Ray Middleton in the pilothouse in *Lady from Louisiana.*

Wayne heads for deep sea disaster in *Reap the Wild Wind*.

Wayne helps Joan Blondell achieve her goal in *Lady for a Night*.

Joan   John
BLONDELL · WAYNE
in
LADY for a NIGHT
A RE-RELEASE
with
RAY MIDDLETON
PHILIP MERIVALE · BLANCHE YURKA · EDITH BARRETT
LEONID KINSKEY and THE HALL JOHNSON CHOIR
A REPUBLIC PICTURE

R50 136

The Spoilers (1942), UNIVERSAL

1. What is Wayne's film billing?
2. In what city does the film take place?
3. Name the actress who plays Cherry Malotte.
4. Name the actor who plays the gold commissioner, McNamara.
5. Who are "The Spoilers?"
6. Name the actor who plays Bronco.
7. Name the actor who plays Wayne's partner, Dextry.
8. What is the name of Wayne's mine?
9. What is Wayne's food fetish?
10. What is Wayne's favorite drink?
11. Who does Wayne show attraction for, other than Cherry?
12. What is the disguise Wayne and his men use to rob the bank?
13. Why is Wayne arrested?
14. What is used to crash through the barricade?
15. What does Wayne do with his pistol before the final fight starts?
16. Where does the fight between Wayne and McNamara take place?
17. Where is the fight eventually finished?
18. Who is the film's director?
19. What star of an earlier *Spoilers* film appears in this version?
20. Who wrote the novel?

AUTHOR'S NOTE: The success of this film was due to the combination of the three stars. This formula would be used again in *Pittsburgh*.

1. Third.
2. Nome, Alaska.
3. Marlene Dietrich.
4. Randolph Scott.
5. They steal the gold illegally from mining claims.
6. Richard Barthelmess.
7. Harry Carey, Sr.
8. Midas Mine.
9. Hard-boiled eggs.
10. Brandy.
11. The judge's niece.
12. Wayne and his men paint themselves black.
13. For shooting the marshal (which he didn't do, of course).
14. A train.
15. He throws it out of Cherry's window.
16. Cherry's room.
17. In front of the saloon.
18. Ray Enright.
19. William Farnum.
20. Rex Beach.

In Old California (1942), REPUBLIC

1. What city is Wayne from?
2. What is Wayne's occupation?
3. In what city does Wayne want to open his business?
4. Who is Wayne's female co-star?
5. What is her character's name?
6. What is her occupation?
7. Name the actor who doesn't want store space rented to Wayne.
8. What is his character's name?
9. How does Wayne show his strength to the boys who don't want his tonic?
10. Name the actor who plays Wayne's sidekick, Kegs McKeever.
11. How does Wayne succeed with his store?
12. Name the actress who plays Helga.
13. Which character dies from taking medicine?
14. How is Wayne framed for murder?
15. What news is heard in town as Wayne is to be hanged?
16. What happens in the gold camps?
17. Who shoots Britt Dawson?
18. How does Wayne save the day?
19. How does Helga take her wash down?
20. What experience had helped Wayne play his role?

AUTHOR'S NOTE: The usual norm in a Wayne film is for Wayne to settle accounts with the heavy himself. This film is one of the few in which another character does the heavy in, leaving Wayne to settle accounts in his next film.

1. Boston, Mass.
2. A druggist.
3. Sacramento.
4. Binnie Barnes.
5. Lacey Miller.
6. A dance hall singer.
7. Albert Dekker.
8. Britt Dawson.
9. Wayne bends a coin with one hand.
10. Edgar Kennedy.
11. Barnes goes into partnership with Wayne.
12. Patsy Kelly.
13. Whitey.
14. Poison is poured into one of Wayne's tonics.
15. Gold is discovered.
16. An epidemic occurs and Wayne saves the day.
17. His second in command.
18. He distributes the medicine to stop the epidemic.
19. She shoots the clothes pins off with a gun.
20. Wayne's father was a druggist.

Flying Tigers (1942), REPUBLIC

1. What is the other name of the "Flying Tigers."
2. In what country do they fly missions at the film's start?
3. Name the actor who plays Hap.
4. What does Wayne tell his mechanic caused the bullet holes in his plane?
5. Name Wayne's female co-star.
6. With what organization is she?
7. What "Mouseketeer" appears in the film?
8. Name the actor who plays the new hot-shot pilot, Woody.
9. What is the nickname he gives Wayne?
10. What type of entertainment is heard while Wayne and his female co-star have dinner?
11. How much is the reward for each enemy plane shot down?
12. What is Hap's flaw causing him to be grounded?
13. Where is Woody when Wayne is ready to fly on a night mission?
14. How is Hap killed?
15. What is the shocking radio news broadcast?
16. Name the actor who plays Col. Lindsay.
17. What is the nature of the suicide mission?
18. How is Woody killed as Wayne parachutes to safety?
19. What does Wayne give the new flyer at the film's end?
20. Why is this a significant film in Wayne's career?

AUTHOR'S NOTE: This film grossed well at the boxoffice and the Wayne image was found to be a powerful tool for American morale.

1. American Volunteer Group.
2. China.
3. Paul Kelly.
4. "Termites."
5. Anna Lee.
6. Red Cross.
7. Jimmy Dodd.
8. John Carroll.
9. "Pappy."
10. A record.
11. $500.
12. He has failing eyesight and lacks depth perception.
13. He is having dinner with Anna Lee.
14. He flies into a Jap plane.
15. Pearl Harbor is attacked.
16. Addison Richards.
17. To stop a Japanese supply train.
18. He flies the plane into the supply train after being wounded.
19. Carroll's scarf.
20. This was Wayne's first war film.

Reunion in France (1942), MGM

1. Name the actress who plays Michele de la Becque.
2. Name the actor who plays her lover.
3. What does he eventually become?
4. How does Becque support herself?
5. What is Wayne's film role?
6. Where has Wayne come from?
7. Where is his injury?
8. Which American city is Wayne from?
9. What does Becque use as Wayne's alibi?
10. Where does Becque eventually hope to travel?
11. Name the actor who plays Ulrich Windler.
12. Name the actor who plays Schultz.
13. What group is suspicious of Becque's plan?
14. Who accompanies Wayne and Becque on their escape?
15. What are Wayne and Becque to watch for on their trip?
16. What does Becque eventually discover about her lover?
17. How does Wayne finally escape?
18. Who clears Becque's lover at the film's end?
19. Name the film's director.
20. What opinion did Wayne and Crawford share on this film?

AUTHOR'S NOTE: MGM executives thought the casting of Wayne would give a boost to Crawford's career. It didn't.

1. Joan Crawford.
2. Philip Dorn.
3. A traitor to the French.
4. She becomes a salesgirl.
5. A R.A.F. pilot.
6. A P.O.W. camp.
7. Wayne has a leg wound.
8. Wilkes Barre, Penn.
9. Wayne is her driver and he has lost his papers.
10. To the U.S.
11. John Carradine.
12. Reginald Owen.
13. The Gestapo.
14. Two Nazi generals.
15. They are to watch for three escaped British prisoners.
16. He is really a patriot.
17. By British plane.
18. Crawford.
19. Jules Dassin.
20. They both hated the film.

Randolph Scott gets his comeuppance from Wayne as
Marlene Dietrich watches in *The Spoilers*.

Wayne makes plans to save the day in *In Old
California*.

Wayne tells his mechanic how the holes got in his plane in *Flying Tigers*.

Joan Crawford arranges for Wayne's escape as Henry Daniell (right) watches in *Reunion in France*.

Pittsburgh (1942), UNIVERSAL

1. What was Wayne's occupation in his early days?
2. Name the actor who plays Wayne's partner, Cash Evans.
3. Name the actor who plays the tailor.
4. Name Wayne's female co-star, who plays Josie Winters.
5. Where do Wayne and Evans meet her for the first time?
6. What is Wayne's nickname for her at that time?
7. Who does Wayne con into the fight ring?
8. Whose car is used on the way to the cave-in?
9. What is Josie's nickname from the past?
10. Name the actor who plays Doc Powers.
11. What are Wayne and Evans looking for in his office?
12. What does Josie dare Wayne to do?
13. Who does Wayne eventually marry?
14. Who does Wayne visit on his wedding night?
15. What happens to Wayne when the coal and steel companies merge?
16. What won't Wayne let the union look at, despite his promise?
17. Where do Wayne and Evans have their fight?
18. How is Josie hurt while they fight?
19. What is Wayne's alias when he starts over?
20. What goal do all of the characters share at the film's end?

AUTHOR'S NOTE: Wayne received third billing behind Marlene Dietrich and Randolph Scott. The 1953 re-issue still featured the same order, despite Wayne's success.

1. Coal miner.
2. Randolph Scott.
3. Shemp Howard.
4. Marlene Dietrich.
5. On a street corner in front of the fight hall.
6. "Countess."
7. Scott.
8. Dietrich's.
9. "Hunky."
10. Frank Craven.
11. A drink.
12. To quit his coal mining job.
13. The banker's daughter.
14. Dietrich.
15. Wayne becomes obsessed with power.
16. The company books.
17. A coal mine.
18. The elevator she is in plunges to the bottom of the mine shaft.
19. Charles Ellis.
20. To all work together for the war effort.

A Lady Takes a Chance (1943), RKO

1. Name the actress who plays Wayne's female co-star, Molly Truesdale.
2. What is her occupation?
3. Which state is she from?
4. What does she save her money for?
5. In what city does she see Wayne for the first time?
6. Why is he there?
7. Name the actor who plays Wayne's friend, Waco.
8. What does Wayne care about more than anything else?
9. What is its name?
10. What happens to Wayne when a horse throws him?
11. What is Molly doing when Wayne encounters her?
12. How do they spend the night?
13. Name the actor who plays Smiley Lambert.
14. What does Molly miss because of the excitement?
15. Where does Wayne sleep when he gives Molly his room?
16. Whose blanket does Molly use to keep warm in the desert?
17. What happens because of this?
18. How many suitors does Wayne persuade to leave Molly?
19. Name the actor Wayne punches who vies for Molly's affections.
20. Name the actor from *Big Jim McLain* who appears in this film.

AUTHOR'S NOTE: This was originally titled *Cowboy and the Girl.*

1. Jean Arthur.
2. A bank clerk.
3. New York.
4. A bus tour going out west.
5. Fairfield, Oregon.
6. To enter a rodeo.
7. Charles Winninger.
8. His horse.
9. Sammy.
10. Wayne falls into Arthur's lap.
11. She is taking his picture.
12. Shooting craps, drinking and watching Wayne fight.
13. Phil Silvers.
14. Her bus.
15. On a pool table.
16. The horse's blanket.
17. The horse gets sick.
18. Three.
19. Grant Withers.
20. Hans Conreid.

Wayne and Randolph Scott fight in an elevator shaft in *Pittsburgh*.

Wayne looks in proper form at the rodeo in *A Lady Takes a Chance*.

In Old Oklahoma (1944), REPUBLIC

1. In what year does the film take place?
2. Who is Wayne's female co-star, who plays Catherine Allen?
3. Who is the actor who plays Jim Gardner?
4. In what city does Catherine meet him?
5. In what do they meet?
6. What is Wayne carrying when he boards the train?
7. How does Wayne stop Gardner from hurting a worker?
8. Who is the actor who plays the Indian interpreter?
9. What does Wayne tell the Indians to do about the land offer?
10. What is the new word the Indian chief learns?
11. What are Wayne and Gardner doing while separated by a curtain?
12. Who is the actor who plays the Cherokee Kid?
13. What does he dynamite?
14. How does Wayne know where the Cherokee Kid is hiding in Gardner's office?
15. Who is the actress who plays "Cuddles"?
16. What does Wayne "borrow" from Gardner to reach oil?
17. Which U.S. president appears in the film?
18. Who plays the president?
19. How does Wayne plan to get the oil to market?
20. What oil refinery city is Wayne's destination?

AUTHOR'S NOTE: When *In Old Oklahoma* was reissued in the 1950's, the new title was *War of the Wildcats.* Some writers have believed these two titles to be two different films. They are not.

1. 1906.
2. Martha Scott.
3. Albert Dekker.
4. Sapulpa, Oklahoma.
5. His private train car.
6. His saddle.
7. Wayne trips Dekker with a whip.
8. Gabby Hayes.
9. Wayne tells the Indians to refuse the offer.
10. "Suckers."
11. They are taking a bath in separate tubs.
12. Paul Fix.
13. Wayne's rig.
14. Wayne looks in a mirror.
15. Dale Evans.
16. A portable rig.
17. President Theodore Roosevelt.
18. Sidney Blackmer.
19. By wagons.
20. Tulsa.

The Fighting Seabees (1944), REPUBLIC

1. What is Wayne in the film?
2. What does c.b. stand for?
3. Name Wayne's female co-star, who plays Constance Chesley.
4. What is her occupation?
5. Name the actor who plays Lt. Commander Yarrow.
6. What is Wayne's argument concerning the loss of his men?
7. What type of dance does Wayne do at one of their parties?
8. Why is Constance denied a seat at the table with empty chairs?
9. Name the actor who plays Captain Joyce.
10. Captain Joyce tells Wayne to recruit a battalion of men. How many men are left for Wayne to recruit?
11. What is Wayne's new rank?
12. What woman's name is used on the bulldozer?
13. How does Wayne cause the deaths of some of his men?
14. How is Constance wounded?
15. Name the actor who plays Wayne's good friend, killed by a sniper.
16. What is he doing when he is shot?
17. What is placed on the bulldozer to destroy the fuel tanks?
18. What is the purpose of this act?
19. How does Wayne meet his fate?
20. Who are the two actors from *In Old Oklahoma* who appear in this film.

AUTHOR'S NOTE: This would be the first Wayne film in which he would fight the Japanese on land.

1. A construction boss.
2. Construction battalion.
3. Susan Hayward.
4. A news reporter.
5. Dennis O'Keefe.
6. The engineers aren't permitted to defend themselves from attack.
7. Jitterbug
8. The empty chairs belong to men who have died.
9. Addison Richards.
10. "1099."
11. Lt. Commander.
12. "Natasha."
13. A crossfire is set up as Wayne attacks, causing heavy losses.
14. A Japanese soldier shoots her.
15. William Frawley.
16. He is opening a valve on the first oil flow going into the tanks.
17. Dynamite.
18. To flood the valley with fuel, destroying the Japanese.
19. Wayne is shot by a sniper as the bulldozer rams into a fuel tank.
20. Grant Withers and Paul Fix.

Tall in the Saddle (1944), RKO

1. What is the name of the town Wayne arrives in at the film's start?
2. Wayne's new job is to be foreman of what ranch?
3. What has happened to the man who originally sent for him?
4. Who is the actress who plays Arly Harolday?
5. Why does Wayne refuse the job?
6. What is the name of Arly's ranch?
7. Why doe she want Wayne hired?
8. Why does the heiress Clara write Wayne a letter?
9. Who is the actor who plays the stage driver?
10. During the poker game Wayne leaves and returns with his gun. Why?
11. After the girl shoots at Wayne, where does he go to escape?
12. Who is the actor who intimidates Wayne at the bar?
13. Where is Wayne then sent to work?
14. Who does Clara's aunt want to handle her legal affairs?
15. Why do Wayne and the judge have a fight?
16. Where does this fight take place?
17. What character eventually kills the film's bad guy?
18. What is Wayne actually discovered to be at the film's end?
19. Which film co-star wrote the script?
20. This was the first film Wayne worked in with what producer, who would later become his partner.

AUTHOR'S NOTE: Wayne liked the script written by Paul Fix. Wayne was making career decisions with the assistance of Robert Fellows.

1. Santa Inez.
2. KC Ranch.
3. He was killed mysteriously.
4. Ella Raines.
5. The new ranch owners are female.
6. Santee.
7. So Raines can fire him immediately.
8. She wants Wayne's help.
9. Gabby Hayes.
10. He is accused of cheating.
11. The saloon.
12. Paul Fix.
13. A line camp.
14. Ward Bond.
15. Wayne finds marked cards in Bond's office.
16. Bond's office.
17. Tala the Bodyguard.
18. The nephew of the murdered man.
19. Paul Fix.
20. Robert Fellows.

Flame of Barbary Coast (1945), REPUBLIC

1. Which state is Wayne from?
2. What is his film role?
3. Which city is the film's background?
4. Why does Wayne travel there?
5. Name the actor who plays Tito Morell.
6. What is the name of the place Morell owns?
7. Name the actress who plays Flaxen.
8. By what name is Flaxen also known in the film?
9. Why does she give Wayne a good time while gambling?
10. What does Flaxen give Wayne after his money is gone?
11. How does Wayne make money in order to return?
12. What new knowledge has he acquired?
13. Name the actor who plays Wayne's teacher.
14. What does Wayne do with his winnings?
15. What is the name Wayne gives to the business?
16. Who wants all of the gambling stopped on the Coast?
17. What event occurs while Flaxen sings?
18. What injury does she incur?
19. Where do Wayne and Flaxen journey at the film's end?
20. What star of *Gone With the Wind* appears in this film.

AUTHOR'S NOTE: Republic Pictures celebrated its 10th anniversary with the release of *Flame of Barbary Coast.*

1. Montana.
2. A cattleman and rancher.
3. San Francisco.
4. To collect money that is owed him.
5. Joseph Schildkraut.
6. The El Dorado.
7. Ann Dvorak.
8. "Flame of the Barbary Coast."
9. She wants to make Morell jealous.
10. A ticket back home.
11. Wayne sells his cattle.
12. Wayne has learned about cards and luck.
13. William Frawley.
14. Wayne opens a gambling palace.
15. The Silver Dollar.
16. The newspaper editor.
17. The San Francisco earthquake occurs.
18. She is paralyzed for a short time.
19. Back to Montana.
20. Butterfly McQueen.

Paul Fix gets the drop on Wayne as Albert Dekker and Martha Scott watch *In Old Oklahoma.*

Wayne proposes protection of his men to Addison Richards as Dennis O'Keefe listens in *The Fighting Seabees.*

Wayne is taken out of action for a short time in *Tall in the Saddle*.

Wayne tells Ann Dvorak his opening is on schedule in *Flame of Barbary Coast*.

Back to Bataan (1945), RKO

1. What is Wayne's military objective in the film?
2. Who is Wayne's co-star, who plays Andres Bonifacio?
3. Who is the actress who plays the school teacher?
4. During the first battle, what happens to Wayne?
5. What happens to the school principal?
6. Why?
7. Who is the character actor who plays the principal?
8. What happens to the Jap officer who hanged the principal?
9. What is the relation of Andres to the original guerrilla leader?
10. Who is the actor who plays the cook?
11. What is the character name of the boy pupil who wants to fight?
12. What is his idea of freedom?
13. How does Andres's ex-girlfriend aid the Japanese?
14. In what city does Andres discover she is with the allies?
15. What is the name of the Jap colonel who is after Wayne?
16. What is Maximo's grief?
17. How do the Japs find Wayne's headquarters?
18. What does Wayne give Maximo before he dies?
19. What is the name of the society Wayne wants?
20. What do the Filipinos wait for on the beach?

AUTHOR'S NOTE: This would be Wayne's last war film during the final months of World War II.

1. To organize guerrilla activities.
2. Anthony Quinn.
3. Beulah Bondi.
4. Wayne is blown out of a foxhole.
5. He is hanged.
6. He refuses to lower the American flag.
7. Vladimir Sokoloff.
8. He is hanged by Wayne's forces.
9. He is the grandson.
10. Paul Fix.
11. Maximo.
12. A hot dog with mustard and relish.
13. By radio broadcasting advising the Filipinos to surrender.
14. Manila.
15. Kuroki.
16. His brother had been killed by the Japs.
17. Maximo is tortured by the Japs.
18. Wayne's colonel's Silver Eagle.
19. Katipunan.
20. A submarine with Wayne, supplies and good news.

They Were Expendable (1945), MGM

1. What is Wayne's billing in the film?
2. Who wrote the film's screenplay?
3. Name the actor who plays Lt. John Brickley.
4. What is the PT boat duty after Pearl Harbor is bombed?
5. Where is the PT boat squadron based?
6. What is the first target?
7. Why doesn't Wayne go on the mission?
8. Name the character actor who appears with Wayne in the hospital.
9. Name the actress who plays nurse Lt. Sandy Davyss.
10. What does Wayne kick to curb his frustration?
11. What are the orders that shorten Wayne's romance?
12. How does Wayne communicate with Davis the last time?
13. From what island are the officers evacuated?
14. Name the main officer they evacuate.
15. Where are the officers to be delivered?
16. How does Wayne lose his PT boat in action?
17. Name the actor who plays "Boats."
18. What group eventually takes charge of the PT boats?
19. Why are Wayne and Lt. Brickley sent to the states?
20. Name the film's director.

AUTHOR'S NOTE: The war was over when this film was released. In December, 1945, the public tried to forget the war and movies made about the war. The film flopped.

1. Wayne is billed second.
2. Frank Wead (Spig).
3. Robert Montgomery.
4. Messenger duty.
5. Manila Bay.
6. A cruiser in Subic Bay.
7. Wayne has an infected hand.
8. Louis Jean Heydt.
9. Donna Reed.
10. A bucket

11. To evacuate officers.
12. By phone.
13. Corregidor.
14. General MacArthur.
15. Mindanao.
16. The boat is machine-gunned by a plane.
17. Ward Bond.
18. The army.
19. To organize PT boat squadrons.
20. John Ford.

Dakota (1945), REPUBLIC

1. What is the occupation of Wayne's future father-in-law?
2. Who is Wayne's female co-star, playing Sandy Poli?
3. Where does she decide that they should settle?
4. What is her plan?
5. How does she obtain money for the honeymoon?
6. What is the stagecoach destination of Wayne and Sandy?
7. Who is the actor traveling with them, named Jim Bender?
8. What town do the bad guys almost own?
9. Who is the character actor who plays Big Tree Collins?
10. Who is blamed for the land burnings?
11. What is the name of the boat Wayne and Sandy travel on?
12. Who is the actor who plays Captain Bounce?
13. What is the character name of his first mate?
14. Who are the two actors who steal Wayne's money?
15. Why doesn't Wayne's gun fire as he attempts to shoot them?
16. With what group does Wayne team up to save Dakota?
17. Who eventually restores order?
18. How does Ward Bond meet his fate?
19. What does Sandy invest the money in at the film's end?
20. What is Wayne's intended destination?

AUTHOR'S NOTE: This was the first teaming of Wayne and Vera Hruba Ralston. Ralston was the main female lead at Republic Pictures.

1. He is a railroad tycoon.
2. Vera Hruba Ralston.
3. North Dakota.
4. To buy land options and sell to the railroad at profit.
5. She sells her father's paintings.
6. Fort Abercrombie.
7. Ward Bond.
8. Fargo.
9. Mike Mazurki.
10. The Indians.
11. *The River Bird.*
12. Walter Brennan.
13. Nicodemus.
14. Grant Withers and Paul Fix.
15. His wife took the bullets out of his gun.
16. The wheat farmers.
17. The cavalry.
18. Mazurki shoots him.
19. Brennan's new riverboat.
20. California.

Without Reservations (1946), RKO

1. Why is Claudette Colbert going to Hollywood?
2. What is Colbert's pen name?
3. What is the name of her book?
4. What is Wayne in the film?
5. Colbert is in the upper train berth. Who is in the lower berth?
6. What is Wayne's opinion of the book.
7. What does she see in Wayne?
8. Who is the actor who plays Wayne's friend Dink?
9. What is the city Colbert switches trains in?
10. What comedian receives an autograph from Colbert?
11. What is the comical interlude in the coach?
12. After all three are kicked off the train, how do they travel?
13. Where do Wayne and Colbert say they love each other?
14. Why is Colbert arrested?
16. Who aids Colbert when her identity is known?
17. At what final destination do Wayne and Dink arrive?
18. Who is the columnist who portrays herself in the film?
19. Who is the movie actor who plays himself in the film?
20. Who is the film's director?

AUTHOR'S NOTE: Wayne would work with Mervyn LeRoy again. In 1967, Wayne had an eye inflammation that hampered some of his directorial duties on *The Green Berets*. LeRoy was brought in to aid with the filming until Wayne recovered.

1. To write the screen version of her book.
2. Christopher "Kit" Madden.
3. *Here is Tomorrow.*
4. A marine flyer.
5. Wayne, of course.
6. He despises it.
7. He is the ideal hero to play the lead in the movie.
8. Don DeFore.
9. Chicago.
10. Jack Benny.
11. Wayne teaches Colbert how to fly by propping furniture up in the guise of a plane.
12. By used car.
13. In a haystack.
14. She writes a bad check.
15. They sell the car.
16. A Hollywood producer.
17. The San Diego Marine Base.
18. Louella Parsons.
19. Cary Grant.
20. Mervyn LeRoy.

Wayne heads for the nearest foxhole in *Back to Bataan*.

Wayne takes a phone call as Robert Montgomery listens in *They Were Expendable*.

Mike Mazurki (in background) watches as Wayne gets punched in *Dakota*.

Wayne has a chat with a senorita in *Without Reservations*.

Angel and the Badman (1947), REPUBLIC

1. What is the film's first scene?
2. Name the actress who plays the "Angel."
3. Where does Wayne travel to at the film's start?
4. What is the last name of the Quaker family who aid Wayne?
5. What is the "Angel's" first name?
6. Whose deputy was Wayne at one time?
7. Whom does Wayne talk of in his sleep as he recovers?
8. What has the Quaker's neighbor done to their crops?
9. What is the character name of Wayne's best friend?
10. Name the actor who plays Marshal Wistful McLintock.
11. Name the actor who plays Laredo Stevens.
12. What is the dispute Wayne has with him?
13. What is wrong with Wayne's gun as he questions Stevens?
14. What is Wayne given at the prayer meeting?
15. From what are Wayne and the "Angel" returning when they're ambushed?
16. Where does Stevens await Wayne before the gunfight?
17. What happens to Wayne's gun before the gunfight?
18. Who eventually kills Stevens and his gang?
19. What happens to Wayne?
20. In what way was this film a first for Wayne.

AUTHOR'S NOTE: While on the Republic Pictures backlot, Wayne was always "Duke" to everybody. Since he was producer for the first time on this film, the crew thought Wayne should be addressed as "Mr. Wayne." The problem was solved on the shooting's first day when someone said "Mr. Wayne" four times before receiving an answer from "Duke." Wayne was always "Duke," no matter what level he attained.

1. Wayne is fanning his pistol.
2. Gail Russell.
3. The telegraph office.
4. Worth.
5. Penelope.
6. Wyatt Earp.
7. The other women he has known.
8. He has dammed the water so the crops can't grow.
9. Randy McCall.
10. Harry Carey, Sr.
11. Bruce Cabot.
12. Cabot had killed Wayne's foster father.
13. His pistol is empty.
14. A Bible.
15. They are returning from an outing.
16. The saloon.
17. The girl takes the gun from Wayne.
18. The marshal.
19. The pistol is dropped in the street and Wayne retires.
20. Wayne was film producer for the first time.

Wayne holds Bruce Cabot and friends at bay as Gail
Russell watches in *Angel and the Badman*.

Wayne, Paul Fix and the crew aid a fallen comrade in
Tycoon.

Tycoon (1947), RKO

1. What is Wayne's occupation?
2. Name the actor who plays the wealthy railroad owner.
3. What does he want built?
4. What does Wayne want to build instead?
5. What mountain chain is the film's backdrop?
6. Name Wayne's female co-star.
7. Where does Wayne follow her the first time he sees her?
8. Name the actor who plays her cousin.
9. Where do Wayne and the girl go for secrecy?
10. What happens to Wayne's jeep while they are there?
11. Where do they spend the night?
12. What is the name of the boy character in Wayne's camp?
13. What happens when the tunnel roof collapses?
14. What is Wayne's vengeance?
15. How many days extension is Wayne given to finish the bridge?
16. How does Wayne cut costs while building the bridge?
17. Name the actor who plays the dynamiter.
18. Who brings Wayne's friends back to him?
19. What threatens to destroy the bridge at the film's end?
20. What prevents the bridge from collapsing?

1. A tunnel and bridge builder.
2. Sir Cedric Hardwicke.
3. He wants a tunnel built through the mountains.
4. Wayne wants to build a bridge.
5. Andes.
6. Laraine Day.
7. To church.
8. Anthony Quinn.
9. The jungle.
10. The jeep runs out of gas.
11. By an Inca ruin.
12. Chico.
13. One of Wayne's friends dies.
14. Wayne dynamites the tunnel.
15. 90 days.
16. He disregards safety regulations.
17. Paul Fix.
18. Laraine Day.
19. A rainstorm brings flood waters.
20. A train engine adds support.

Fort Apache (1948), RKO

1. What is the name of Henry Fonda's character?
2. Who is the actress who plays Fonda's daughter?
3. What is the dance for at the film's start?
4. Who is the actor who plays the lieutenant accompanying Fonda?
5. What is the first difference between Wayne and Fonda?
6. Who is the actor who plays Meacham the Indian Agent?
7. What does Wayne tell the four sergeants to destroy in the warehouse?
8. Who is the actor who accompanies Wayne to the Indian parley?
9. What did Wayne rescue him from at the fort?
10. Who is the Indian chief Wayne wants to parley with?
11. As Wayne returns from the parley, what is happening in the fort?
12. Who plays the captain who is awaiting the message that comes too late?
13. What does Fonda accuse Wayne of before the final battle?
14. How does Wayne answer this accusation?
15. Where is Wayne during the attack?
16. Where is Fonda wounded during the battle?
17. What does Fonda request from Wayne before the final battle?
18. Whose portrait is on the wall after the attack?
19. What does Wayne see as he looks out the window?
20. What does Wayne wear that belonged to Fonda?

AUTHOR'S NOTE: *Fort Apache* is the first film of the John Ford cavalry trilogy. *She Wore a Yellow Ribbon* and *Rio Grande* would follow shortly.

1. Colonel Owen Thursday.
2. Shirley Temple.
3. To celebrate Washington's Birthday.
4. John Agar.
5. The number of men and ammunition needed for a burial detail.
6. Grant Withers.
7. The whiskey shipment.
8. Pedro Armendariz.
9. Shoveling manure.
10. Cochise.
11. The Non-Commissioned Officer's Dance.
12. George O'Brien.
13. Cowardice.
14. Wayne throws his gauntlet in front of Fonda.
15. Wayne is with the supply wagons in safety.
16. In the head.
17. Wayne's horse and saber.
18. Fonda's portrait.
19. The image of the dead troopers.
20. His kepi (hat).

Wayne and Pedro Armendariz enter the Apache camp in *Fort Apache.*

Wayne kicks Montgomery Clift in the climactic fight of *Red River*.

Red River (1948), UNITED ARTISTS

1. Name the actress who plays Fen.
2. What does Wayne find on the Indian he killed with a knife?
3. Who first falls victim to Wayne when he arrives in Texas?
4. How many years have passed since the film's start?
5. Name the actor who plays Matt.
6. What do Matt and Cherry Valance discuss as they test their shooting skills?
7. What is the original destination of the cattle drive?
8. What is the first crisis on the trail drive?
9. What is Wayne's intention towards Kenneally after the funeral?
10. Where is Wayne wounded when he shoots the mutineers?
11. Who is the actor who shoots Wayne's gun out of his reach?
12. What is the new destination after the mutiny?
13. Name the actress who plays Tess Millay.
14. Name the actress briefly seen during the dance sequence after the Indian attack.
15. Where does Millay hide her gun while talking with Wayne?
16. Name the actor who plays the Abilene cattle buyer.
17. Which character tries to stop Wayne from shooting Matt?
18. Where does he wound Wayne?
19. Where does Wayne shoot Matt in the showdown?
20. Who wrote the original story?

AUTHOR'S NOTE: In the *Red River* script, there was a scene where Wayne cuts a finger and the finger has to be amputated. Wayne said this scene wasn't right and refused to film. The scene was used four years later in *The Big Sky*. It was one of the film's highlights. Upon seeing the film, Wayne told Director Howard Hawks the idea was good.

1. Coleen Gray.
2. The bracelet Wayne had given Fen.
3. A Mexican gunman.
4. "Fourteen, near to fifteen."
5. Montgomery Clift.
6. The value of a good Swiss watch and a woman from anywhere.
7. Missouri.
8. A stampede.
9. Wayne wants to whip him for starting the stampede.
10. In the leg.
11. Noah Beery, Jr.
12. Abilene, Kansas.
13. Joanne Dru.
14. Shelley Winters.
15. In her sling.
16. Harry Carey, Sr.
17. Cherry Valance.
18. The left side of the waist.
19. The right cheek.
20. Borden Chase.

Three Godfathers (1948), MGM

1. What is the tribute at the film's start to Harry Carey, Sr.?
2. What is the name of the town in which Wayne and company arrive?
3. What is Wayne's plan?
4. What happens to the robbers during their escape across the flatlands?
5. What is the name of the watering hole?
6. Name the actress who plays the new mother.
7. Which one of the godfathers delivers the baby?
8. At what train stop does the posse guard the water?
9. How does Wayne comfort the kid before he dies?
10. What brings about Pete's injury?
11. What Bible passage does the wind find for Wayne in the cave?
12. To what town does Wayne bring the baby?
13. What is the name of the saloon to which Wayne brings the baby?
14. On what day does Wayne bring the baby to town?
15. What is Wayne's dinner before the verdict is given?
16. Why doesn't Wayne sign the release for the baby?
17. What is Wayne's prison sentence?
18. Name the actor who plays the judge.
19. What is Wayne's character's middle name?
20. What is Wayne's responsibility on the train?

AUTHOR'S NOTE: During filming, Director John Ford allowed no drinking on the set. One day, Ford told Wayne he wasn't needed for the next day's shooting. That night, Wayne went drinking and Ford heard about it. He reworked the shooting schedule, and the scene where Wayne has the chicken dinner before going to prison was scheduled. Wayne got the call and was told to report for shooting. He had a massive hangover. After shooting the scene with greasy chicken several times, Wayne decided to obey Ford and discontinued the drinking bouts while filming!

1. "The Bright Star of the Early Western Sky."
2. Welcome, Arizona.
3. To rob the bank.
4. Their water bag is shot.
5. Terrapin Tanks.
6. Mildred Natwick.
7. Pedro Armendariz.
8. Mojave Wells.
9. Wayne uses his hat to shield his face from the sun.
10. He breaks his leg when falling into a gopher hole.
11. Matthew 23: 1,2.
12. New Jerusalem.
13. Last Chance Saloon.
14. Christmas Eve.
15. A chicken dinner.
16. He had promised the baby's mother he would care for the baby.
17. One year and one day.
18. Guy Kibbee.
19. Marmaduke.
20. Wayne is to watch the deputy and make sure he gets safely on the right train for home.

Wake of the Red Witch (1948), REPUBLIC

1. What was the cargo of the sunken *Red Witch*?
2. Name the actor who plays Wayne's first mate.
3. What is the character name of the tyrant?
4. What is the name of his trading empire?
5. How do Wayne and the tyrant meet for the first time?
6. What group of islands is Wayne rescued from?
7. Name Wayne's female co-star?
8. How many flashbacks are there in the film?
9. Who relates the first flashback?
10. What is the name of the court at which Wayne must appear?
11. What guards the cavern Wayne must enter?
12. What is Wayne's objective in the cave?
13. Name the actor who plays the French commissioner.
14. How does he meet his fate?
15. What has happened to the tyrant since Wayne saw him last?
16. How many years pass before Wayne sees the heroine again?
17. How does she meet her fate?
18. Why does Wayne make the dive at the film's end?
19. What is occurring as this takes place?
20. What is the last scene in the film?

AUTHOR'S NOTE: Wayne named his production company "Batjac Productions" after the name of the trading empire in *Wake of The Red Witch*. Wayne's company ended in a "c" whereas the one in the film ended in a "k."

1. $5,000,000 in gold bullion.
2. Gig Young.
3. Sidneye.
4. Batjak.
5. Wayne is adrift, tied to a wooden cross. He is rescued by Sidneye.
6. Gilbert Islands.
7. Gail Russell.
8. Two.
9. Adele Mara.
10. Maritime Commission.
11. An octopus.
12. Pearls.
13. Henry Daniell.
14. Wayne knocks him into a ritual fire.
15. He is crippled by a tropical disease.
16. Seven.
17. A tropical disease.
18. To get the gold off of *The Red Witch*.
19. A storm rolls in.
20. The ghostly *Red Witch* sails away.

The Fighting Kentuckian (1949), REPUBLIC

1. In what state is the film set?
2. What type of army is Wayne in?
3. Who is Wayne's female co-star who plays Fleurette DeMarchand?
4. In what city does Wayne meet her at the film's start?
5. Who is the actor who plays Wayne's sidekick Willie Paine.
6. Who is the actor who plays Captain Carroll?
7. Why has the French general brought his people to the south?
8. What group does Grant Withers lead?
9. What gets tossed around at the "free for all"?
10. How does Wayne manage to enter the big party?
11. Who is the actor who plays Beau Meritt?
12. What is the name of the proposed town?
13. What does Willie give Wayne to call on Fleurette?
14. Name the actress who plays Ann Logan.
15. Where is Wayne shot while holding a land marker?
16. What is Ann next to when she meets her fate?
17. What is the swindle that is revealed?
18. Who is the actor imprisoned with Wayne?
19. What is the fate of Withers?
20. Who comes to the rescue of Wayne and everyone concerned?

AUTHOR'S NOTE: This was the first film in which Chuck Roberson doubled as a stunt man for John Wayne. In Roberson's book *The Fall Guy,* he explains how the meeting of Wayne would change his life as he would double Wayne throughout his career. Roberson did appear in *Wake of The Red Witch* in a fight sequence not involving Wayne.

1. Alabama.
2. A Kentucky Regiment.
3. Vera Hruba Ralston.
4. Mobile.
5. Oliver Hardy.
6. Jack Pennick.
7. The French want to settle the area.
8. The rivermen.
9. A whiskey jug.
10. Wayne pretends to be a fiddler.
11. Paul Fix.
12. Demopolis.
13. His dress hat.
14. Marie Windsor.
15. His left hand.
16. By an empty safe as some coins pour onto the floor.
17. The French markers for the survey have been moved.
18. John Howard.
19. His own horsemen trample him to death.
20. Wayne's army comrades.

Harry Carey, Jr. and Pedro Armendariz make preparations as Wayne holds the baby in *Three Godfathers.*

"The Red Witch" comes between Wayne and Gail Russell in *Wake of The Red Witch.*

Wayne and Hugo Haas appear to be museum pieces in *The Fighting Kentuckian*.

She Wore a Yellow Ribbon (1949), RKO

1. Whose death does Wayne discuss with his wife in the graveyard?
2. How many years has Wayne's wife been dead?
3. Who will get command of the fort when Wayne retires?
4. Name the actor who plays Major Allshard.
5. Name the actress the two lieutenants fight over.
6. What is the name of the Confederate trooper who dies?
7. Name the character actor who plays the bugler.
8. What is the sergeant's fond name for Wayne?
9. Why is the sergeant incarcerated?
10. What is the present Wayne receives at his final troop review?
11. Name the two actors who are with Wayne when the gunrunners are killed.
12. What is Wayne doing when the gunrunners are killed?
13. What is the name of the Indian chief Wayne has known for years?
14. Who does Wayne take to the Indian camp with him?
15. What does Wayne study in the Indian camp?
16. What is Wayne's plan?
17. What is the army dispatch Wayne receives at the film's end?
18. What is his new rank?
19. What does Wayne take to his wife's grave?
20. Who did the Academy Award-winning photography?

AUTHOR'S NOTE: Wayne said in many interviews that this film was his favorite. Wayne was in his early 40's when he played the part of a 65-year-old army officer. This acting challenge contributed to Wayne's role.

This was the first film in which Wayne had a moustache. The other three films in which he had a moustache are *Rio Grande, The Conqueror* and *The Shootist.*

1. General Custer, Captain Keough and the others killed at Little Big Horn.
2. Nine.
3. John Agar.
4. George O'Brien.
5. Joanne Dru.
6. Private Smith.
7. Frank McGrath.
8. "Captain Darling."
9. So he can receive a peaceful retirement due in two weeks.
10. A silver watch.
11. Ben Johnson and Harry Carey, Jr.
12. Chewing tobacco.
13. Pony-That-Walks.
14. Sgt. Tyree (Ben Johnson).
15. Where the horses are picketed.
16. To stampede the Indian horses and humiliate the Indians.
17. Notification that he is made Chief Of Scouts
18. Lt. Colonel.
19. Flowers.
20. Winton Hoch.

Sergeant Victor McLaglen tells Wayne his retirement day is at hand in *She Wore a Yellow Ribbon*.

1704 X54

Wayne, Director John Ford and Ward Bond discuss a
scene on the set of *The Wings of Eagles*.

THE 1950's

Sands of Iwo Jima (1950), REPUBLIC

1. What is Wayne's military rank?
2. In which branch of the service is Wayne?
3. Name the actor who plays Corporal Al Thomas.
4. Name the actor who plays Private First Class Conway.
5. Name the actor who plays Private First Class Charlie Bass.
6. Name the actor Wayne trains to use a bayonet properly.
7. Name the actor who plays Private First Class Dan Shipley.
8. On what island is the squad's first battle?
9. Which squad member is killed attemping to destroy a bunker?
10. What is Wayne's heroic act?
11. Which squad member calls for Wayne on the battlefield at night?
12. Why does Wayne start a fight with Corporal Thomas?
13. Name the actress who Conway marries.
14. What causes Wayne to be wounded in the grenade throwing area?
15. What is the character name of the prostitute Wayne encounters?
16. What does Wayne discover in her bedroom?
17. How does Wayne meet his fate?
18. Which squad member gets revenge?
19. What does Conway read that Wayne started?
20. Where is the flag raised when the battle is over?

AUTHOR'S NOTE: Wayne had his footprints placed at Grauman's Chinese Theatre for the opening of *Sands of Iwo Jima*. The sand used for the event was literally from Iwo Jima. Two 100 pound sacks were used for the footprints and handprints.

Sands of Iwo Jima was released briefly in 1949 to qualify for the Academy Awards of 1949. The general release was in 1950.

1. Sergeant.
2. Marine Corps.
3. Forrest Tucker.
4. John Agar.
5. James Brown.
6. Hal Baylor.
7. Richard Webb.
8. Tarawa.
9. Shipley.
10. Wayne throws a satchel charge into a bunker, destroying it.
11. Bass.
12. Tucker delayed returning to his friends, which resulted in their deaths. When Wayne discovers this, he fights Tucker.
13. Adele Mara.
14. While Agar is reading a letter from his wife, a grenade lands by him and Wayne pushes him out of the way.
15. Mary.
16. A baby boy.
17. He is shot in the back by a sniper.
18. Bass.
19. Wayne's unfinished letter to his son.
20. Mt. Suribachi.

Rio Grande (1950), REPUBLIC

1. What appears on Wayne's face for the first time in this film?
2. What is the incident Wayne and Maureen O'Hara share from the past?
3. Who was the actor who burned O'Hara's plantation?
4. How many years have Wayne and O'Hara been separated?
5. Why does O'Hara arrive at Wayne's fort?
6. Who is the actor who plays Wayne's son Jeff?
7. Why does he enlist in the army?
8. What medicine is he given after fighting with a fellow soldier?
9. Who arrives after dinner to serenade O'Hara?
10. What is O'Hara's duty while she is at the fort?
11. Who is the actor who plays General Sheridan?
12. What are his unofficial orders to Wayne?
13. What does he promise Wayne before the mission?
14. Why does Actor Ben Johnson elude the law?
15. What do the Indians take after stopping the wagon train?
16. Who is the volunteer sent to find Wayne after the kidnapping?
17. Who is the scout sent to the Indian camp to prepare the escape?
18. Who are Johnson's two volunteers for the mission?
19. Where are the children being held?
20. Where is Wayne wounded?

AUTHOR'S NOTE: In the synopsis of the *Rio Grande* pressbook, (a manual theatre owners use for advertising and promotion of a film) a sequence is mentioned that occurs after the heroes are given medals. Wayne is sent to the Court of St. James's as U.S. Military attache in England. This trip to England brings Wayne and O'Hara closer together. This sequence was edited out and deservedly so. The present film ending serves well.

1. A moustache and small lower lip growth, together.
2. Wayne ordered the burning of O'Hara's plantation.
3. Victor McLaglen.
4. Fifteen.
5. O'Hara wants to buy her son out of the army.
6. Claude Jarman, Jr.
7. He had failed at West Point.
8. Castor oil.
9. The Regimental Singers (Sons of The Pioneeers).
10. A Laundress.
11. J. Carrol Naish.
12. To cross the Mexican border and defeat the Indians.
13. To personally select the court martial board.
14. To help save his sister's reputation.
15. The children leaving the fort.
16. Jarman.
17. Ben Johnson.
18. Harry Carey, Jr., and Jarman.
19. An old church.
20. In the chest, by an arrow.

Operation Pacific (1951), WARNER BROTHERS

1. What different part of the service is depicted in this film?
2. What is Wayne doing in his first scene?
3. What is the name of the film's submarine?
4. Who is the actor who plays Wayne's C.O.?
5. Who is Wayne's female co-star?
6. Why does she dislike Wayne?
7. Why is there a barrier between the two?
8. What is the nickname she calls Wayne?
9. Who plays the young flier she likes?
10. What is the tie between Wayne and the flier?
11. Why does a freighter force the sub to dive?
12. Why is there resentment between Wayne and the flier?
13. What is the sub plot of the film (the other story line)?
14. Who is the actor who plays the chief?
15. Who is the actor who plays Jonesy?
16. Where does the crew receive leave?
17. Why is the crew arrested?
18. What is the sub's new duty?
19. Who rescues the flier Wayne dislikes?
20. Where is Wayne wounded?

AUTHOR'S NOTE: *Operation Pacific* was the first film Wayne did with Warner Brothers since the 1930's. This was the beginning of a long string of films that brought Warner Brothers and Wayne quite hefty sums of money.

1. The submarine service.
2. Wayne is carrying a baby out of the jungle.
3. *Thunderfish*.
4. Ward Bond.
5. Patricia Neal.
6. Neal is Wayne's ex-wife of four years.
7. Their infant son had died.
8. "Big Ape."
9. Phillip Carey.
10. Bond is Carey's older brother.
11. The seemingly innocent freighter opens fire.
12. Bond drowned because Wayne ordered the sub to dive.
13. Submarine torpedos are defective.
14. Jack Pennick.
15. Paul Picerni.
16. Hawaii.
17. They are blackmailed by shady merchants.
18. To rescue downed pilots.
19. Wayne's sub.
20. Upper right side of the chest.

Flying Leathernecks (1951), RKO

1. Who is Wayne's co-star in the film who plays Captain Carl Griffin?
2. What type of fighting unit does Wayne command?
3. What is the resentment Wayne receives from the crew?
4. At what land area is Wayne training the pilots?
5. What is Wayne's basic argument in the film?
6. What is Griffin's argument in the film?
7. What does every squadron flier have that identifies him?
8. When does Wayne know when to write a letter home about a downed pilot?
9. Who is the actor who plays Griffin's brother-in-law?
10. Who is the actor who plays the scrounger Master Sergeant Clancy?
11. What does he repair for Wayne every time it breaks down?
12. What is on the recording that Wayne likes to hear?
13. What does Clancy steal from the navy on Guadalcanal?
14. Why does he keep getting busted in the film?
15. What does Wayne give his son on a short visit home?
16. What well-known phrase does Griffin quote to Wayne?
17. What popular TV actor plays the ground control officer?
18. How do Wayne and Griffin bury the hatchet?
19. Where does Wayne leave the squadron at the film's end?
20. What injury has Wayne as he departs?

AUTHOR'S NOTE: While working on the film, Wayne asked a marine sergeant about the origin of the word "Leatherneck." The sergeant said this was part of a marine uniform worn around the throat made of black leather. This was used as protection from a "Snickersnee." Wayne then asked what that was. The sergeant said that it was a large knife used to slit the throat.

1. Robert Ryan.
2. A marine flier fighter squadron.
3. The crew and Ryan thought Ryan would be placed in charge.
4. Guadalcanal.
5. That squadron's planes should fly low for ground support.
6. That the planes should fly at higher altitudes and save lives.
7. Each flier has a coffee cup with his name on it.
8. A returning pilot would place a dead pilot's coffee cup on Wayne's desk.
9. Don Taylor.
10. Jay C. Flippen.
11. A record player.
12. The voices of his wife and son.
13. A generator.
14. He keeps getting caught for scrounging.
15. A Japanese sword.
16. "No Man Is an Island."
17. Milburn Stone (Doc Adams of *Gunsmoke*).
18. They get drunk.
19. Okinawa.
20. His arm is in a cast.

Maureen O'Hara and Wayne rekindle the past in *Rio Grande*.

Wayne gives Hal Baylor a bayonet lesson as the squad takes note in *Sands of Iwo Jima*.

Wayne thunders orders as the Japanese close in in
Operation Pacific.

Wayne tightens the formation as danger closes in in
Flying Leathernecks.

The Quiet Man (1952), REPUBLIC

1. Why does Wayne leave the U.S.?
2. Name Wayne's female co-star who plays Mary Kate Danaher?
3. What is she doing when Wayne sees her for the first time?
4. Name the actor who plays Michaeleen Flynn.
5. Name the actor who plays Will Danaher.
6. What does Wayne want to purchase?
7. Who does Wayne find when he returns home on a windy night?
8. What makes her scream as she starts to run away?
9. What does she see going into Wayne's cottage the next day?
10. What is her concern throughout the film?
11. What is the plot to get Mary Kate married?
12. What does Wayne discard on their first outing?
13. Where do they find shelter during a rainstorm?
14. What happens when Wayne is punched at the reception?
15. What does she do on their wedding night that angers Wayne?
16. Where does Wayne sleep on his wedding night?
17. What does Wayne discover about Reverend Playfair?
18. What does a woman give Wayne when he takes Mary Kate to Danaher?
19. What does Mary Kate finally do with the dowry?
20. Who does Wayne bring home to dinner after the fight?

AUTHOR'S NOTE: Republic Pictures Boss Herbert Yates told Director John Ford he wanted the film to last two hours. Ford's final running time was 129 minutes. Yates wanted nine minutes cut. During a screening for Republic distributors, Yates noticed the film hadn't been recut. Ford said nine minutes were gone. During the film's climax, the screen went white. Ford couldn't decide what to edit, so he cut the ending. Yates went with Ford's 129 minute print.

1. Wayne had killed a fighter in the ring.
2. Maureen O'Hara.
3. She is tending a flock of sheep.
4. Barry Fitzgerald.
5 Victor McLaglen.
6. The cottage that was Wayne's birthplace.
7. O'Hara is cleaning inside the cottage.
8. She sees her reflection in a mirror.
9. A double bed.
10. Her dowry must be claimed when she is married.
11. If O'Hara marries Wayne, Danaher could marry the widow.
12. His hat and gloves.
13. A graveyard.
14. A flashback occurs in which Wayne killed a boxer.
15. She bolts the bedroom door.
16. Wayne spends the night in his sleeping bag.
17. He was a prizefighter.
18. A switch.
19. O'Hara opens a furnace door and Wayne burns the dowry.
20. Danaher.

Big Jim McLain (1953), WARNER BROTHERS

1. Whose spirit is heard at the film's start?
2. Where is the hearing room for criminals?
3. Which House committee is the background?
4. What is a Communist guilty of after 1945?
5. Where is Wayne sent to expose the Communists?
6. Name the actor who plays Wayne's partner Mel Baxter.
7. Why are Wayne and Baxter sent to Hawaii?
8. What was Baxter in the past?
9. What is the cover Wayne and Baxter use?
10. Name the actor who plays the Communist leader.
11. What does actress Veda Ann Borg call Wayne?
12. What is the first case in the film?
13. Name Wayne's female co-star.
14. What name does Wayne use as an alias when he meets her?
15. Name the actor coming for the trunk as Wayne talks with Borg.
16. What tips Wayne on how to find ten more Communist agents?
17. How does Wayne discover that the man next to him at the beach restaurant is an agent?
18. Wayne questions a nurse on an island for ———.
19. Where does Wayne see Baxter for the last time?
20. What does Wayne say his condition is when rescued at the film's end?

AUTHOR'S NOTE: Wayne's Americanism is at its peak in *Big Jim McLain*. One would expect no less from the man on the issue of Communism.

1. Daniel Webster.
2. The House of Representatives.
3. Un-American Activities.
4. Treason.
5. Hawaii.
6. James Arness.
7. To expose the Communist spy network.
8. A Korean War hero.
9. A vacation.
10. Alan Napier.
11. "Seventy-six. (That's a lot of man)."
12. An economics professor is sending out microfilm.
13. Nancy Olson.
14. Jim Marshall.
15. Hal Baylor.
16. Unusual insurance policies.
17. The man acts as if he is deaf and disregards the tapping on Wayne's table, which a deaf person would sense.
18. Lepers.
19. The morgue.
20. "Fine. Just fine."

Trouble Along the Way (1953),

WARNER BROTHERS

1. Who is the actor who plays Father Burke?
2. What is Wayne doing when first approached by the Father?
3. Why is Wayne hired?
4. Who is the actress who plays Wayne's daughter?
5. What is the name of the college?
6. How much is the college in debt?
7. Why does Wayne take the job?
8. Who plays Alice Singleton, who according to Wayne, has nice legs?
9. What company is she with?
10. Who is the actress who plays Wayne's ex-wife?
11. Who is the actor who plays Father Malone?
12. Who is the actor who plays Father Provincial?
13. Who is the actor who plays Wayne's buddy Stan?
14. By what method does Wayne get football uniforms?
15. What does Wayne promise the players?
16. How will Wayne get the money?
17. What does Wayne's daughter attend with Alice that causes them to leave early?
18. What is the name of the school the team plays on the field?
19. What does the Father do when he discovers Wayne's plan?
20. Who directed the film?

AUTHOR'S NOTE: Television sets were on the market in 1953. *Trouble Along the Way* disappeared quickly and was one of the lowest grossing Wayne films.

1. Charles Coburn.
2. Wayne is playing pool.
3. To be the football coach.
4. Sherry Jackson.
5. St. Anthony's.
6. $170,000.
7. To justify raising his daughter.
8. Donna Reed.
9. Probation Bureau.
10. Marie Windsor.
11. Tom Tully.
12. Leif Erickson.
13. Chuck Conners.
14. Through blackmail.
15. A piece of the action.
16. By parking charges, selling pennants, etc.
17. A birthday party.
18. Santa Carla.
19. He cancels the rest of the season.
20. Michael Curtiz.

Wayne and Maureen O'Hara strike an unusual wedding pose in *The Quiet Man*.

The climactic fight between Wayne and Victor
McLaglen is almost over in *The Quiet Man*.

Wayne comes out swinging in *Big Jim McLain*.

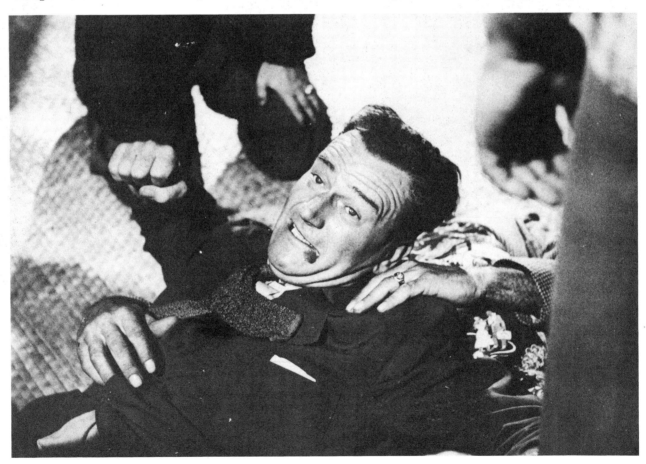

Sherry Jackson looks to Donna Reed as Wayne watches in *Trouble Along the Way*.

Island in the Sky (1953), WARNER BROTHERS

1. What type of plane does Wayne pilot?
2. What type of pilot is Wayne?
3. For what organization does Wayne fly?
4. What is the factory name of Wayne's plane?
5. Where is Wayne's plane forced to land?
6. On what does Wayne's plane land?
7. Name the actor who plays Wayne's co-pilot Lovatt?
8. How many crew members are there on Wayne's plane?
9. How long will the food last?
10. How cold is the weather?
11. Name the actor who plays Col. Fuller back at the base.
12. Name the actor who plays Wayne's friend Stutz.
13. Name the actor who plays McMullen.
14. Who is the "Our Gang" member seen in the film?
15. How are transmitting signals sent from the plane?
16. Who wanders away from the plane and dies?
17. Why do the search planes return to base?
18. What is the decision made by the pilots after returning to the base?
19. What happens during the second sweep of the plane?
20. Who are Wayne's thoughts of in his final scene?

AUTHOR'S NOTE: *Island in the Sky* does not appear on television regularly. I recently viewed the film and found the production to be quite good. The black-and-white photography creates an eerie atmosphere.

1. A four-engine transport plane.
2. Civilian pilot.
3. Army Transport Command.
4. Corsair.
5. North of Labrador.
6. On a frozen lake.
7. Sean McClory.
8. Five.
9. Six-days.
10. −40 degrees.
11. Walter Abel.
12. Lloyd Nolan.
13. James Arness.
14. Alfalfa.
15. By the last battery.
16. McClory.
17. The planes are low on fuel.
18. To fly back over previous flown territory or branch out into a new area. (They decide to fly back over where they had previously searched.)
19. Wayne and company are found.
20. His family.

Hondo (1953), WARNER BROTHERS

1. What is Wayne doing in his first scene?
2. What is Wayne's occupation?
3. Name the actress who plays Angie Lowe.
4. What is the name of Wayne's dog?
5. How does Angie discover Wayne's identity?
6. How does Wayne teach her son to swim?
7. Of whom does Wayne remind Angie?
8. Name the actor who plays Major Sherry.
9. Name the actor who plays Buffalo.
10. Name the actor who plays Angie's husband, Ed Lowe.
11. Why do the Indians show off for Angie?
12. Name the actor who plays Vittoro.
13. How is the boy made blood brother to the Apaches?
14. What is Wayne forced to do to Lowe?
15. How is Wayne tortured by the Apaches?
16. What does Angie tell Vittoro about Wayne?
17. Why is Wayne's life spared?
18. Name the actor who plays Wayne's rival, Lennie.
19. What does Lennie want that belongs to Wayne?
20. What is Wayne's plan for the wagon train's survival?

AUTHOR'S NOTE: Warner Brothers had hoped that Wayne's popularity would help save the floundering 3-D concept. Cinemascope (a wide-screen process) was around the corner and 3-D was on borrowed time. *Hondo* was originally released in 3-D. The film fared decent grosses, but its timeless story has made it a western classic.

1. Walking out of the desert.
2. An army dispatch rider.
3. Geraldine Page.
4. Sam.
5. She sees Wayne's name plate on the rifle butt.
6. Wayne throws the boy into the water and tells him to start grabbing.
7. Wayne's deceased Indian wife.
8. Paul Fix.
9. Ward Bond.
10. Leo Gordon.
11. So Angie can select one Indian for a husband.
12. Michael Pate.
13. His thumb is cut and this is pressed against the Indian's thumb.
14. Wayne shoots him in self defense.
15. Hot coals are placed on Wayne's palms.
16. That Wayne is her husband.
17. Wayne has the boy's picture he took off Lowe's body.
18. James Arness.
19. His rifle.
20. The wagons are to form a circle, then move out, form a circle again, etc. This is designed to disrupt the Apaches.

Wayne peers out of the corsair in *Island in the Sky.*

Wayne approaches Lee Aaker and Geraldine Page in *Hondo.*

The High and the Mighty (1954),

WARNER BROTHERS

1. What is Wayne's role?
2. What is Wayne's personal crisis?
3. Who died in that crisis?
4. What is Wayne holding briefly before he falls to the ground?
5. What is Wayne's permanent injury as a result of the crisis?
6. Name the actor who plays the pilot, Sullivan.
7. From what city does the plane depart?
8. What city is the plane's destination?
9. Name the actor who plays Ed Joseph.
10. Name the actress who plays May Holst.
11. Name the actress who plays Sally McKee.
12. Name the actor who plays Pardee.
13. Name the actor who plays Ken Childs.
14. What is done to lighten the load and save fuel?
15. Name the actor who plays the airport manager, Garfield.
16. What does Paul Fix give the stewardess for safekeeping?
17. What does Wayne wrap carefully in plastic?
18. What does Wayne do to Sullivan to prevent a watery landing?
19. How many gallons of gas does the plane have left?
20. What does Garfield call Wayne as Wayne departs the airport?

AUTHOR'S NOTE: Wayne had endorsed Robert Cummings for the part of Sullivan. Director William Wellman wanted Robert Stack for the part. Stack's role concept was approved and he got the part. When Wayne and Stack met, Wayne said: "Mr. Cummings, I believe." Wayne and Stack became good friends.
The High and the Mighty was the first Wayne film in a Cinemascope (wide-screen) process.

1. Wayne is the co-pilot.
2. Wayne was the only survivor of a plane crash.
3. His wife and son.
4. A teddy bear.
5. A limp.
6. Robert Stack.
7. Honolulu.
8. San Francisco.
9. Phil Harris.
10. Claire Trevor.
11. Jan Sterling.
12. Robert Newton.
13. David Brian.
14. The baggage is thrown out.
15. Regis Toomey.
16. His watch.
17. A picture of his family.
18. Wayne slaps Stack, causing Stack to land the plane.
19. 30 gallons.
20. "So long you ancient pelican."

Wayne checks the back of the plane before disaster strikes in *The High and the Mighty*.

The Sea Chase (1955), WARNER BROTHERS

1. Who is Wayne's female co-star playing Elsa Keller?
2. What is the name of Wayne's ship?
3. What flag does Wayne fly under?
4. Name the actor who plays the British Commander Napier.
5. What harbor does Wayne leave at the film's start?
6. What is the name of the British vessel in pursuit?
7. What is Wayne's destination?
8. How is Wayne's ship disguised?
9. What does Wayne put an axe to on the ship?
10. Who is the actor who plays the German Kirchner?
11. What is the the name of the shipwreck station?
12. Whom does Kirchner murder?
13. How is one of Wayne's officers injured while swimming?
14. What is the officer's fate?
15. Who is the actor who physically matches Wayne in the film?
16. Who is the actor he slashes with an axe?
17. Who is the actor who plays the sentry on the hill?
18. What does Wayne want placed on the lifeboat at the film's end?
19. How is the ship eventually sunk?
20. How does Napier discover Wayne is innocent of the murders?

AUTHOR'S NOTE: Wayne was married to his third wife, Pilar, during the filming of *The Sea Chase* in Hawaii.

1. Lana Turner.
2. *Ergenstrasse.*
3. The German flag.
4. David Farrar.
5. Sidney, Australia.
6. Rockhampton.
7. Valparaiso.
8. As a Panamanian banana boat.
9. The lifeboats.
10. Lyle Bettger.
11. Auckland Island.
12. Six fishermen.
13. He is attacked by a shark.
14. He commits suicide.
15. James Arness.
16. Claude Akins.
17. Paul Fix.
18. Wayne's log.
19. By British shelling.
20. Bettger confessed he was guilty of the killings in the log.

Blood Alley (1955), WARNER BROTHERS

1. What imaginary person does Wayne talk to during the film?
2. What is she?
3. What is Wayne doing when he first meets the ship's engineer?
4. Who is Wayne's female co-star who plays Cathy Grainger?
5. Who is the actor who plays Big Han?
6. How many people are trying to escape?
7. From what area do the people try to escape?
8. What is their destination?
9. What straits must the boat travel through?
10. What is the type of vessel Wayne commands?
11. What is the profession of Cathy's father?
12. Where does Wayne hide the ship charts before they leave?
13. Who plays the Chinese elder?
14. What does the elder look at when in a car?
15. What is the fate of Cathy's father?
16. What is in the graveyard the boat passes through?
17. What happens to the food supply aboard the ship?
18. What does Actor Paul Fix want to be saved from burning?
19. Who is the unrecognized actress who has a minor role?
20. This was Wayne's first venture with what production company?

AUTHOR'S NOTE: The ferry boat used in the film was built by the army as a tow boat for barges at a cost of $200,000. Batjac purchased it from war surplus and added a superstructure disguising the Diesel engine, making it appear as a woodburner.

1. "Baby."
2. She is a composite of all the girls Wayne has known.
3. Wayne is taking a bath.
4. Lauren Bacall.
5. Mike Mazurki.
6. 180.
7. Red China.
8. Hong Kong.
9. Formosa Straits.
10. A ferry boat.
11. A doctor.
12. A hollow bed post.
13. Barry Kroeger.
14. A view master.
15. He is stoned to death.
16. Sunken ships.
17. It is poisoned.
18. Ancient carved wood.
19. Anita Ekberg.
20. Batjac.

The Conqueror (1956), RKO

1. What is Wayne doing in his first scene?
2. Name the actor who plays Wayne's brother Jamuga.
3. Name the actress who plays Bortai.
4. Name the actress who plays Wayne's mother.
5. What tribe does Wayne hate?
6. Why does Wayne want to destroy that tribe?
7. Name the actor who plays Chepei.
8. Name the actor who plays Kasar.
9. What divides Wayne's camp when he returns with Bortai?
10. How does Wayne kill Bortai's betrothed Targutai?
11. What does Bortai throw at Wayne after her seductive dance?
12. How is Wayne wounded in battle?
13. Where does Wayne hide after he is wounded?
14. Name the actor who plays Wayne's enemy Kumlek.
15. How is Wayne restrained as Kumlek's prisoner?
16. What is Wayne's signal for his men to capture the Khan's city?
17. How does Wayne kill Kumlek?
18. What is Jamuga's death wish?
19. What is the meaning of "Genghis Khan"?
20. Where did the location filming take place?

AUTHOR'S NOTE: Wayne's view of his role in *The Conqueror* was that he saw Genghis Khan as a western gunfighter. This "oriental western" didn't fare well at the boxoffice.
Wayne was very good friends with RKO boss Howard Hughes. They shared many outdoor interests.

1. Wayne is on horseback riding down a hill, holding a hunting bird.
2. Pedro Armendariz.
3. Susan Hayward.
4. Agnes Moorehead.
5. The Tarters.
6. The Tarter chief had killed his father.
7. Lee Van Cleef.
8. William Conrad.
9. Wayne wants to take Hayward for his wife.
10. Wayne kills him with a broken spear.
11. A sword.
12. By an arrow.
13. In a cave.
14. Ted de Corsia.
15. Tied to a yoke.
16. By flaming arrow.
17. A knife.
18. To be killed.
19. "Perfect Warrior."
20. St. George, Utah. (Nearby Yucca Flat, Nevada, was used as an atomic testing range. Of the 220 cast and crew members, 91 have contacted cancer since filming. Whether this is coincidence or not is still a mystery. Eleven test explosions occurred a year before filming on *The Conqueror* began.

Wayne takes an axe to the lifeboats to stop the mutiny in *The Sea Chase*.

Mike Mazurki (left) and Wayne eye trouble in *Blood Alley*.

Wayne is wounded in *The Conqueror*.

The Searchers (1956), WARNER BROTHERS

1. What weapon does Wayne keep after the Civil War?
2. Why did Wayne leave home before the war?
3. Name the actress who plays Debbie as a young girl.
4. Name the actor who plays Martin Pawley?
5. Name the actor who plays the Reverend Samuel Clayton.
6. What does Martha fondle that indicates her feeling for Wayne?
7. Name the actor who plays Chief Scar.
8. What happens to the Edwards home?
9. Name the actress who plays Laurie Jorgensen.
10. Name the actor who plays the third searcher.
11. What happens to Wayne's niece Lucy?
12. What does Wayne leave behind to bury her in?
13. What is enclosed with a letter awaiting Wayne?
14. What is the name of Martin's Indian wife?
15. What does Martin take to the fort where the captives are held?
16. Name the actress who plays Debbie grown.
17. What does Wayne ask Martin to read after finding Debbie the first time?
18. What does Mose Harper want while telling where Chief Scar is located?
19. How many years does the search take?
20. What does Wayne take from Scar's body?

AUTHOR'S NOTE: During filming, a two-year-old Navajo Indian girl baby became critically ill with double pneumonia and also incurred an advanced case of measles. The nearest doctor was the crew location doctor. The only thing that could save the girl was an oxygen tank in a hospital 100 miles away. When Wayne heard this, he offered his plane as transport so the girl could enter the hospital. The girl arrived in time. Wayne became the real life hero of the Indians and received a new name: "The Man with the Big Eagle."

1. His army saber.
2. He was in love with his brother's wife.
3. Lana Wood (she appeared in *Diamonds Are Forever*).
4. Jeffrey Hunter.
5. Ward Bond.
6. His army coat.
7. Henry Brandon.
8. It is burned by Comanches.
9. Vera Miles.
10. Harry Carey, Jr.
11. She is raped and murdered by the Comanches.
12. His army coat.
13. A piece of material from Debbie's dress.
14. Look.
15. A doll.
16. Natalie Wood.
17. His will.
18. A rocking chair and a roof over his head.
19. Five.
20. His scalp.

Wayne is almost sworn in by Ward Bond in *The Searchers*.

An embittered Wayne knows what he must do on the trail of vengeance as Jeffrey Hunter watches in *The Searchers*.

The Wings of Eagles (1957), MGM

1. What is the name of Wayne's squadron at the film's start?
2. Name the actor who plays Wayne's friend Carson.
3. Name the actor who plays the army officer who flies with Wayne?
4. What do they fly through?
5. What is Carson's function for Wayne?
6. Where does the plane eventually land?
7. Name the actor who is always with Carson.
8. How many more children do Wayne and Maureen O'Hara have after their son dies?
9. Where do O'Hara and the kids see Wayne with goggles.
10. What is the prize for the airplane race?
11. What prompts Wayne's tragedy on the steps at home?
12. Where does Carson hide the liquor in Wayne's hospital room?
13. How does Wayne see the carrier in the harbor?
14. Name the actor who plays director John Dodge.
15. What doesn't he know about Wayne before he sees him?
16. What does he want Wayne to write about?
17. What film clip is shown in the screening room?
18. What stops the final reconciliation between Wayne and O'Hara?
19. What is Wayne's forgotten idea that he finally remembers?
20. What is the World War II battle Wayne is in?

AUTHOR'S NOTE: Wayne spent about four hours being suspended 40 feet over the water for the final scene. Two ships were 80 yards apart while Wayne was on a breeches buoy.

1. First Regular Flying Class.
2. Dan Dailey.
3. Ken Tobey.
4. A hangar.
5. A mechanic.
6. In a swimming pool at the Admiral's Tea Party.
7. Tige Andrews.
8. Two.
9. In a theatre newsreel.
10. The Schneider Cup.
11. One of Wayne's daughters wakes up crying. As Wayne goes to her, he misses his footing and falls down the steps.
12. Behind a dresser on hangers.
13. In a wheelchair.
14. Ward Bond.
15. He is crippled.
16. To write about navy people.
17. *Hell Divers*
18. Pearl Harbor is attacked.
19. Jeep carriers.
20. Kwajalein.

Jet Pilot (1957), RKO/UNIVERSAL

1. Name the actress who plays the Russian air pilot Anna.
2. .Why does Anna leave Russia?
3. What is her rank in the Russian Air Force?
4. What is Wayne's air force rank?
5. What flying group is represented in the film?
6. To what U.S. state does Anna fly?
7. To what airfield is she taken?
8. Name the actor who plays Wayne's buddy, Major Rexford.
9. Name the actor who plays the interrogater, Major General Black.
10. What does Anna want in the U.S.?
11. For what organization is Wayne to find information from Anna?
12. What information is Wayne to obtain from Anna?
13. What military information is Wayne to give Anna?
14. What is Wayne ordered to show her of the U.S.?
15. In what city do Wayne and Anna have a romantic interlude?
16. What does Wayne do that irks his superiors?
17. What is the plan behind this?
18. To what Russian city does Wayne accompany Anna?
19. Name the actor who plays the Russian Colonel Matoff.
20. How does the film end?

AUTHOR'S NOTE: More than 16 months of actual aerial footage was filmed. No stock footage shots were used in the film. Cameramen flew more than 40,000 miles and spent over 250 hours in the air.

Wayne filmed *Jet Pilot* after *Sands of Iwo Jima*. The filming took place as an RKO production under Howard Hughes. The film wasn't released until 1957. Universal released the film at that time. The original filming took place in 1949.

1. Janet Leigh.
2. She didn't want to be shot for disobedience, so she defected.
3. Lieutenant.
4. Colonel.
5. "Hell's Angels."
6. Alaska.
7. Palmer Field.
8. Paul Fix.
9. Jay C. Flippen.
10. Political asylum.
11. The FBI.
12. Information on the Russian Air Force.
13. Secrets of U.S. planes that are out of date.
14. Luxuries of American life.
15. Palm Springs.
16. He marries Leigh.
17. For Anna to convince Wayne to defect from the U.S.
18. Moscow.
19. Hans Conreid.
20. Wayne and Leigh fly back to the U.S. after stealing a Russian plane.

Legend of the Lost (1957), UNITED ARTISTS

1. Where is Wayne at the film's start?
2. What is the name of the city he is in?
3. Who does Rossano Brazzi ask to find the best guide?
4. Why is Wayne in jail?
5. For what reason is Wayne hired to go into the desert?
6. What is the name of Sophia Loren's character?
7. What is Wayne's transportation in the desert?
8. What is Brazzi's mission?
9. What does their route take them through?
10. What does Brazzi want to build?
11. What is in front of Loren as she bathes?
12. What does she hit Wayne with during a fight?
13. What is the name of the city they find?
14. What do they find in one of the ruins?
15. Why had they died?
16. Where do Wayne and Loren find Brazzi in the desert?
17. What does Brazzi do to Wayne when his back is turned?
18. What is Wayne doing at that time?
19. How is Brazzi killed?
20. What saves Wayne and Loren at the film's end?

AUTHOR'S NOTE: Wayne took his first camel ride in this film. After riding for about half an hour, Wayne said, "My kingdom for a horse."

1. In jail.
2. Timbuktu.
3. Kurt Kasznar.
4. Wayne was celebrating the Fourth of July too loudly.
5. A guide.
6. Dita.
7. By mule.
8. To locate the jewels found by his father.
9. Sahara Desert.
10. A medical center dedicated to his father.
11. A mule.
12. A frying pan.
13. Timgad.
14. The bodies of Brazzi's father and a guide.
15. They had fought over a woman.
16. By a dry river bed.
17. He stabs Wayne in the back with a knife.
18. He is digging for water.
19. Loren shoots him with Wayne's gun.
20. A passing caravan.

Ken Tobey and Wayne have their cake in a different way in *The Wings of Eagles*.

Wayne looks at home as the pilot in *Jet Pilot*.

Sophia Loren gives Wayne a surprise haymaker in *Legend of the Lost*.

I Married a Woman (1957), RKO

1. Who is the male star of the film?
2. Who is Diana Dors's favorite movie star?
3. Who is one of the film's stars Wayne will appear with again?

1. George Gobel.
2. John Wayne, of course.
3. Angie Dickinson.

Wayne appears as himself on the movie screen in *I Married a Woman*.

The Barbarian and the Geisha (1958),
20TH CENTURY-FOX

1. Which U.S. president sends Wayne to the Orient?
2. What is Wayne's official title?
3. Who is the actor who plays Wayne's interpreter?
4. What type of building is Wayne quartered in?
5. Why does Wayne keep getting headaches?
6. What is the name of the geisha's character?
7. What is Wayne forced to take down by his temple?
8. Wayne has a fight with a samurai, but who defeats Wayne?
9. What does Wayne stand in front of as a ship appears?
10. What disease has broken out on the ship?
11. Why does Wayne set fire to the village?
12. One lord asks Wayne if there are archers in the U.S. What is Wayne's reply?
13. Where is one of Wayne's supporters assassinated?
14. What is the ancient capital of Japan?
15. In the Emperor's Court how does Wayne amuse a boy?
16. What is the naval instrument Wayne gives the Emperor?
17. What is the piece of furniture Wayne gives the Emperor?
18. What does Okichi do to spare Wayne's life?
19. After Wayne's murder attempt fails, what does the Japanese lord do?
20. What does Okichi leave Wayne at the film's end?

AUTHOR'S NOTE: While filming the interiors, Wayne made the floors creak because of his massive weight. The sound man complained. A second floor had to be constructed for support, which solved the sound problem.

1. Pierce.
2. A Consul General.
3. Sam Jaffe.
4. A derelict temple.
5. He bumps his head on the rafters because he is too tall.
6. Okichi.
7. The American flag.
8. A small judo expert defeats Wayne.
9. A cannon.
10. Cholera.
11. To kill the epidemic.
12. Wayne refers to the Southwest Indians.
13. At an archery game.
14. Yedo (Tokyo).
15. Wayne wiggles his ears and the kid does the same.
16. A brass telescope.
17. A rocking chair.
18. She sleeps in Wayne's bed.
19. The lord kills himself.
20. A comb and mirror.

Rio Bravo (1959), WARNER BROTHERS

1. Director Howard Hawks made *Rio Bravo* because he didn't like what popular western film?
2. What is Dean Martin doing when Wayne is seen the first time?
3. Name the actor who plays Wayne's friend, Pat Wheeler.
4. Name the actor who plays Colorado.
5. Name the actor who plays Stumpy.
6. Name the actor being held prisoner in jail.
7. Name the actress who plays Feathers.
8. What does she see Wayne looking at in Carlos's room?
9. Where is Wheeler's killer hiding when Martin enters the saloon?
10. How does Martin discover where the killer is hiding?
11. What was the occupation of Feathers' husband?
12. What items from the past does Wayne return to Martin?
13. Name the actor who plays Nathan Burdette.
14. Why does Stumpy hate Burdette?
15. What Mexican music is played when Colorado tells Wayne of its origin?
16. Why does Wayne carry a rifle?
17. What does Feathers throw through a window to save Wayne?
18. What signals Martin's salvation?
19. What is Martin doing when Wayne is taken prisoner in the hotel?
20. What character throws the dynamite for Wayne at the film's end?

AUTHOR'S NOTE: I asked Harry Carey, Jr., at The Memphis Film Festival in August 1982 why his name appears in the film credits of *Rio Bravo*. Carey is not seen in the film. A sequence was filmed where Carey offers his services as deputy to Wayne. Wayne declines the offer as he does those of the other characters in the film. The killer hiding in the saloon rafters was reported to have been Carey. He said this was not true. The sequence with Carey ended on the cutting room floor.

This was the first film in which Wayne wore his *Red River* "D" belt buckle (the letter "D" is for Dunson and the two wavy lines represent a river). This was given to him by director Howard Hawks in commemoration of the brand used in *Red River*. Wayne wears the belt buckle in *Rio Bravo, North to Alaska, Hatari, McLintock, Circus World, The Sons of Katie Elder, El Dorado, The War Wagon* and *Rio Lobo*.

1. *High Noon.*
2. Martin is reaching for a coin in a spittoon.
3. Ward Bond.
4. Ricky Nelson.
5. Walter Brennan.
6. Claude Akins.
7. Angie Dickinson.
8. A pair of red pants for Carlos's wife.
9. He is hiding in the saloon rafters.
10. The killer is bleeding into a glass on the bar.
11. A gambler.
12. Martin's two guns, which he had sold.
13. John Russell.
14. Burdette took Stumpy's land.
15. The De Guella, which was playing during the Alamo siege.
16. Because he has met others faster with a handgun than he.
17. She throws a flower pot.
18. He pours whiskey back into a bottle without spilling a drop when he hears the Mexican music.
19. He is taking a bath.
20. Stumpy.

The Horse Soldiers (1959), UNITED ARTISTS

1. Which Civil War general gives Wayne his mission orders?
2. What town is Wayne's military objective?
3. What will Wayne's fate be if he fails?
4. Name the actor who plays the surgeon, Major Kendall.
5. What is Wayne's decision when his plan is discovered by the rebels?
6. Name the actress who plays Hannah Hunter.
7. What is the name of her plantation?
8. What occupation does Wayne reveal he had before the war?
9. How does Hannah overhear Wayne's battle plan?
10. What does Hannah do to Wayne after she is revived by having water thrown on her?
11. Name the two actors who play the rebel deserters.
12. What is the confession Wayne tells Hannah at a bar?
13. What prompts the fight between Wayne and Kendall?
14. What occurs during the fight?
15. Where is Wayne wounded?
16. What is the cost of Wayne's boots?
17. What city will be Wayne's destination?
18. What is Kendall's decision?
19. What does Wayne take from Hannah before he leaves?
20. How do Wayne and company escape?

AUTHOR'S NOTE: The bridge used in the climax of *The Horse Soldiers* was 200 feet long and was constructed at a cost of well over $50,000.

1. Grant.
2. Newton Station.
3. Andersonville Prison.
4. William Holden.
5. Wayne splits his command, sending one-third back.
6. Constance Towers.
7. Greenbriar.
8. A railroad construction engineer.
9. By listening through a heating duct.
10. Hannah punches him.
11. Strother Martin and Denver Pyle.
12. His wife had died because of an incorrect diagnosis.
13. A soldier Holden operated on died.
14. The rebels launch an attack.
15. The right leg, by the calf.
16. $20.00.
17. Vicksburg.
18. To stay with the wounded and then face incarceration in Andersonville Prison.
19. Her scarf.
20. Wayne lights a fuse causing a bridge to explode.

Wayne takes a gamble for American diplomacy in
The Barbarian and the Geisha.

Ricky Nelson tells Wayne and Dean Martin the tale
of the saloon music in *Rio Bravo*.

Wayne gets the drop on his adversary in *Rio Bravo*.

Wayne sees rebel trouble coming his way as Willis Bouchey takes note in *The Horse Soldiers*.

Wayne is the victim of William Holden's wrath in *The Horse Soldiers*.

Wayne as he appears in *The Green Berets*.

106

THE 1960's

The Alamo (1960), UNITED ARTISTS

1. Name the actor who plays Sam Houston.
2. Name the actor who plays Colonel Travis.
3. Name the actor who plays Jim Bowie.
4. Name the actor who plays Beekeeper.
5. Where do Wayne and Travis meet the first time?
6. What do Wayne and the character Bull place on their noses?
7. What does Wayne offer Travis before his "Republic speech"?
8. Name the actress who plays Flaca.
9. Where does Wayne and Bowie find stored guns and powder?
10. What is Bowie's idea of fighting?
11. What does Wayne tell Travis his major worry is?
12. What legendary person supposedly fought Crockett for three days?
13. What character brings Wayne a wagon so Flaca can leave?
14. What is destroyed by the Mexican cannon that disturbs Beekeeper?
15. Why does Bowie hit Wayne after seeing Smitty?
16. What is the comment Wayne makes as Bowie starts to read his message?
17. What bad news does Bowie receive?
18. Name the actor who arrives with the bad news from Goliad.
19. What is Wayne thinking about the night before the final battle?
20. How is Wayne killed in the finale?

AUTHOR'S NOTE: Magnetic Video has released *The Alamo* on video tape. The two-tape package runs 161 minutes. The roadshow engagement running time was 192 minutes in 1960. Because of only fair boxoffice business, the film was recut for the regular theatrical release. The film was cut to 161 minutes for the spring release of 1961.

Here is a list of the cut sequences, totaling 31 minutes: 1. A drunken Bowie finds Major Travis (now Colonel Travis) in charge. 2. Travis and Captain Dickinson discuss Jeffersonian democracy. 3. The merchant Emil is killed by Crockett, who confronts Flaca with the news. 4. Flaca and a character named Mrs. Guy talk as the settlers leave. 5. Bowie defends Smitty. 6. Crockett and Bowie discuss pyrotechnics. 7. Crockett tells Flaca about a ridgepole. 8. Travis and Bowie argue as messenger Bonham arrives with news of reinforcements. 9. A patrol suffers casualties, reinforcements arrive, and a birthday party for Lisa Dickinson takes place. 10. The parson dies as Crockett prays. 11. Religious beliefs are discussed before the battle. 12. A line of dialogue spoken by Bowie is missing as the north wall falls. Other cuts included the overture, intermission music, and end music.

The rawhide rifle cover Wayne uses in *The Alamo* was previously used by Wayne in *The Searchers*.

1. Richard Boone.
2. Laurence Harvey.
3. Richard Widmark.
4. Chill Wills.
5. The cantina.
6. A feather.
7. A cigar.
8. Linda Cristal.
9. In the church cellar.
10. "Cut, slash and run."
11. 23 Tennesseeans.
12. Mike Fink.
13. The Parson.
14. The keg he is dispensing liquor from is destroyed.
15. Wayne had gotten Widmark drunk so he would stay and fight.
16. "Maybe Santa Anna's surrendered."
17. His family had died.
18. Patrick Wayne.
19. "Not thinking, just remembering."
20. He is bayoneted by a Mexican lance.

Wayne and Richard Widmark are going to have a drink or eight or ten after their first encounter in *The Alamo*.

Wayne and Richard Widmark make plans to destroy the Mexican cannon in *The Alamo*.

Wayne pulls his stuntman "Bad Chuck" Roberson off the mighty Cocaine in *The Alamo*.

Wayne faces the final Mexican assault in *The Alamo*.

North to Alaska (1960), 20TH CENTURY-FOX

1. Who sings the title song, "North to Alaska"?
2. Name the actor who plays Wayne's partner George Pratt.
3. At what city do Wayne and George strike it rich?
4. Name the actor who plays George's brother.
5. What city is Wayne's destination?
6. Why will Wayne travel there?
7. What is the name of Wayne's dog?
8. Name the actor who plays the con man Frankie Canon?
9. What does the dog prevent Canon from taking during the saloon fight?
10. What does Canon use as a con on Wayne in the shower room?
11. What does Wayne discover when he reaches his destination?
12. Name the actress who plays Michelle.
13. What is the other name Wayne calls her?
14. What do Wayne and the girl attend before leaving for Alaska?
15. What event does Wayne enter?
16. Why does Wayne bring the girl back for George?
17. What accident befalls Wayne that results in the routing of claim jumpers on a neighbor's claim?
18. What does George do to the girl, causing Wayne to become jealous?
19. How does Wayne prove that his mining claim is legitimate?
20. What does Wayne finally admit at the film's conclusion?

AUTHOR'S NOTE: The creek that was used next to Wayne's cabin was fed by the cold 40-degree waters of Mt. Whitney.

1. Johnny Horton.
2. Stewart Granger.
3. Nome, Alaska.
4. Fabian.
5. Seattle, Washington.
6. To bring back the girl George wants to marry.
7. Clancy.
8. Ernie Kovacs.
9. The bag full of money from the mining claim.
10. He tries to sell Wayne a ring made of glass.
11. George's girl is married.
12. Capucine.
13. Angel.
14. The Logger's Picnic.
15. The pole climbing contest.
16. To console George on losing his girl.
17. Wayne is climbing on a wagon when the brake malfunctions, forcing the wagon and Wayne onto a collision course with the mining claim.
18. Granger tickles Capucine's foot.
19. A fight in the muddy street enables Wayne to get the confession from Kovacs that he stole Wayne's claim.
20. That he loves Capucine.

The Comancheros (1961), 20TH CENTURY-FOX

1. Name the actor who plays the gambler Paul Regret.
2. Name the actress who plays Pilar.
3. What is Wayne's Texas ranger rank?
4. For what is Paul Regret wanted?
5. With what does Regret hit Wayne at the burial site?
6. Name the actor who plays Major Henry.
7. What was Wayne's gunrunner alias?
8. What is the name of the town where Wayne is to meet the contact?
9. Name the actor who plays the contact, Tully Crowe.
10. Crowe offers Wayne snuff, but Wayne says he is what kind of man.
11. What are Wayne and Crowe doing before Wayne kills him?
12. To what does Wayne handcuff Regret at the weigh station?
13. How are Wayne and company rescued from the Comancheros?
14. Name the actor who plays the judge who frees Regret.
15. Name the actor who follows Wayne and signals the rangers as to Wayne's location.
16. To what does Wayne tell Regret Indians can be compared?
17. What is the wagon marker the Comancheros watch for awaiting the rifles?
18. What is missing from the rifles Wayne brings into the camp?
19. Name the actor who plays the Comancheros leader.
20. What does the character Pilar tell Wayne as he rides away?

AUTHOR'S NOTE: The Tombstone, Arizona, western street on the 20th Century-Fox backlot was destroyed after *The Comancheros* filming. This town was used as Sweetwater in the film. A new development was to take its place.

1. Stuart Whitman.
2. Ina Balin.
3. Captain.
4. Extradition on a murder charge for killing a man in a duel.
5. A shovel.
6. Bruce Cabot.
7. Ed McBain.
8. Sweetwater.
9. Lee Marvin.
10. "A cigar man."
11. Playing poker.
12. An anvil.
13. Regret, who had escaped, brings a company of rangers to Wayne's rescue.
14. Edgar Buchanan.
15. Patrick Wayne.
16. A rattlesnake.
17. A lance with feathers.
18. The firing pins.
19. Nehemiah Persoff.
20. "We kind of gotten used to you."

The Man Who Shot Liberty Valance (1962),

PARAMOUNT

1. Name the actor who plays Link Appleyard.
2. Name the actor who plays the lawyer Ransom Stoddard.
3. Name the actress who plays his wife Hallie.
4. Why does Stoddard arrive in town?
5. Name the actor who plays Liberty Valance.
6. What is Wayne doing in his first scene?
7. Name the actor who plays Pompey.
8. What advice does Wayne give Stoddard?
9. Name the town in which the film takes place.
10. What is the name of the town's newspaper.
11. Name the actor who plays the newspaper editor, Dutton Peabody.
12. What present does Wayne give Hallie at the diner?
13. What falls on the floor when Valance trips Stoddard in the diner?
14. What is the main issue at the town meeting?
15. Who does Stoddard nominate for a candidate?
16. What happens when Stoddard faces Valance in the street?
17. What does Wayne discover when he sees Stoddard and Hallie after the shooting?
18. What does Wayne then destroy?
19. What is the confession that Wayne makes to Stoddard?
20. What does Hallie place on Wayne's coffin at the film's end?

AUTHOR'S NOTE: During the filming of this last Wayne black-and-white western, James Stewart said, director John Ford was always giving Wayne trouble. Stewart never had a run-in with Ford. Filming was almost completed when the funeral scene was next. Woody Strode was in make-up and Ford asked Stewart what his thoughts were. Stewart said Strode looked like Uncle Remus. Stewart realized his mistake as Ford called for the crew telling them "Stewart didn't like Uncle Remus." Afterwards, Wayne told Stewart: "You thought you were going to make it through, didn't you!"

The advertising material on *The Man Who Shot Liberty Valance* carried Stewart's name first and the prints of the film carried Wayne's name first. Wayne and Stewart or Stewart and Wayne could not have cared less who was billed first.

1. Andy Devine.
2. James Stewart.
3. Vera Miles.
4. To attend Wayne's funeral.
5. Lee Marvin.
6. He is bringing Stewart into town.
7. Woody Strode.
8. To learn how to use a gun.
9. Shinbone.
10. Shinbone Star.
11. Edmond O'Brien.
12. A cactus rose.
13. Wayne's supper.
14. Statehood.
15. Wayne. He declines.
16. Stewart is wounded, but he manages to kill Marvin.
17. That Stewart and Miles are in love.
18. Wayne burns his house down.
19. Wayne actually shot Marvin to save Stewart.
20. A cactus rose.

Wayne and Stewart Granger celebrate their new found wealth in *North to Alaska*.

Wayne goes into action, triggered by an attack of *The Comancheros*.

Lee Van Cleef (left) watches Lee Marvin size up
Wayne as James Stewart is caught between them in
The Man Who Shot Liberty Valance.

Wayne is on the receiving end of James Stewart's
haymaker in *The Man Who Shot Liberty Valance.*

James Stewart finds out from Wayne how to solve his problems out west in *The Man Who Shot Liberty Valence.*

Hatari (1962), PARAMOUNT

1. What does Hatari mean?
2. In what country was the film photographed?
3. Who plays the Indian?
4. How is he injured at the film's start?
5. What does the character "Chips" have that the Indian needs?
6. Who is the actor who plays the doctor?
7. Who does Wayne find in his bed when he comes home drunk?
8. Who is the actress who plays "Dallas"?
9. What is her profession?
10. Why do Wayne and company catch the animals?
11. Who is the actor who plays "Pockets"?
12. How does Wayne test "Chips's" shooting skills?
13. What goes into the bathroom as "Dallas" bathes?
14. What does Wayne protect "Dallas" from at the watering hole?
15. What type of animal is caught when "Pockets" uses a rocket?
16. What is the nickname "Dallas" is given by the natives?
17. How many elephants are there in Wayne's troupe?
18. What is the last animal to be caught in the film?
19. Where does the film end?
20. Who did the film's score?

AUTHOR'S NOTE: The Momella "Game Farm" used in the film was located by Mt. Mero, twin of Mt. Kilimanjaro.

1. In Swahili it means danger.
2. Tanganyika, Africa.
3. Bruce Cabot.
4. He is gored by a rhino.
5. The same blood type as the Indian, for a transfusion.
6. Eduard Franz.
7. "Dallas."
8. Elsa Martinelli.
9. A photographer.
10. To restock world zoos.
11. Red Buttons.
12. By shooting at moving bottles.
13. A cheetah.
14. An elephant.
15. Monkeys.
16. "Mama Tembo."
17. Three.
18. The rhino.
19. In Wayne's bedroom.
20. Henry Mancini.

The Longest Day (1962), 20TH CENTURY-FOX

1. Which division does Wayne command?
2. Who is the actor who plays Wayne's C.O.?
3. What does Wayne tell him his immediate concern is?
4. Where had Wayne landed on the practice mission?
5. One click must be answered by what?
6. What does Wayne do when he receives word about the invasion?
7. In what direction does Wayne tell his men to move if they miss the drop zone?
8. What happens to Wayne when he lands in France?
9. How far is Wayne from his drop zone?
10. What does Wayne commandeer to be carried on?

AUTHOR'S NOTE: Wayne is shown eight times in the film:
1. In the parachute room talking to Steve Forrest.
2. Talking to Ryan in Ryan's office.
3. Receiving the word about the invasion.
4. Addressing the troops.
5. On a plane with last minute instructions.
6. In the swamp.
7. On the ammo carrier going to St. Mere Eglise.
8. Entering St. Mere Eglise.
When the 8 sequences are tabulated, Wayne appears in the film for 12 minutes and 15 seconds.

1. 82nd Airborne.
2. Robert Ryan.
3. The placement of the drop zones.
4. Wayne landed in a convent courtyard.
5. Two clicks.
6. He throws his coffee cup across the parachute room.
7. North by east.
8. He sprains his ankle in the airdrop.
9. Five miles.
10. An ammo carrier.

How the West Was Won (1963), MGM

1. Which general does Wayne play?
2. What battle is the backdrop for the Civil War sequence?
3. What does Wayne ask the sentry for before he talks with Grant?
4. Who is the actor who plays General Grant?
5. Who plays the rebel soldier who tries to kill Grant?
6. What actor saves Wayne and Grant from being shot?

AUTHOR'S NOTE: Wayne is seen in the film for only 3½ minutes.

1. Sherman.
2. Shiloh.
3. A lantern.

4. Harry Morgan.
5. Russ Tamblyn.
6. George Peppard.

Wayne, Katharine Hepburn, and Richard Romancito escape the bad guys in *Rooster Cogburn*.

Wayne in his final gunfight in *The Shootist*.

A father's confession brings Wayne and son Gary Grimes closer in *Cahill, U.S. Marshal.*

Wayne takes aim at a hit man in *Brannigan.*

Wayne confronts the kidnappers in *Big Jake*.

Wayne says kind words for a fallen trailhand in *The Cowboys*.

James Caan, Wayne, and Robert Mitchum "make some music" in *El Dorado*.

Jim Hutton and Wayne are a tough breed in *Hellfighters*.

UNIVERSAL PRESENTS
**JOHN WAYNE
KATHARINE ROSS
JIM HUTTON**
in
"HELLFIGHTERS"u
TECHNICOLOR®   PANAVISION®

Steve Forrest and Wayne prepare for an assault in *The Longest Day*.

Earl Holliman, Wayne, and Dean Martin await blazing guns in *The Sons of Katie Elder*.

Wayne faces a fortified position in *The Horse Soldiers*.

Wayne as Davy Crockett takes aim in *The Alamo*.

Ethan Edwards realizes his family is in danger in *The Searchers*.

The poster to Howard Hawks's *Rio Bravo*.

Maureen O'Hara and Wayne cope with married life in *The Quiet Man*.

David Brian talks with Wayne as Claire Trevor listens in *The High and the Mighty*. Jan Sterling is at left.

Donovan's Reef (1963), PARAMOUNT

1. What is Donovan's Reef?
2. What is Wayne's nickname in the film?
3. What is the name of Lee Marvin's character?
4. Who is the actor who plays the governor?
5. What do Wayne and Marvin both have in common besides the navy?
6. Who is the actress who plays Amelia?
7. Where is she from?
8. What is the name of the boat on which she arrives?
9. What item sits on the bar?
10. What is the item that never works in the bar?
11. Who is the actress Wayne throws out of his bedroom?
12. Why do Wayne and company go to the mountains?
13. What does Amelia find there?
14. What does the priest need money for that he never repairs?
15. What is the church occasion near the film's end?
16. Who plays the Australian lieutenant?
17. Who is "The King of the United States" in the pageant?
18. What does Marvin get for Christmas from Amelia?
19. What does Amelia hit Wayne with on Christmas Day?
20. What is Marvin carrying in the film's last scene?

AUTHOR'S NOTE: In the bar is a slot machine that pays off near the film's end. The priest puts in a silver dollar and the machine pays out 2700 silver dollars. These were borrowed from The Bank of America and observed by five armed guards. This was shot on the Paramount back lot in Hollywood.

1. A bar.
2. "Guns."
3. "Boats" Gilhooley.
4. Cesar Romero.
5. They both have the same birthday.
6. Elizabeth Allen.
7. Boston.
8. Innisfree.
9. A record player with a crank.
10. A slot machine.
11. Dorothy Lamour.
12. To get a Christmas tree.
13. A monument to the dead queen.
14. The leaky church roof.
15. A Christmas pageant.
16. Patrick Wayne.
17. Marvin
18. An electric train.
19. Her umbrella.
20. A piano stool.

Wayne faces a new adversary, a rhino in *Hatari*.

Final orders are given by Wayne before the parachute jump, as Steve Forrest listens in *The Longest Day*.

Wayne urges Harry Morgan not to resign in *How the West Was Won.*

The slot machine delivers the goods as a stunned Lee Marvin and Wayne watch in *Donovan's Reef.*

McLintock (1963), UNITED ARTISTS

1. Name the actor who plays Drago.
2. What does Wayne watch the children do as he leaves for town?
3. Name the actor who plays Bunny Dull.
4. Name the actor who plays Mr. Birnbaum.
5. Name the actor who plays Devlin Warren.
6. Name the actress who plays Wayne's wife, Katherine McLintock.
7. What is Wayne's full character name?
8. What does Wayne's wife hand him in the hotel room?
9. What does Wayne eat that will test a new cook's capabilities?
10. Name the actress who plays the new cook, Mrs. Warren.
11. Name the actor who plays the Indian agent Agard.
12. What does Wayne say to Leo Gordon after Wayne takes a shotgun from him?
13. What occurs after this?
14. Name the actress who plays Wayne's daughter Becky.
15. What is Wayne asked to read as the governor listens at a hearing?
16. What decision does Mrs. Warren tell Wayne when he comes home drunk?
17. What is Wayne's decision after falling down the stairs several times drunk?
18. What holiday is the background for the film's conclusion?
19. What does Wayne do to his wife when he catches her?
20. What is the film's last scene.

AUTHOR'S NOTE: The free-for-all mud sequence in *McLintock* cost $50,000. Bentonite was used for mud. This is a chalk derivative used in drilling oil wells and in chocolate syrup. Two tons were required. Mixed with water, the bentonite was continually reheated.

In *McLintock*, there is a sequence involving a horse race. Not only did the winner have to cross the finish line first but he had to deliver an unbroken egg that was in his mouth. Wayne had $50.00 for the winner: Stuntman Chuck Hayward.

1. Chill Wills.
2. They climb onto a roof to retrieve Wayne's hat on a weathervane.
3. Edgar Buchanan.
4. Jack Kruschen.
5. Patrick Wayne.
6. Maureen O'Hara.
7. George Washington McLintock.
8. Divorce papers.
9. A biscuit.
10. Yvonne DeCarlo.
11. Strother Martin.
12. "Now. We'll all calm down...I'm gonna use good judgment. I haven't lost my temper in 40 years. But, pilgrim, you caused a lot of trouble this morning, mighta got somebody killed and somebody oughta belt you in the mouth. But I won't. I won't. The hell I won't."
13. A fist fight with all concerned falling down a mud slide.
14. Stefanie Powers.
15. Indian grievances.
16. She is going to marry the sheriff and quit working for Wayne.
17. To fall down the stairs drunk only twice.
18. July the 4th.
19. Wayne spanks her.
20. Wayne's hat on the weathervane.

Circus World (1964), PARAMOUNT

1. What is Wayne looking at when he is first seen?
2. Who plays Cap Carson?
3. Who is the actress who plays Wayne's daughter, Toni Alfredo?
4. What does she see in the tent before disaster strikes?
5. What are the two bad omens that occur before the voyage?
6. Who is the actor who plays Wayne's younger partner, Steve McCabe?
7. What is the midget's character name?
8. When Toni hexes Steve, what does he roll with the dice?
9. At what city does the ship sink?
10. While on the ship, what animal does Wayne put back in a cage?
11. Whose circus show does Wayne work for after he loses his?
12. What is the publicity stunt Wayne creates in the parade?
13. Who is the actor who plays Toto the Clown?
14. What does Wayne want the German to work with in Wayne's new circus?
15. Who is the actress who plays Lili Alfredo, who Wayne wants to find?
16. What does Wayne find in her room?
17. Where does Wayne finally meet Lili?
18. What does Toni tell Wayne she won't wear again?
19. What crisis brings all of the characters together?
20. In which city does the finale occur?

AUTHOR'S NOTE: During the fire sequence, Wayne got injured when the special effects became too effective. His injuries were minor, and this event was marked in the newspapers.

1. The empty highwire.
2. Lloyd Nolan.
3. Claudia Cardinale.
4. A bird is flying in the tent top.
5. Wayne breaks a mirror and places his Stetson on a bed.
6. John Smith.
7. Goliath.
8. "Snake eyes."
9. Barcelona.
10. A lion.
11. Colonel Purdy.
12. Wayne stops a runaway stagecoach.
13. Richard Conte.
14. Tigers instead of lions.
15. Rita Hayworth.
16. Empty liquor bottles.
17. In a small bar.
18. Bloomers.
19. A fire.
20. Vienna.

Stefanie Powers and Patrick Wayne witness the
spanking of Maureen O'Hara by Wayne in *McLintock*.

Wayne takes control of the fire as his circus is in
danger in *Circus World*.

The Greatest Story Ever Told (1965),

UNITED ARTISTS

1. What is Wayne's military rank in the film?
2. What is his one line of dialogue?
3. Why did he agree to do this film?

AUTHOR'S NOTE: During the filming of *Circus World*, Wayne did his guest stint in *The Greatest Story Ever Told*. His total time on this film was three weeks. Also, Wayne did not accept a paycheck for the film because of George Stevens' reputation in the film world.

Wayne appears in a 13-minute sequence but is seen for 2:51 minutes.

1. A centurion in the Roman legions.
2. "Truly this man was the son of God."
3. As a favor to director George Stevens.

Wayne trails Max Von Sydow in *The Greatest Story Ever Told*.

In Harm's Way (1965), PARAMOUNT

1. What is Wayne's nickname in the film?
2. What is the nickname for Wayne's ship?
3. Name the actor who plays Wayne's executive officer, Eddington.
4. Why does Wayne stop the zig-zag pattern?
5. Name the popular TV star who plays Lt. Commander Burke.
6. What is Wayne's injury?
7. Name Wayne's female co-star.
8. Name the actor who rooms with Wayne.
9. Name the actor who plays Wayne's son.
10. What is the length of time Wayne has not seen his son?
11. Name the actress who plays the plane watcher?
12. Name the actor who plays the Australian coast watcher.
13. Name the actor who gives Wayne his promotion.
14. Who plays the public relations officer?
15. What is the military operation's code name?
16. Name the actor who is Wayne's military rival?
17. How does Wayne change the operation without the brass knowing?
18. What does Wayne give his son after the nurse commits suicide?
19. What battleship does Eddington report he sees before he is shot down?
20. How long was Wayne in the coma at the film's end?

AUTHOR'S NOTE: A crew of 40 spent one month and $1,000,000 recording the final battle that lasts five minutes on the screen.

1. The Rock.
2. "Old Swayback."
3. Kirk Douglas.
4. To conserve fuel.
5. Carroll O'Connor.
6. His right arm is broken.
7. Patricia Neal.
8. Burgess Meredith.
9. Brandon de Wilde.
10. Eighteen years.
11. Paula Prentiss.
12. Stanley Holloway.
13. Henry Fonda.
14. Patrick O'Neal.
15. "Skyhook."
16. Dana Andrews.
17. Wayne throws a rock out of a plane to the troops below, with his new plan tied to it.
18. An engagement ring Wayne's son had given the nurse.
19. *Yamato*
20. Three weeks.

The Sons of Katie Elder (1965), PARAMOUNT

1. Name the actor who plays Tom Elder.
2. Name the actor who plays Matt Elder.
3. Name the actor who plays Bud Elder.
4. What will the Elders attend?
5. Name the man who plays the gunfighter Curley, who gets off the train.
6. Name the actor who plays the villain Morgan Hastings.
7. Name the actress who plays Mary Gordon.
8. Where is Wayne when the funeral occurs?
9. Name the actor who plays Sheriff Billy Wilson.
10. What does Wayne want to investigate?
11. What is Tom Elder's idea for a monument for his mother?
12. What decision does Wayne make in the saloon confrontation?
13. What is Wayne's plan after the Elder brothers fight against each other?
14. What happens to Sheriff Billy Wilson?
15. What does the deputy decide to do with the Elder brothers?
16. Where is an ambush set up to kill the Elders?
17. What happens after the explosion that Wayne tries to prevent?
18. What is Wayne's vengeance at this point.
19. Where does Wayne encounter Hastings in the climax?
20. What is the last scene?

AUTHOR'S NOTE: Director Henry Hathaway wanted to make sure Wayne was able to do the film with its vigorous locations. Wayne had his cancer operation four months before filming started. Hathaway decided to film the sequence in which the Elder brothers are being transported to another town when the bad guys attack. This sequence has the most action in the film and Wayne came through with flying colors.

This was the last film in which Wayne would wear a double-breasted shirt. He wore this type of shirt in *Stagecoach, The Dark Command, Angel and the Badman, Red River, Fort Apache, Rio Grande, The Searchers, Rio Bravo, The Horse Soldiers, North to Alaska, The Comancheros, The Man Who Shot Liberty Valance, McClintock* and *Circus World.*

1. Dean Martin.
2. Earl Holliman.
3. Michael Anderson, Jr.
4. Their mother's funeral.
5. George Kennedy.
6. James Gregory.
7. Martha Hyer.
8. In the hills watching.
9. Paul Fix.
10. The circumstances of his father's death.
11. A statue of a horse.
12. Not to pick up a gun off the bar that Kennedy wants Wayne to use.
13. To sell horses to the miners so Bud can go to college.
14. He is shot by Hastings at the Elder's house.
15. To move the Elders to another town for a fair trial.
16. At a bridge.
17. Holliman is killed.
18. He fires two six guns simultaneously, then a rifle, routing the bad guys.
19. In Hasting's gun shop.
20. Katie's rocking chair.

Wayne and Kirk Douglas face a changing navy during World War II in *In Harm's Way*.

Wayne is still quick on the draw in *The Sons of Katie Elder*.

Cast a Giant Shadow (1966), UNITED ARTISTS

1. What is Wayne's rank in the film?
2. What does Kirk Douglas throw at Wayne while in a jeep?
3. What camp do Wayne and Douglas enter in the flashback?
4. What does Wayne call Douglas as the camp is liberated?
5. After the war, where is Wayne stationed?

AUTHOR'S NOTE: During the filming of the sniper sequence, Wayne incurred a slipped disc. The news releases said this was caused by a fight between Wayne and Kirk Douglas in the sequence. There was no such fight. Wayne got out of the jeep too fast, causing the problem. He was hospitalized for a short while. Wayne appears in six sequences totaling 11 minutes.

1. A two-star general and a three-star general.
2. A bouquet of flowers.
3. Dachau.
4. "An insubordinate s.o.b."
5. The Pentagon.

Wayne and Kirk Douglas enter a concentration camp in *Cast a Giant Shadow.*

El Dorado (1967), PARAMOUNT

1. What is Wayne doing when Robert Mitchum finds him at the film's start?
2. Name the TV star who plays the film's villain.
3. Name the actor who plays the sentry Wayne is forced to shoot.
4. Name the actress who shoots Wayne.
5. Name the actor who plays Mississippi.
6. What is Wayne playing when Mississippi enters the saloon?
7. What is the character's name who Mississippi avenges?
8. What is Mississippi's first weapon in the film?
9. What is the name of the character played by Christopher George?
10. What does he offer Wayne?
11. What two pieces of advice does Wayne give Mississippi?
12. Why doesn't Wayne shoot him on the way to El Dorado?
13. Which author does Mississippi quote to Wayne on their journey?
14. What does Wayne discover about Mitchum?
15. Where is the character Bull shot when the church attack occurs?
16. Where in the saloon is the killer hiding?
17. Name the actor who plays Charlie the bartender.
18. What happens to Wayne when he corners Milt and Pedro?
19. How does Wayne receive assistance from Mississippi in the final gunfight?
20. How is Wayne wounded in the showdown?

AUTHOR'S NOTE: *El Dorado* was filmed in the fall of 1965. Paramount, who released the film, didn't want this and their film *Nevada Smith* both released in the summer of 1966. It was decided that *Nevada Smith* was to be released in 1966 and *El Dorado* was released in June, 1967.

During the filming of *El Dorado* in Old Tucson, Arizona, Wayne had the "John Wayne Drive" named after him through official delegation.

1. Wayne is shaving.
2. Ed Asner.
3. Johnny Crawford.
4. Michele Carey.
5. James Caan.
6. Dominoes.
7. Johnny Diamond.
8. A knife.
9. Nelse McLeod.
10. The job Wayne turned down months before.
11. To get rid of his hat and use a gun.
12. Wayne recognizes his hat at a distance.
13. Poe.
14. He is a drunk and hasn't been sober for quite awhile.
15. In the bugle.
16. Behind the piano.
17. John Mitchum.
18. Wayne's side goes numb.
19. He assumes a Chinese disguise to gain entrance in the back of the saloon.
20. By Mississippi's shotgun.

The War Wagon (1967), UNIVERSAL

1. How long was Wayne in prison?
2. What is Wayne's plan?
3. Name the actor who plays Lomax.
4. What is Wayne doing when Lomax shoots at him at the film's start?
5. What is Lomax's other occupation besides gunfighter?
6. What does Wayne use to show Lomax his plan?
7. Name the actor who plays Levi Walking Bear.
8. Name the actor who plays Billy Hyatt.
9. Name the actor who plays the film's villian, Frank Pierce.
10. How long is the War Wagon from lead horse to back end?
11. Name the actress who deals cards in the saloon.
12. What prevents the impending saloon gunfight between Wayne and Lomax?
13. What is the new addition to the War Wagon?
14. Where do Wayne and Hyatt place nitro bottles?
15. How do Wayne and Lomax board the War Wagon?
16. How is Pierce killed?
17. Where is the money hidden during the getaway?
18. What does Lomax take from Wayne at this time?
19. How long will Lomax have to wait for his share?
20. What is the new item Wayne wears in this film for the first time?

AUTHOR'S NOTE: The world premiere of *The War Wagon* was held at the Majestic Theatre in Dallas, Texas on Saturday May 27, 1967.

El Dorado was filmed in the fall of 1965. *The War Wagon* was filmed in the fall of 1966. *The War Wagon* was released in May and *El Dorado* in June 1967.

1. Two years.
2. To obtain his ranch and land that was stolen from him.
3. Kirk Douglas.
4. He is starting to light a cigarette in the saloon.
5. A safecracker.
6. A chopstick.
7. Howard Keel.
8. Robert Walker, Jr.
9. Bruce Cabot.
10. Forty-seven and one-half feet long.
11. Joanna Barnes.
12. Keel enters and forces a fight with Wayne that leads to a brawl and Wayne's escape.
13. A gatling gun.
14. Under a bridge.
15. A piece of wood suspended by ropes is cut loose by Wayne and Douglas, causing it to crash into the driver's seat. This slows the wagon so Wayne and Douglas can board.
16. Cabot shoots a guard, who in turn shoots him.
17. In flour barrels.
18. Wayne's horse.
19. Six months.
20. A gold bracelet Wayne received in Vietnam.

The Green Berets 1968, WARNER BROTHERS

1. What is Wayne's military rank?
2. Name the actor who plays George Beckworth, the news correspondent.
3. Name the actor who plays Sgt. Muldoon.
4. Name the actor who plays Sgt. Petersen.
5. What is Wayne doing when he tells Petersen he is a sergeant?
6. What is Petersen's function?
7. Name the actor who plays Col. Morgan, who Wayne will replace in Vietnam.
8. Name the actor who plays Col. Cai.
9. What is the nickname of the army camp in Nam?
10. What is the camp number?
11. What is the character name of the Vietnamese camp boy?
12. Name the actor who plays Col. Nim.
13. What does Wayne tell Beckworth what due process is, as a prisoner is being tortured?
14. Name the actor who plays the leader of the Seabees.
15. What is Wayne's code word for trouble?
16. What is Wayne's code name?
17. What destroys the V.C. in Wayne's camp after the withdrawal?
18. What is Sgt. Provo's death wish?
19. What is Wayne's new secret mission?
20. What does Wayne tell the boy at the film's end?

AUTHOR'S NOTE: During the Vietnam war, Wayne visited the American troops in 1966. He vowed to make a film about the war effort and bought the rights to Robin Moore's *The Green Berets*. Wayne went from studio to studio, getting turned down. Warner Brothers eventually backed Wayne and the film went into production at Fort Benning, Georgia.

1. Colonel.
2. David Janssen.
3. Aldo Ray.
4. Jim Hutton.
5. Shooting skeet.
6. The scrounger.
7. Bruce Cabot.
8. Jack Soo.
9. Dodge City.
10. Camp A 107.
11. Hamchunk.
12. George Takei.
13. "Out here due process is a bullet."
14. Patrick Wayne.
15. "Tabasco."
16. "Bulldog."
17. "Puff the Magic Dragon."
18. "Provo's Privy."
19. To kidnap a North Vietnamese general.
20. "You let me worry about that Green Beret. You're what this is all about."

Robert Mitchum and Wayne both have physical injuries, but they will get the job done in *El Dorado*.

Wayne discusses with Kirk Douglas his plan for taking back what was his in *The War Wagon*.

Wayne leads the assault in *The Green Berets*.

Wayne cuts down the V.C. flag as Aldo Ray (left) and Edward Faulkner (right) watch in *The Green Berets*.

Hellfighters (1968), UNIVERSAL

1. Name the real person on whom Wayne's character is based.
2. What is Wayne's role?
3. Name the actor who plays Wayne's friend, now an oil executive.
4. Name the actor who plays Greg Parker.
5. Name the actor who plays Joe Horn.
6. How is Wayne injured after the film's first fire?
7. Name the actress who plays Wayne's daughter, Tish.
8. What does Wayne request when he regains consciousness?
9. Why does Wayne punch Greg at the hospital?
10. What news does Wayne hear at the hospital?
11. Name the actress who plays Madelyn Buckman.
12. What had caused the friction between Wayne and his wife?
13. To what Asian area does Wayne travel?
14. What is the type of fire there?
15. Name Wayne's lady friend there.
16. What is the comic relief Wayne hears at the board meeting?
17. In what South American country does the film conclude?
18. How many fires are there that must be extinguished?
19. What is Wayne's plan?
20. What does Tish say her mother needs at the film's end?

AUTHOR'S NOTE: Universal had to pay $300.00 per minute per well during the filming of *Hellfighters*.

1. Red Adair.
2. Wayne extinguishes oil well fires.
3. Jay C. Flippen.
4. Jim Hutton.
5. Bruce Cabot.
6. He is sandwiched between two bulldozers.
7. Katharine Ross.
8. His pants.
9. Hutton allowed Ross to remain at an oil well fire.
10. That Ross and Hutton got married.
11. Vera Miles.
12. Her fear of Wayne's job and impending possible death.
13. Malaysia.
14. A poison oil well fire.
15. Madame Loo.
16. Debate on what color to paint restroom interiors.
17. Venezuela.
18. Five.
19. To extinguish the first and fifth fire simultaneously, and then extinguish the remaining three.
20. A tin hat.

True Grit (1969), PARAMOUNT

1. Name the actress who plays Mattie Ross.
2. Name the actor who runs the funeral parlor.
3. What is Wayne doing in his first scene?
4. Name the actor who plays the Texas Ranger La Boeuf.
5. Name the actor who plays the horse dealer.
6. What is the name of Mattie's horse?
7. How many men had Wayne killed in the line of duty?
8. Name the actor who plays Judge Parker.
9. What is the name of Wayne's cat?
10. What does the drunken Wayne shoot while Mattie watches after supper?
11. What is the character name of Mattie's lawyer?
12. What food item had Chen Lee provided Wayne?
13. Name the actor who plays Quincy.
14. What is the character name of Wayne's ex-wife?
15. What is the character name of Wayne's son?
16. Name the actor who plays Lucky Ned Pepper.
17. How many gunmen does Wayne fight in the meadow?
18. What does Mattie want from Chaney's body?
19. What is Wayne's final film scene?
20. Where was the film's location shooting done?

AUTHOR'S NOTE: In *True Grit*, Wayne wears Gary Cooper's silver and leather western hatband. This was a gift to Director Henry Hathaway from Cooper, a close friend.

Wayne was furnished with a new eyepatch every day during the filming of *True Grit*.

1. Kim Darby.
2. Hank Worden.
3. He is unloading prisoners from the territory.
4. Glen Campbell.
5. Strother Martin.
6. Little Blackie.
7. "Counting them two Whartons, 23."
8. James Westerfield.
9. General Sterling Price.
10. A rat.
11. J. Noble Daggett.
12. Corn dodgers.
13. Jeremy Slate.
14. Nola.
15. Horace.
16. Robert Duvall.
17. Four.
18. Her father's pistol and gold piece.
19. Wayne is on horseback, jumping over a fence.
20. Montrose, Colorado.

The Undefeated (1969), 20TH CENTURY-FOX

1. What does Wayne discover after the first battle?
2. Name the actor who plays Colonel Langdon.
3. Name the actor who plays his sergeant.
4. Name the actor who plays Big George.
5. Name the actress who plays Colonel Langdon's wife.
6. Name the actor who plays Wayne's army commander.
7. Name the actor who plays Short Grub.
8. Name the actor who plays Blue Boy.
9. What are Wayne and Short Grub playing while they wait for Blue Boy?
10. Name the actor who plays McCartney the cook.
11. What is the name of his cat?
12. Who is waiting at the stage stop to buy Wayne's horses?
13. What friendly warning does Wayne give Col. Langdon when they meet?
14. Name the actor who plays the Mexican bandit leader.
15. What is the phrase Wayne speaks to the character Ann Langdon?
16. What holiday is the background for the friendly fight?
17. What city had Wayne's wife moved to when she left him?
18. Name the actress who stops the brawl between the soldiers.
19. What does Wayne say he is going to give the Mexicans a taste of?
20. What song is eventually agreed upon by everyone for Harry Carey, Jr., to play on the harmonica.

AUTHOR'S NOTE: *The Undefeated* featurette shows how the final stampede sequence is staged. What looks complex on film is less effective when shown at different angles. Wayne and Hudson are in separate rows, as are the horses. A camera can't film depth, so Wayne and Hudson appear to be meshed with the action, but in actuality they aren't, thanks to the wizardry of the special effects people.

1. The war had ended three days before.
2. Rock Hudson.
3. Bruce Cabot.
4. Merlin Olsen.
5. Lee Meriwether.
6. Paul Fix.
7. Ben Johnson.
8. Roman Gabriel.
9. Checkers.
10. Dub Taylor.
11. High Bread.
12. Two Mexicans.
13. Mexican bandits are getting ready to attack.
14. Pedro Armendariz, Jr.
15. "Windage and elevation, Mrs. Langdon."
16. The Fourth of July.
17. Philadelphia.
18. Marian McCargo.
19. General Sherman's War.
20. "Yankee Doodle."

Wayne looks in place as he battles oil well fires in *Hellfighters.*

Wayne serves "a rat writ, writ for a rat" by shooting a rat as Kim Darby watches in *True Grit.*

Wayne is looking for signs at close hand in *True Grit*.

Bruce Cabot is the victim of Wayne's haymaker in *The Undefeated.*"

Wayne and Director Howard Hawks look at home on
the set of *Rio Lobo*.

THE 1970's

Chisum (1970), WARNER BROTHERS

1. What is Chisum's full name?
2. Chisum is King of the ———.
3. Where does he take stock of his land?
4. Name the actor who plays his friend Pepper.
5. Name the actor who runs the stage depot.
6. What does Wayne say he brought to buy back his horses from the rustlers?
7. What does Wayne allow the character Juan to use?
8. Name the actor who plays Henry Tunstall.
9. Name the actor who plays Billy the Kid.
10. From what city is Chisum's niece?
11. Name the actor who plays L.G. Murphy.
12. What type of drinking man is Chisum?
13. Name the actor who plays Pat Garrett.
14. What is the character name of Chisum's Indian friend?
15. What does Wayne offer the army sergeant?
16. What does Chisum tell the sergeant?
17. What does Wayne use for cover to enter town in the finale?
18. By what unorthodox method does Wayne confront Murphy?
19. How does Murphy meet his fate?
20. Where is Chisum in the film's final scene?

AUTHOR'S NOTE: The television prints of *Chisum* do not show how Forrest Tucker's character meets his fate. When Wayne looks at Tucker, the scene showing Tucker's body, gored by cattle horns, has been cut.

1. John Simpson Chisum.
2. Pecos.
3. On horseback atop a hill.
4. Ben Johnson.
5. Hank Worden.
6. "Just lead."
7. To water his horses on Wayne's land.
8. Patric Knowles.
9. Geoffrey Deuel.
10. Baltimore.
11. Forrest Tucker.
12. "A bourbon man—on the inside."
13. Glenn Corbett.
14. White Buffalo.
15. A cigar.
16. "You touch White Buffalo again and I'll kill ya."
17. By cattle stampede.
18. He rides through a window on horseback.
19. He is gored by a pair of cattle horns.
20. Atop his hill looking over his land.

Rio Lobo (1971), NATIONAL GENERAL

1. What is Wayne doing while the train robbery occurs?
2. How is Wayne later taken prisoner?
3. How does Wayne plan the arrest of the rebel officer?
4. Why does Wayne want the traitor?
5. Name the actress who plays Shasta.
6. Name the actor who attempts to shoot Wayne from behind in the saloon gunfight.
7. What does Shasta want from Rio Lobo?
8. Who does Wayne find next to him when he awakens on the trail?
9. Name the actor who plays the Rio Lobo sheriff, Hendricks.
10. Name the actor who plays the dentist.
11. How much money does Wayne give the dentist when he leaves?
12. What is Wayne's response when the dentist asks Wayne his name?
13. Name the actor who plays Phillips.
14. Name the actor who plays Ketchum.
15. What is Wayne's plan in Rio Lobo?
16. What thwarts this plan?
17. What does Wayne exchange before the trade?
18. What does Wayne take from Ketchum at the exchange point?
19. Where is Wayne wounded in the finale?
20. Who composed the film's music score?

AUTHOR'S NOTE: While working on *Rio Lobo*, Wayne won his Academy Award. He was to appear on the set the next day for a 10:00 call. Wayne was greeted by the film company of about 200, each wearing an eyepatch.

1. Waiting for the train to arrive unharmed.
2. Wayne is knocked off his horse and struck in the head.
3. Wayne bends a branch and releases it, causing havoc. This affects Wayne's rescue and the arrest of the officer.
4. A junior officer Wayne liked died the next day after the robbery and the theft of the money.
5. Jennifer O'Neill.
6. George Plimpton.
7. A medicine wagon.
8. O'Neill. (She tells Wayne she chose him because he was "comfortable.")
9. Mike Henry.
10. David Huddleston.
11. Four bits.
12. "It doesn't matter."
13. Jack Elam.
14. Victor French.
15. To rescue Chris Mitchum from jail and join him there with Ketchum as prisoner.
16. One of Wayne's men is held prisoner in exchange for Ketchum.
17. Wayne exchanges rifles, using his own.
18. His belt.
19. The left leg.
20. Jerry Goldsmith.

Forrest Tucker gets his just desserts from Wayne in
Chisum.

Wayne strikes a familiar doorway pose in *Rio Lobo*.

Big Jake (1971), NATIONAL GENERAL

1. Name the actor who plays the lead villain, John Fain.
2. Name the actor who plays Little Jake McCandles.
3. Name the actress who plays Martha McCandles.
4. Name the actor who plays the ranch foreman, Bert Ryan.
5. What is the amount of ransom requested for Little Jake?
6. What is Wayne doing in his first scene?
7. What is Wayne's dog's name?
8. Name the actor who plays James McCandles.
9. What happens to Wayne when the motorcycle rider arrives?
10. Name the actor who plays Michael McCandles.
11. Name the actor who plays Sam Sharpnose, the Indian scout.
12. What incident befalls the Texas Rangers.
13. What does Wayne do to his son James that causes James pain?
14. What does Wayne offer Fain when Fain rides into camp?
15. Where does Wayne dispose of his intended killer?
16. What happened to the ransom box in the hotel room?
17. What does Wayne say to Fain when Fain opens the ransom box?
18. What weapon does Wayne give Little Jake?
19. How many times is Wayne wounded?
20. Who saves Wayne and Little Jake at the film's end?

AUTHOR'S NOTE: In the climax of *Big Jake,* the arched courtyard of Don Luis Flores is utilized. Historically this courtyard was used by Pancho Villa and his men where they slaughtered 750 persons.
The original shooting title for *Big Jake* was *The Million Dollar Kidnapping.*

1. Richard Boone.
2. Ethan Wayne.
3. Maureen O'Hara.
4. John Agar.
5. $1,000,000.
6. Watching a sheep herder about to be hanged.
7. "Dog."
8. Patrick Wayne.
9. The motorcycle spooks Wayne's horse and Wayne falls into a mud puddle.
10. Christopher Mitchum.
11. Bruce Cabot.
12. An ambush set up by Fain.
13. Wayne pulls shotgun pellets out of Patrick Wayne's backside.
14. A peach.
15. A shower stall.
16. The lock is broken by a gun blast, revealing there isn't any ransom money, just news clippings.
17. "Now you understand. Anything goes wrong, anything at all, your fault, my fault, nobody's fault. It don't matter. I'm gonna blow your head off. It's as simple as that.... No matter what else happens. No matter who gets killed. I'm gonna blow your head off."
18. A derringer.
19. Twice (left leg and left arm).
20. Mitchum.

Wayne protects his grandson (actually his youngest son, Ethan) from impending trouble in *Big Jake*.

The Cowboys (1972), WARNER BROTHERS

1. Which film composer did the score?
2. Name the film's director.
3. Why do Wayne's cowhands leave his ranch?
4. Name the actor who plays Wayne's friend Anse.
5. What is the school teacher's character name?
6. What dissuades Wayne from hiring the school boys?
7. What does Wayne do when he thinks he will not find any cowhands?
8. What is the name of the horse the cowboys must ride to prove themselves?
9. How many sons did Wayne have?
10. What is the total number of miles on the trail drive?
11. What is the name of the town's destination?
12. How is the smallest boy accepted when Wayne leaves the school?
13. Name the actor who plays Jebediah Nightlinger.
14. Name the actor who plays Long Hair.
15. What historical landmark is passed on the drive?
16. Name the actress who plays the madam, Kate.
17. What does Wayne tell Long Hair before their fight starts?
18. Who wins the fist fight?
19. How does Wayne meet his fate?
20. What words are on the monument at the film's end.

AUTHOR'S NOTE: Wayne enjoyed working with the young cast and director Mark Rydell.

1. John Williams.
2. Mark Rydell.
3. They go gold prospecting.
4. Slim Pickens.
5. Ellen Price.
6. The boys try to scare the girls with a frog.
7. He frees his livestock.
8. Crazy Alice.
9. Two.
10. 400
11. Belle Fouche, Montana.
12. Wayne draws a line on a blackboard just high enough so that when it is lowered, the small boy will be the right height for the cattle drive.

13. Roscoe Lee Browne.
14. Bruce Dern.
15. Little Big Horn.
16. Colleen Dewhurst.
17. "I'm 30 years older than you are. I've had my back busted once, my hip twice, and on my worst day I could beat the hell out of you."
18. Wayne, of course.
19. He is shot from behind by Dern.
20. "Beloved Father and Husband"

Wayne proceeds to beat Bruce Dern to a pulp in *The Cowboys.*

Cancel My Reservation (1972),
WARNER BROTHERS

1. What is Wayne's one line in the film?

AUTHOR'S NOTE: This is a Bob Hope film. There is a sequence in which Hope is in jail. While there, he imagines he is going to be hanged. Wayne appears and utters his one line of dialogue.

1. "I'd like to help ya, but it's not my picture."

The Train Robbers (1973), WARNER BROTHERS

1. In what town does the film start?
2. Name the actor awaiting Wayne by the train track who plays Jesse.
3. Name the actor who plays Grady.
4. How many days late is Wayne?
5. Name Wayne's female co-star, who plays Mrs. Lowe.
6. How much money is hidden?
7. How much is the reward for the stolen money?
8. In what is the gold buried?
9. What does Wayne tell Mrs. Lowe to do with her shirt?
10. Which actor tells her about Wayne's past?
11. How long had Wayne been married before his wife died?
12. Who is the leader of the bad guys?
13. What gets stolen from Wayne's camp the first night?
14. What incident brings the group together during the thunderstorm?
15. From what do Wayne and Jesse rescue Mrs. Lowe?
16. Why does Wayne get her drunk?
17. What is Wayne's response when she suggests they turn back?
18. What is Wayne's plan after they find the gold in the desert?
19. How does Wayne save the day in the finale?
20. Name the actor who plays the Pinkerton agent.

AUTHOR'S NOTE: During the filming, Wayne discovered Ann-Margret had a fear of horses. Wayne noticed she was nervous during a night shot. She explained her fear to him. Wayne, an expert horseman, took her under his wing and allayed her fear.

During the filming of *Train Robbers*, Ben Johnson and Ann-Margret wanted to attend the 1972 Academy Awards Ceremony. Johnson was nominated for *The Last Picture Show* and Ann-Margret for *Carnal Knowledge*. No planes were available because of the desert filming. Wayne loaned his personal plane to them so they could both attend the ceremony. Johnson won but Ann-Margret lost. They both flew back for location filming the next day.

1. Liberty, Texas.
2. Ben Johnson.
3. Rod Taylor.
4. One day.
5. Ann-Margret.
6. One-half million dollars.
7. $50,000.
8. In a train engine boiler.
9. To boil it.
10. Johnson.
11. One year.
12. There isn't one (surprise).
13. Their mule packed with dynamite.
14. A tree falls onto Chris George's horse and they all free the horse.
15. Drowning.
16. To make her reveal where the gold is.
17. "When I start plying a woman with whiskey, it's time to throw the key in the water bucket and ride on."
18. To stay by the train with the empty strong box in the open, so the bad guys will know they have the gold."
19. He throws dynamite into the buildings where the bad guys are from a train.
20. Ricardo Montalban.

Cahill: U.S. Marshal (1973), WARNER BROTHERS

1. What does Wayne do first when he rides into the outlaw camp?
2. Name the actor who plays Wayne's Indian friend.
3. How many bad buys are there in the camp?
4. Where is Wayne wounded?
5. What song does Wayne sing on the way to town?
6. What is the name of the town Wayne is marshal of?
7. Name the actor who watches Wayne's sons.
8. Who plays Charlie Smith, the town drunk?
9. Name the two actors who play Wayne's sons.
10. Name the actor who plays the heavy, Abe Fraser.
11. Why are he and Wayne's older son in jail?
12. How does Wayne sleep on a train while guarding the prisoners?
13. Name the actor who plays Hank, the deputy.
14. Name the actress who runs the boarding house.
15. Why does a mob wait for Wayne at the river?
16. Name the actor Wayne does some horse dealing with.
17. What does Wayne end up riding at that point?
18. At what does Wayne shoot to make sure Fraser is dead?
19. Where is Wayne wounded at this point?
20. What is Wayne's advice to his sons?

AUTHOR'S NOTE: *Wednesday Morning* was the original shooting title.

1. He puts his marshal's badge on his coat.
2. Neville Brand.
3. Four.
4. Upper part of the left chest.
5. "Streets of Laredo."
6. Valentine, Texas.
7. Denver Pyle.
8. Jackie Coogan.
9. Gary Grimes and Clay O'Brien.
10. George Kennedy.
11. They were involved in a saloon fight.
12. Peacefully with a cocked shotgun.
13. Harry Carey, Jr.
14. Marie Windsor.
15. To lynch Wayne's prisoners.
16. Royal Dano.
17. A mule.
18. Kennedy's hat.
19. Upper part of the left chest.
20. "Don't rob banks."

McQ (1974), WARNER BROTHERS

1. What is McQ's first name?
2. In what city does the film take place?
3. On what does Wayne live?
4. Who does Wayne think caused the cop killings?
5. Name the actor who plays Wayne's superior, Captain Kosterman.
6. Who does he suspect of the murders?
7. How does Wayne silence the agitator?
8. Name the actor who plays Santiago.
9. Name the actress who plays Wayne's ex-wife.
10. Name the actress who plays the cocktail waitress, Myra.
11. Name the actor who plays Wayne's cover after Wayne leaves the force.
12. Where does the drug theft take place in the police station?
13. What does Wayne encounter two of during the car chase?
14. What does Wayne shoot to test the Ingram?
15. Where does Wayne conceal the Ingram?
16. What does Santiago receive instead of the drugs?
17. How does a surrounded Wayne escape from the car pound?
18. What has an unaware Wayne been carrying in his car?
19. Where does Wayne confront Santiago in the finale?
20. What does Kosterman return to Wayne at the film's end?

AUTHOR'S NOTE: Stunt driver Gary McLarty performed the film's final car stunt in a 1973 four door Chevy Impala. 50-50 shocks and air bags were used. The cannon, the firing device, measured 12 × 36 inches and weighed 400 pounds. Reinforced tie rods prevented the car from collapsing and wheels from folding. The steering wheel was turned to the right with the left hand, starting the stunt. The brakes were then rammed. Both of these actions caused the car to raise at a 45 degree angle. The cannon was detonated with the right hand, catapulting the car into the air at 75 mph. The car flipped over six times, covering some 40 yards in 4½ seconds.

1. Lon.
2. Seattle, Washington.
3. A boat.
4. A drug mogul named Santiago.
5. Eddie Albert.
6. Radicals.
7. Wayne kicks him in the shin.
8. Al Littieri.
9. Julie Adams.
10. Colleen Dewhurst.
11. David Huddleston.
12. The incinerator room.
13. Laundry trucks, one of which has the drugs.
14. A garbage can full of water.
15. In his gym bag.
16. Powdered sugar.
17. Wayne hot wires a police car.
18. The drugs.
19. Along a Pacific Ocean beach coast.
20. His badge.

Brannigan (1975), UNITED ARTISTS

1. In which American city is Wayne a cop?
2. Who is Wayne looking for when we first see him?
3. Name the actor who plays Wayne's captain.
4. Name the actor who plays Wayne's nemesis, Larkin.
5. Name the actress who plays Wayne's London partner, Jennifer.
6. Why had Wayne been in London years before?
7. What had Jennifer's father told her about the Yanks that applies to Wayne?
8. Name the actress who receives a visit from the hit man.
9. Name the actor who plays Sir Charles Swann.
10. What is Wayne given when he enters The Garrick Club?
11. What is Wayne's weapon?
12. What nickname does Wayne give the mail switch?
13. Where does Wayne find the second trap in his flat after he escapes the shotgun blast?
14. What kind of beer does Wayne order in the bar sequence?
15. What type of car does Wayne use to chase the hit man?
16. What is "that item" Wayne is to surrender after his partner is almost shot?
17. What do the police receive in the mail to show the kidnappers have Larkin?
18. Name the actor Wayne suspects of assisting Larkin.
19. What is the occupation of Wayne's son in Chicago?
20. How does Wayne discover where the kidnappers are at the film's end?

AUTHOR'S NOTE: On the set of *Brannigan*, Director Douglas Hickox called the British actors "Darling" or "Love." It was always "Duke" for Wayne.

1. Chicago.
2. A counterfeiter.
3. Ralph Meeker.
4. John Vernon.
5. Judy Geeson.
6. World War II.
7. The yanks were "overpayed, oversexed and over here."
8. Lesley-Anne Down.
9. Richard Attenborough.
10. A tie.
11. 38 caliber Diamond Back Colt.
12. A "Murphy."
13. The toilet.
14. Guinness.
15. A Capri.
16. His gun.
17. A finger.
18. Mel Ferrer.
19. The Assistant D.A. of Cook County.
20. Wayne had hidden a mike in the ransom money.

Wayne leads Ann-Margret and Ben Johnson in *The Train Robbers*.

Wayne's prowess with a six gun is still up to par in *Cahill: U.S. Marshal*.

Wayne prepares to take aim at a hit man in *McQ*.

Another hit man will soon fall victim to Wayne in *Brannigan*.

160

Rooster Cogburn (1975), UNIVERSAL

1. What is the name of the criminal Wayne catches at the film's start?
2. Name the actor who plays Judge Parker.
3. What is a lustrum?
4. What does Wayne lose in court?
5. Name the actor who plays the villain, Hawk.
6. What does he steal?
7. Name the actor who plays Breed.
8. Name the actress who plays Eula Goodnight.
9. What tragedy befalls her?
10. Where does Wayne first meet Eula?
11. What name does Eula call Wayne?
12. What is Wayne's plan to regain the stolen goods?
13. What does Wayne shoot at when he is drunk?
14. Of what incident from his past does Wayne tell Eula and Wolf?
15. Of what does Eula approve that Wayne does after supper?
16. What is the weapon used on Hawk's men when they try to recapture the wagon from Wayne?
17. Name the actor who plays the ferry operator, McCoy.
18. At what does Wayne shoot to dispose of the bad guys?
19. What is Eula's new destination after Wayne is reinstated?
20. What book and chapter does Wayne refer to Eula about his drinking?

AUTHOR'S NOTE: On the first day of shooting, the crew members displayed some homemade bumper stickers that read: "God Bless John Wayne. And Sister Kate, Too."

1. Pecos.
2. John McIntire.
3. Five years.
4. His marshal's badge.
5. Richard Jordan.
6. A wagonload of nitroglycerine.
7. Anthony Zerbe.
8. Katharine Hepburn.
9. Her father is killed by Hawk's men.
10. At the grave site of Eula's father.
11. Reuben.
12. To set up an ambush and take the wagon.
13. Corn dodgers and an empty whiskey bottle.
14. The time he shot Lucky Ned Pepper's gang.
15. Smoking a cigar.
16. A gatling gun.
17. Strother Martin.
18. The nitro cases floating on the river.
19. California.
20. "Rooster Cogburn, 1880."

The Shootist (1976), PARAMOUNT

1. Which Wayne film clips are shown in the montage at the film's start?
2. At what town does Wayne arrive?
3. What famous person's death does Wayne read about in the paper?
4. Name the actor who plays Doc Hostetler.
5. What does Hostetler tell Wayne?
6. Name the actress who plays Bond Rogers.
7. Name the actor who plays her son, Gilliam Rogers.
8. What is the name of Wayne's horse?
9. What type of pistol does Wayne use?
10. Name the actor who plays Marshal Thibido.
11. What item does the blacksmith find that shows Wayne's identity?
12. Name the actor who plays Pulford the faro dealer.
13. Name the actor who plays Mike Sweeney.
14. What businessman does Wayne allow to take advantage of his death?
15. Name the actress who plays Serepta.
16. What does Wayne give the trolley car driver before the gunfight?
17. What is Wayne's plan?
18. What is Wayne's fate?
19. What is Wayne's silent request?
20. Name the film's director.

AUTHOR'S NOTE: Of *The Shootist*, Wayne said: "This is the kind of picture you wait for. They don't come by often so when they do, you grab fast."

The actor who plays Murray, the bartender, is Michael Currie. He has since appeared in *Firefox* and *Sudden Impact*.

Wayne's horse Dollor was owned by Terry Bush of Williamsburg, Iowa, from October 1982 to November 1983. Dollor, as of July 1985, is a 19-year-old Quarter Horse. Wayne thought so much of him that he had him written into his contracts. The horse has appeared at many public functions and has been seen in *Dynasty* on TV. The word Dollor is from the Spanish *dolor*, meaning pain or sorrow. He is presently owned by Dave Pelham and co-owners of Dallas, Texas. He is kept near the town of Midlothian, located approximately 25 miles southwest of Dallas, and is currently for sale for $50,000. He appeared in *True Grit*, *Big Jake*, *The Cowboys*, *The Train Robbers*, *Rooster Cogburn* and *The Shootist*.

1. *Red River*, *Hondo*, *El Dorado* and *Rio Bravo*.
2. Carson City, Nevada.
3. Queen Victoria.
4. James Stewart.
5. Wayne is dying of cancer.
6. Lauren Bacall.
7. Ron Howard.
8. Old Dollor.
9. An ivory-handled .44.
10. Harry Morgan
11. A label under Wayne's saddle with his name on it.
12. Hugh O'Brien.
13. Richard Boone.
14. The barber.
15. Sheree North.
16. His pillow.
17. To kill the three men in the saloon awaiting him, and for them to kill Wayne.
18. Wayne is shot in the back with a shotgun by Murray, the bartender.
19. Ron Howard shoots Murray. Afterwards Wayne sees Howard throw the gun across the floor, appalled by the killing, and Wayne dies.
20. Don Siegel.

Katharine Hepburn and Wayne take on the bad guys in *Rooster Cogburn*.

Wayne in the climactic gunfight from *The Shootist*.

PART THREE

JOHN WAYNE THE MAN

So You Think You Know All About John Wayne

This contest is designed for the John Wayne connoisseur. Match the film titles with the character John Wayne played in that film. So ride tall and shoot right through the answers, pilgrim. The answers are on page 168.

1. How the West Was Won
2. In Old California
3. Three Godfathers
4. The Searchers
5. Tall in the Saddle
6. The Horse Soldiers
7. Operation Pacific
8. The Shootist
9. The Dark Command
10. Pittsburgh
11. Sands of Iwo Jima
12. Blood Alley
13. The Undefeated
14. Circus World
15. Stagecoach
16. The Sea Chase
17. Hatari
18. Lady for a Night
19. Trouble Along the Way
20. The Comancheros
21. Allegheny Uprising
22. Tycoon
23. The Train Robbers
24. Reunion in France
25. Fort Apache
26. Island in the Sky
27. The Green Berets
28. A Man Betrayed
29. Dakota
30. Flying Leathernecks
31. The Long Voyage Home
32. Jet Pilot
33. The Cowboys
34. Three Faces West
35. The Barbarian and the Geisha
36. Back to Bataan
37. The High and the Mighty

38. The War Wagon
39. Cancel My Reservation
40. Seven Sinners
41. North to Alaska
42. A Lady Takes a Chance
43. The Fighting Kentuckian
44. I Married a Woman
45. Cast a Giant Shadow
46. Lady From Louisiana
47. Angel and the Badman
48. The Wings of Eagles
49. True Grit
50. Flying Tigers
51. The Longest Day
52. The Shepherd of the Hills
53. Without Reservations
54. The Quiet Man
55. Rio Lobo
56. The Conqueror
57. Flame of Barbary Coast
58. Rio Grande
59. Hellfighters
60. Reap the Wild Wind
61. Legend of the Lost
62. They Were Expendable
63. The Spoilers
64. The Greatest Story Ever Told
65. Red River
66. War of the Wildcats
67. She Wore a Yellow Ribbon
68. The Fighting Seabees
69. El Dorado
70. Rio Bravo
71. Wake of the Red Witch
72. The Alamo
73. In Harm's Way
74. The Man Who Shot Liberty Valance

The Wayne Characters

A. Chance Buckman
B. Lynn Hollister
C. Wilder
D. Sean Mercer
E. Matt Masters
F. Rocklin
G. Joe January
H. Ringo Kid
I. John Wayne
J. Duke Gifford
K. Bob Seton
L. Charles Markham
M. Robert Hightower
N. John Phillips
O. Rusty Thomas
P. Jake Cutter
Q. Sean Thornton
R. Lt. Dan Brent
S. John Devlin
T. Dan Roman
U. Jim Gordon
V. Col. John Marlowe
W. Sgt. John M. Stryker
X. "Spig" Wead
Y. Lt. Rusty Ryan
Z. Jack Morgan
a. Col. Joseph Madden
b. Roy Glennister
c. Gen. Mike Randolph
d. Lane
e. Jim Smith
f. Dan Somers
g. Johnny Munroe
h. Lt. Col. Benjamin Vandervoort
i. John Breen
j. Ole Olsen
k. John Bernard Books

l. Tom Doniphon
m. Ethan Edwards
n. Lt. Col. Kirby Yorke
o. John Reynolds
p. Will Andersen
q. Cole Thornton
r. Pat Talbot
s. Sam McCord
t. Duke Fergus
u. Cord McNally
v. Davy Crockett
w. Matt Matthews
x. Wedge Donovan
y. Townsend Harris
z. Tom Craig
I. Capt. Rockwell Torrey
II. Capt. Jack Stuart
III. Col. Shannon
IV. Steve Williams
V. Capt. Kirby York
VI. Duke Hudkins
VII. John T. Chance
VIII. Col. John Henry Thomas
IX. Quirt Evans
X. Major Dan Kirby
XI. General William Sherman
XII. Capt. Karl Ehrlich
XIII. Rooster Cogburn
XIV. Capt. Ralls
XV. Col. Mike Kirby
XVI. John Wayne
XVII. Capt. Dooley
XVIII. Roman Centurion
XIX. Genghis Khan
XX. Capt. Nathan Brittles
XXI. Taw Jackson
XXII. Tom Dunson

Answers

1. XI
2. z
3. M
4. m
5. F
6. V (vee)
7. J
8. k
9. K
10. L
11. W
12. C
13. VIII
14. E
15. H
16. XII
17. D
18. Z
19. IV
20. P
21. e
22. g
23. d
24. r
25. V (five)
26. XVII
27. XV
28. B
29. S
30. X (ten)
31. j
32. III
33. p
34. N
35. y
36. a
37. T
38. XXI
39. I or XVI (letter i)
40. R.
41. s
42. VI
43. i
44. XVI or I (letter i)
45. c
46. o
47. IX
48. X (the letter)
49. XIII
50. U
51. h
52. w
53. O
54. Q
55. u.
56. XIX
57. t
58. n
59. A
60. II
61. G
62. Y
63. b
64. XVIII
65. XXII
66. f
67. XX
68. x
69. q
70. VII
71. XIV
72. v
73. I (one)
74. l

DID YOU KNOW THAT ...

Did You Know That...

1. Some of Wayne's hobbies were playing chess, bridge, poker and going on deep sea fishing cruises?
2. Wayne had a size 18 neck and wore size 11 boot?
3. Wayne had a perforated eardrum?
4. Wayne collected walking canes?
5. Wayne had a bad memory and couldn't remember names?
6. Wayne was a compulsive gambler?
7. Wayne was a practical joker and was always involved in some gag?
8. Wayne loved to clip coupons and obtain mail order items like little gadgets he sent away for in the mail.
9. Wayne was an excellent ballroom dancer?
10. Wayne considered talking with moviegoers good public relations?
11. Robert Frost was one of Wayne's favorite poets?
12. Tom Mix helped Wayne get his start in the movie business?
13. Wayne's favorite singer was Frank Sinatra?
14. Wayne liked country music?
15. Wayne's favorite country and western singer was Charley Pride?
16. Wayne's photographic equipment was worth over $10,000?
17. Wayne was a soft touch?
18. Wayne owned a Cessna plane?
19. Wayne's first movie hero was Douglas Fairbanks, Sr.?
20. Wayne was a crack pistol and rifle shot?
21. Wayne wore his watch crystal inwards?
22. Wayne hated telephones and eating fish?
23. Wayne had a box at Dodger Stadium but rarely used it?
24. Wayne owned shrimp boats out of Panama?
25. Wayne owned a custom-built Winnebago?
26. Wayne's star appears at 1541 Vine Street in front of the Merv Griffin Theatre?
27. Wayne collected comic books, Kachina western dolls, and cowboy outfits?
28. Wayne owned a share of Al Capp's comic book publishing company?
29. Wayne had a television set mounted in his bedroom ceiling?
30. Wayne watched all of Lucille Ball's television shows?
31. Wayne's favorite crime show was *Hawaii Five-O*?
32. Wayne defended *Sanford and Son* and *All in the Family* because these shows made us laugh at ourselves?
33. Wayne didn't watch his old movies because of the editing, and the westerns lost effect on small television screens?
34. Wayne believed that pay television would save the film and television industry?
35. Wayne was in the 91% tax bracket?
36. Wayne sprinkled his eggs with celery salt?
37. Wayne liked to cook?
38. Wayne averaged a 94 grade in all of his high school subjects?
39. Wayne would screen movies in his home projection room?
40. Wayne's yacht "Wild Goose" was used in Director Otto Preminger's *Skidoo*?

41. Wayne had a 20 volume set of *The North American Indian* by Edward S. Curtis?
42. Wayne's director's chair was black and tan with the name *Duke* embellished on the back of the chair?
43. Wayne had mining interests in Nigeria?
44. Wayne owned oil wells in Texas?
45. Wayne's favorite western writer was Emmet Rhodes?
46. Wayne smoked Camel Cigarettes?
47. Wayne did full page magazine ads for Camel Cigarettes in the 1950's?
48. Wayne liked to have accordionist Danny Borzage on the set?
49. Wayne's favorite make-up man was Webb Overlander?
50. Wayne's favorite photo of himself was a publicity shot taken of him when he was 23 years old on the set of *The Big Trail*?
51. A life-like wax figure of Wayne as *Hondo* appears at the Movieland Wax Museum in Buena Park, California?
52. Wayne's favorite drink was tequila with lemon? He preferred Commemorativo Tequila.
53. Wayne and Maureen O'Hara were close friends?
54. Wayne always gave autographed cards to autograph seekers? He would sign many of these in advance.
55. Screenwriter Frank Nugent said of Wayne: "Having Wayne put his arm on your shoulder is like having somebody drop a telephone pole on you"?
56. Wayne had a bumper sticker on his station wagon that read: "The Marines Are Looking For Strong Men"?
57. Wayne had his boots made by Lucchese Boot Company in San Antonio, Texas?
58. On a hunting trip, Wayne accidentally shot Ward Bond in the back with Bond's shotgun? Wayne carried Bond quite a distance to the hospital. Bond recovered from the wounds. After Bond passed away in 1960, Wayne was willed the shotgun.
59. Wayne and Janet Leigh both had the same last name of Morrison before becoming stars?
60. Wayne owned some Remington sculpture?
61. George Montgomery did a bronze of Wayne called "The Legend."
62. Harry Jackson did a sculpture of Wayne from *True Grit*, a bronze casting weighing 75 pounds? It measured three feet in height and four feet in length.
63. Wayne had a Charles Russell sculpture "Changing Outfits" on his desk in his study? Wayne's study was the largest room in his home.
64. Wayne learned to swim in an irrigation ditch?
65. Wayne rode a horse named Jenny to school?
66. Wayne Wayne received his nickname "Duke" from the Glendale Fire Department? He had an Airedale named "Duke" and the firemen called the dog "Big Duke." Wayne was "Little Duke." As Wayne became taller, the firemen called him "Duke."
67. Wayne's first job was picking apricots on his summer vacations?
68. Wayne spent a night in jail for stowing away on the U.S.S. *Malolo*, bound for Hawaii?
69. Wayne worked on an ice truck while in college? He was a Sigma Chi.
70. One of Wayne's biggest disappointments was when he lost his appointment to Annapolis? This is one reason why he liked to play military-related roles.
71. Duke Morrison won The Southern California Shakespeare Oratory Contest for his recital of Cardinal Wolsey's farewell speech in *Henry VIII*?
72. Wayne earned $35.00 a week as a prop boy moving furniture on movie sets?
73. Wayne herded geese on the set of John Ford's *Mother Machree*?
74. Playing pitch was an early interest of Wayne's and Ford's? This was the beginning bond of their friendship.

75. The first article written about Wayne appeared in the December, 1930, issue of *Photoplay*?
76. Paul Fix was an early acting coach for Wayne?
77. Wayne and Yakima Canutt developed screen fighting?
78. Wayne hated the song "Granada"?
79. Wayne was a true perfectionist and had little patience with sloppiness and carelessness in others?
80. Wayne's favorite horse was named Banner? He was used in every Wayne western from 1940-1954.
81. Wayne was always ready to offer encouragement and thoughtful suggestions on the set?
82. Wayne made personal appearances during World War II?
83. Wayne was always meticulously tailored and barbered, and possessed savoir-faire?
84. Wayne couldn't whistle?
85. Wayne had the most fun making *The Quiet Man*?
86. Some of Wayne's heroes were Buck Jones, Douglas MacArthur and Harry Carey, Sr.?
87. Wayne knew everybody's job on the set because he was interested enough when he started in the business to ask questions about the production?
88. Wayne was going to become a lawyer before the movies turned him into a star?
89. George Montgomery got his start as a stand-in for Wayne?
90. Wayne's films have grossed over $700,000,000?
91. At a SHARE Benefit for mentally disturbed children, Wayne sang "Home on the Range"?
92. Wayne had a seven-inch bubble installed over the front seat of his station wagon so he could wear his ten gallon hat?
93. Wayne's birth certificate says Wayne was born Marion Robert Morrison, not Marion Michael Morrison? The certificate was in error.
94. Glenn Strange did the voice of "Singin' Sandy"?
95. Wayne and Lee Marvin appeared in three films together?
96. Wayne and Kirk Douglas appeared in three films together?
97. When Richard Boone agreed to do a film with Wayne, he never signed a contract? A handshake was the agreement.
98. Some of Wayne's favorite films were *Stagecoach, Red River, She Wore a Yellow Ribbon, Sands of Iwo Jima, The Alamo, Hatari, True Grit* and *The Shootist*?
99. One of Merv Griffin's favorite jokes was that Wayne defeated so many Indians in his films that he got hate mail from Jane Fonda?
100. It was rare for Wayne to do more than three takes?
101. Wayne gift-wrapped a statue of himself and sent it to Arizona as a birthday present for Barry Goldwater?
102. Wayne had a ranch in Durango, Mexico called La Joya, "The Jewel"?
103. Wayne presented Joanne Woodward with her Academy Award for *Three Faces of Eve*?
104. Wayne would walk and jog in the mornings?
105. Director Andrew McLaglen once drove 200 miles out of his way to have dinner with Wayne?
106. Wayne owned "26 Bar Ranch" in Stanfield, Arizona, consisting of 17,000 acres? It was headquartered in Springerville, Arizona.
107. Parts of Wayne's ranch was used in the filming of *Who'll Stop the Rain*?
108. *Time* Magazine said of Wayne: "Go west and turn right," and "Wayne is as much in demand in Hollywood as unlimited bank credit"?
109. Batjac Productions owns the rights to: *Island in the Sky, Plunder in the Sun, Hondo, The High and the Mighty, Ring of Fear, Man in the Vault, Seven Men from Now* and *McLintock!*?
110. Before Wayne worked on director Raoul Walsh's *The Big Trail*, he was told to take acting lessons? After three lessons, the acting coach said he couldn't do anything with Wayne.
111. After *Stagecoach*, Wayne was earning $6,000 a film?

112. Wayne helped found The Motion Picture Alliance for the Preservation of American Ideals?

113. Wayne received a *"Red River 'D'"* belt buckle from Director Howard Hawks?

114. Director John Ford was so pleased with Wayne's performance in *Red River* that he gave Wayne a birthday cake with one candle to mark the first anniversary of being an actor of maturity?

115. Wayne was 33rd in the list of top film stars in the country in 1948?

116. Wayne succeeded Robert Taylor as president of The Motion Picture Alliance for the Preservation of American Ideals in 1948? Wayne served three terms.

117. *John Wayne Adventure Comics* were first printed in the winter of 1949? The last issue was #31, printed in May, 1955. These were printed by "Toby Press."

118. Wayne appeared on the *Motion Picture Herald*'s Poll from 1949–1973? Wayne was always in the top ten, 1958 being the exception. In 1950, Wayne was number one. Wayne appeared 23 times in the top five and 25 times in the top ten.

119. Wayne was named favorite actor by *Photoplay* with a "Gold Medal Award" in 1950.

120. A set of six pocket-size giveaways were distributed through the mail as a set in 1950 by Oxydol Dreft? Only #4 had Wayne on the cover.

121. *Flying Leathernecks* was the film in which Wayne started the custom of giving coffee cups to fellow workers?

122. Wayne was paid $301,000 by Howard Hughes for *Flying Leathernecks*? A John Wayne coloring book costing ten cents appeared about this time in 1951.

123. Wayne appeared on the cover of *Time* Magazine on March 3, 1952?

124. Wayne's make-up man Webb Overlander was told he was not needed for the filming of *The Quiet Man*? When Wayne heard this he refused to film until Overlander was on the set. Overlander arrived and filming got under way.

125. In 1953, Wayne accepted Academy Awards for Gary Cooper and John Ford?

126. Wayne appeared on a "Milton Berle Show" to promote *Hondo* in 1953? He had an electric sign on his back and when he turned around, pulled a switch and the word *Hondo* was lit. Wayne did not like doing this.

127. During a poker game on *Hondo,* Wayne won Lassie from Rudd Weatherswax? Wayne felt bad about it and returned the dog.

128. Wayne was hospitalized in 1955 for a strained back during the filming of *Blood Alley*?

129. When Wayne did his bathtub scene for *Blood Alley,* director William Wellman ordered the set closed to all females? Wellman said: "I just thought it was time someone returned the dirty trick."

130. Paul Mantz, the stuntman pilot who died during the filming of *Flight of the Phoenix,* was used in the same capacity in *The Wings of Eagles*? He flew the seaplane through the hangar and crash dived into the swimming pool at The Admiral's Tea Party.

131. Six war airplanes had to be built for *The Wings of Eagles,* as this type of plane no longer existed?

132. Two giant-sized cakes were needed for filming during *The Wings of Eagles*? Director John Ford had six stand-in cakes made. Wayne and actor Ken Tobey had perfect aim on their first takes. The crew ate cake for quite some time.

133. The aircraft carrier USS *Philippine Sea* was used in *The Wings of Eagles*?

134. Wayne's family dog Blackie, a Dachshund, saved Wayne's family from a house fire in 1958 in Encino? At that time, Wayne was on location in Japan for *The Barbarian and the Geisha.* When Wayne returned he gave the dog a hero's medal.

135. Wayne's wife, Pilar, saved Wayne's battered cowboy hat from the fire and other movie mementos?

136. During the filming of *Legend of the Lost,* Wayne injured his right foot and was on crutches?

137. Wayne was given an award at "The Headliner's Banquet" in Texas in 1959?

138. Wayne dominated shooting conferences and the script?
139. In the 1960's, Wayne was earning $750,000 per film?
140. Wayne helped finish directing *The Comancheros* because director Michael Curtiz was taken ill before the filming was completed?
141. Wayne and Bruce Cabot were partners with Prince Bernhard of The Netherlands? "The Prince's Scotch" became available in the U.S. because of the partnership.
142. During the filming of *Hatari*, Wayne actually roped a 450-pound wildebeest in 36 seconds?
143. The filming of *Hatari* lasted for six months? Five months of filming were needed on the various African locations.
144. When the filming of *Hatari* was completed, Wayne stopped in England to present Princess Margaret with a $7500 Texas saddle?
145. Wayne's home at Newport Beach cost $175,000? The French provincial house has 11 rooms and seven bathrooms.
146. Wayne purchased *The Wild Goose* in 1962? This converted minesweeper is 136 feet long and was the pride and joy of Wayne.
147. Wayne earned $250,000 for four days filming on *The Longest Day*?
148. The crews on *The Longest Day* consumed 63,000 meals, drank 145,000 bottles of wine, beer and soft drinks. These costs came to $968,000 during the shooting. This was almost one-tenth of the $10,000,000 budget.
149. Wayne worked for six days and earned $25,000 on *How the West Was Won*?
150. Wayne started the trend for actors to be well paid for cameo appearances?
151. More than 12,000 players were used during the filming of *How the West Was Won*? The filming lasted 11 months. The three directors, John Ford, Henry Hathaway and George Marshall, had 149 years of film knowledge between them.
152. Four weeks of exterior filming on the island of Kauai were needed for *Donovan's Reef*?
153. Wayne was made an honorary member of The Kauai Canoe and Racing Club, receiving the official shirt with the club insignia on the front and back?
154. *Donovan's Reef* was the last feature film that Wayne and Director John Ford worked together on?
155. Wayne crossed the Atlantic Ocean in *The Wild Goose* for the filming of *Circus World* in Europe?
156. During Wayne's first cancer operation in 1964, his left lung and part of his right lung were removed, as was a rib? The surgery occurred at Hollywood's Good Samaritan Hospital.
157. The cancer removed was the size of a golf ball?
158. Writer James Bacon reported that Wayne received over 50,000 letters after the operation?
159. While in Chupaderos, Mexico, in 1965, Wayne discovered that local women walked two miles to wash clothes in muddy water? The children had nothing to do. Wayne had a well drilled and a playground built for the children.
160. On September 23, 1965, Wayne appeared on "The Dean Martin Show" in which he and Martin sang, "Everybody Loves Somebody Sometime"?
161. Wayne received a *Photoplay* "Special Editors Award" in 1965?
162. The Appaloosa stallion Wayne rode in *El Dorado* belonged to Director Howard Hawks?
163. One day on the set of *El Dorado*, James Caan tried to enter his dressing room? The door was locked. He had to break into his room. Chairs were stacked throughout the room and garbage cans were piled high in the center of the room. A sign said: "Courtesy Mr. Wayne."
164. Wayne and Lassie were presenters at "The Golden Globe Awards" on February 21, 1966?
165. Sally Field's most embarrassing moment was when she presented an award at a "Golden Globe" ceremony? At that time, she was popular on television's *Flying Nun*. She entered the stage by wires. The wires couldn't hold and Wayne, who was on stage, caught her as she fell. She landed in his arms.

166. On a USO handshaking trip to Vietnam in June, 1966, bullets came within 17 yards of Wayne?

167. The USO trip lasted three weeks?

168. Wayne received a brass ring from the Montagnards while in Vietnam?

169. On October 27, 1966, Wayne appeared again on "The Dean Martin Show"? Wayne and Martin sang "I'm an Old Cowhand."

170. Director Robert Aldrich offered Wayne the role Lee Marvin eventually accepted for *The Dirty Dozen*? Wayne declined the role because the military was shown in a different light than Wayne wanted.

171. Wayne made a campaign trailer for Ronald Reagan during the filming of *The War Wagon*?

172. Wayne was a partner on the television series *Hondo* which premiered in September, 1967, opposite "The CBS Friday Night Movies"? On one week, *The Man Who Shot Liberty Valance* was shown and the next week *McLintock* was shown. The films did well in the ratings and after 13 weeks *Hondo* left the air. Wayne not only shot Liberty Valance but *Hondo* as well.

173. During the filming of *The Green Berets*, 1500 blackpowder bombs were used and 6,000 rounds of blank ammunition? The average war film used only 500 blackpowder bombs. The camp used in the film was turned over to the military after filming was completed.

174. The filming of *The Green Berets* lasted 70 days?

175. Actress Vera Miles worked on *The Green Berets* for one morning? She didn't want to be paid, so Wayne used her in *Hellfighters*.

176. On August 1, 1968, *The Green Berets* was under attack in Paris by leftists?

177. *The Green Berets* was pulled in Stockholm, Sweden, after three days of demonstrations and was climaxed with a smoke bomb explosion? It was referred to as "The Paid American Aggression in Indochina."

178. Wayne and James Stewart attended Governor Reagan's Inaugural in 1968? A picketer waved a Vietnamese flag. Stewart's son had been killed in Vietnam. When Wayne saw the picketer, he left Stewart's side and destroyed the flag. Wayne didn't harm the youth.

179. *Hellfighters* was the first film in which Wayne earned a million dollars?

180. Wayne was willing to pay $300,000 to purchase the unpublished galleys of *True Grit* in 1968?

181. Stuntman Chuck Hayward doubled for Wayne on the horsefall in *True Grit*?

182. Wayne had said the best scene he ever did appears in *True Grit*? The scene occurs in the mountains where Wayne tells the heroine about himself, showing a different side of the Wayne persona.

183. When Wayne made the "Laugh-In" television appearances, he was paid union scale wages at $210.00?

184. During the filming of *The Undefeated*, Wayne fell off of his horse and dislocated his shoulder. He called this a "jinx" film.

185. Three thousand horses were used during the filming of *The Undefeated*? This was the largest number of horses used in a film at that time.

186. In 1969 Wayne was named "Favorite Actor" in a *Photoplay* Award?

187. Wayne was made Admiral in the "Texas Navy" on April 17, 1969?

188. Wayne was in Salt Lake City, Utah, for the 100th anniversary of the joining of the Union Pacific Railways?

189. Wayne arranged for the *True Grit* premiere in Cuernavaca, Mexico, as a benefit for an orphanage? The youngsters gave Wayne on location a trophy they won as soccer champions.

190. On August 8, 1969, a statue of Wayne as Rooster Cogburn appeared on the cover of *Time* Magazine?

191. Wayne presented Joan Crawford with the Cecil B. DeMille Award at The Golden Globe Awards on February 3, 1970?

192. Wayne appeared in an advertising supplement on Sunday March 1, 1970, of the Sunday

newspapers across the country? The ad read: "Take the Duke's Grand Tour of Southern California."

193. On April 17, 1970, Wayne became Dr. Wayne as a honorary Ph.D. by Pima College in Tuscon, Airzona, while filming *Rio Lobo*?

194. Wayne and his wife sponsored "Our Little Brothers and Sisters" Orphanage in Cuernavaca, Mexico?

195. In May, 1970, Wayne had some 30 guns stolen from his home? Eventually all of the guns were recovered. One of the rifles was used in *Hatari*.

196. At the *Chisum* World Premiere on June 24, 1970, in Dallas, Texas, Wayne received "The American Academy of Achievement Gold Plate"?

197. In 1970 Wayne was in Dallas at The Cotton Bowl for "Action Now," a drug abuse rally?

198. On July 30, 1970, Wayne's first race horse, "Big Roman," won a two-length victory at Bay Meadows?

199. Wayne appeared on "The Chicago TV Forum" with Professor Herman Finer? Film and politics was discussed.

200. "Swing Out, Sweet Land" was the most expensive single show produced for television?

201. The special cost Budweiser roughly $2,000,000?

202. Wayne owned the special after two television runs?

203. 77,000,000 people saw the special?

204. Wayne's salary was the highest paid for hosting a show?

205. On Wednesday December 2, 1970, "Swing Out, Sweet Land" had a 39.3 rating and a 58 share in *Variety* Magazine? The special was number one in the ratings that week.

206. Wayne was master of ceremonies at Governor Ronald Reagan's second inaugural?

207. Wayne was offered *Dirty Harry* but declined because of the violence and the language?

208. In 1971 Wayne was presented with "The Veterans of Foreign Wars National Americanism Gold Medal Award"?

209. On August 25, 1971, Wayne emceed a fashion show at The Newporter Inn where money was raised for "The Local Youth Probation Center"?

210. Wayne purchased silver mines in Colorado in October, 1971?

211. *Photoplay* Magazine named Wayne "Favorite Actor" in 1971? This Gold Medal Award was the fourth *Photoplay* Award Wayne received.

212. In January, 1972, Wayne was at The Radio City Music Hall to promote *The Cowboys*?

213. Bruce Cabot was to have played the role Ricardo Montalban accepted in *The Train Robbers*? Cabot had died before filming started.

214. Wayne was upset about the low price *True Grit* received when it was sold to television? Wayne threatened to sue and an agreeable deal was reached.

215. The television premiere of *True Grit* scored number one in the television ratings the week ending November 12, 1972?

216. Wayne was to have appeared in *The Bridge Wore Blinkers*, with Bing Crosby, Jackie Gleason and Bob Hope? The film was never made. Wayne was to have played an owner of a stud farm.

217. Wayne's record "America, Why I Love Her" was released on March 1, 1973? In the first two weeks, the record sold more than 100,000 copies.

218. *Cahill: U.S. Marshal* had a Seattle world premiere on June 14, 1973, while Wayne was there filming *McQ*?

219. On August 13, 1973, Wayne received "The U.S. Marine Corps Leagues 'Iron Mike Award '"? This is given for Americanism.

220. On October 10, 1973, Wayne refused to allow Director Martin Scorsese to use a film clip from *Donovan's Reef*? This clip was to have been used in Scorsese's *Mean Streets*. A scene from *The Searchers* was substituted without Wayne in the scene.

221. On the "Rowan and Martin Laugh-In" of September 13, 1973, "The Ten Most Wanted Unwanted Singers In America" appeared? The group consisted of Wayne, Howard Cosell, Ernest Borgnine, Jack Carter, Redd Foxx, Glenn Ford, Kent McCord, Martin Milner, Charles Nelson Reilly and Ed Asner.

222. On January 6, 1974, Wayne appeared on the cover of *The National Enquirer* for the first time?

223. Wayne received "The George Washington Award" on February 18, 1974, for recording "America, Why I Love Her"?

224. Wayne appeared in *Newsweek* on January 28, 1974? This was concerning Wayne's trip to Harvard University to accept his "Brass Balls Award." Wayne arrived on an armored personnel carrier.

225. During the filming of *Rooster Cogburn*, Katharine Hepburn said of Wayne, "Duke Wayne is an artist and he is all male—and that's a rarity today"?

226. On May 24, 1975, Wayne offered land acreage for Vietnamese refugees to provide farm workers land?

227. On July 11, 1975, Wayne was in Marion, Illionis, scouting for a possible location for a coal degasification plant? This would remove methane gas from coal and leave oil as a by-product.

228. Wayne promoted an oil-water separator system to fight sea pollution? This is used by oil tankers when the emptied tanks are cleaned.

229. When Universal first released *Rooster Cogburn*, Wayne was in the original ad campaign looking at Hepburn with a look of disbelief and shock? The campaign was then changed showing Wayne with a clenched jaw and grin. This was referred to as a "Rooster Booster."

230. Wayne wanted the original ending of *The Shootist* changed because he felt the script was too graphic about the cancer, and the character Gilliam took unfair advantage of the death of Wayne's character?

231. The saloon used in *The Shootist* cost $150,000 to build.

232. Wayne appeared on the cover of *The National Enquirer* on March 16, 1976, with his secretary Pat Stacy? This was the second time Wayne appeared on the cover.

233. Wayne attended the Super Bowl in 1976?

234. The character Schneider in *One Day at a Time* has a wall poster of Wayne on his closet door?

235. Wayne was named "All Time Favorite Star" by *Photoplay* Magazine in 1976? This was the fifth *Photoplay* Award Wayne received.

236. In 1977, Wayne signed a multimillion-dollar contract with ABC?

237. In 1977, Wayne worked with The American Cancer Society to promote checkups?

238. Wayne was paid $400,000 for two days filming of the Datril commercials?

239. Wayne was involved with DECO (Duke Engineering Company), which reclaimed old tires and yielded petrochemical oil for fuel?

240. On December 27, 1977, Wayne appeared on the cover of *The National Enquirer* with "Lucky," the *Enquirer's* dog? This was the third time Wayne appeared on the cover.

241. Wayne helped write the dialogue and used his own wardrobe on "The Great Western Savings and Loan Association" commercials?

242. From December 1977 to January 1978, "Great Western Financial Corporation" in California had Wayne as the commercial spokesperson for "Great Western Savings and Loan Association"? The ads Wayne did appeared on 26 television stations and were heard on 18 radio stations. Newspaper ads appeared in 24 newspapers. The campaign was only in California.

243. Wayne's home at Newport Beach, California, appeared in the book *Celebrity Homes 11*?

244. While at the Academy Awards on April 3, 1978, Bob Hope wished Wayne well after his open heart surgery? The operation took place in Boston, Massachusetts.

245. Wayne received over 100,000 letters while in the hospital?

246. A letter from Wayne was read on the air by Richard Dawson on "Family Feud" while Wayne

was recovering from surgery? Wayne said he enjoyed watching the show.

247. On Friday April 14, 1978, Wayne sent his best wishes to basketball star John Havilcek, whose nickname is "Hondo"? Wayne's message to him read: "'Hondo' is watching 'Hondo.' Good Luck Forever."

248. When Wayne returned from Boston, a fleet of 500 boats sailed by his home in respect?

249. Upon returning home, Wayne had a "Letters-to-the-Editor" letter published on a page in *The Los Angeles Times* thanking the Californians for his welcome home ovation?

250. "The John Wayne Pavilion" was added to The Variety Children's Hospital in Miami, Florida in June, 1978?

251. Ex-President Ford presented Wayne with a bronze plaque for the Boy Scouts? The award was named "A Tribute To America's John Wayne." The presentation was held on September 21, 1978. The proceeds were used to purchase a 577-acre Scout facility named "The John Wayne Outpost Camp."

252. On October 31, 1978, "Great Western Savings and Loan" said Wayne helped earn $242,000,000 in the extensive media campaigns which utilized his commercials?

253. Wayne declined the General Stilwell role in *1941* and the patriarch role that was intended for him in *Trinity*?

254. Shortly after Wayne's cancer surgery in January 1979, Wayne was cheering up patients on his hospital floor by sharing his gifts and flowers with them?

255. Wayne appeared on the cover of *The National Enquirer* for the fourth time on February 6, 1979?

256. For the Academy Award presentation of 1979, Wayne had a new tuxedo made especially for him because of the massive amount of weight he had lost?

257. On May 22, 1979, Maureen O'Hara appeared before a congressional committee in Washington with Elizabeth Taylor to approve Wayne's gold medal? O'Hara said: "John Wayne is not just an actor, John Wayne is America."

258. On May 23, 1979, Wayne's congressional medal was approved: Public Law 96-15 (s. 631), May 26, 1979?

259. On June 5, 1979, Glenn Ford paid tribute to Wayne on the television special "How the West Was Fun"?

260. The Orange County Airport became "John Wayne Airport, Orange County" on June 20, 1979? The Board of Supervisors passed a Resolution #79-950 to rename the airport.

261. Before Wayne died, he stated The National Cowboy Hall Of Fame in Oklahoma City, Oklahoma, would receive his private collections? Included were Wayne's Kachina doll collection, his collection of western art paintings and western sculptures. Wayne's private and film gun collections were also received. All of these items are on display, as is the letter Wayne sent to the Hall of Fame stating his wishes. Wayne was a board member. A 10' by 15' projection room was built utilizing a video disc system, showing a 10-minute film-clip segment of scenes from *Stagecoach* to *The Shootist*. This concludes with the Academy Award appearance.

262. A "John Wayne Statue" became available in 1979? The statue is 20" high and is a life-like western pose of Wayne.

263. Sculptor Brett-Livingstone Strong unveiled a seven-foot statue of Wayne on Tuesday December 4, 1979? A boulder costing $100.00 became the Wayne likeness. The statue was shown at Mann's Chinese Theatre. Strong sold the 10-ton boulder for $1 million to Tom Murphy of Scottsdale, Arizona.

264. "The Duke T-Shirt" made of blue cotton and poly blend was released in California in 1979? A brown-printed portrait appeared on the shirt front. The shirt sold for $10.00.

265. In 1980, I was able to purchase a coffee cup used during filming of *McQ*? This is the type cup Wayne gave to fellow workers. All of these cups had "Good Luck, John Wayne" inscribed on them. They were made by Ketchum Originals in Long Beach, California.

266. In 1980, "The Official U.S. Mint John Wayne Commemorative Medal 'On A Matching' Belt Buckle" became available? The belt buckle was available in either bronze or genuine silver plate. The bronze belt buckle cost $9.98, with $1.00 for postage and handling. The medal plated with genuine silver buckle cost $12.98, with $1.00 for postage and handling. They can be ordered from The Westport Mint, Dept. WWB-22, 60 Wilton Road, Westport, Connecticut 06887.

267. A radio doll from the east debuted in 1981? A 10" plastic Wayne doll sat atop the radio. The cost was $11.50.

268. Wayne appeared on a limited edition plate of the "Hollywood Greats" series in October 1981? Susie Morton had 27,500 of the plates made. The plate front has a portrait of Wayne from *Circus World* with a western town background. A tribute appears on the plate back. The porcelain plate is trimmed in 22-karat gold at a cost of $29.95.

269. A book entitled *John Wayne Paper Dolls* is now available? The book has two Wayne paper dolls. The first paper doll has 16 costumes from Wayne films from 1930-1949. The second doll has 15 costumes from Wayne films from 1949-1976.

270. "The John Wayne Elementary School" of Brooklyn, New York, is the first school in the country to be named after Wayne? A bronze bust of Wayne was given by the Wayne family to the school on October 27, 1982. PS (Public School) 380 became John Wayne Elementary School.

271. On November 4, 1982, A life-like Wayne statue was dedicated at the John Wayne Airport, Orange County? The statue is located in the terminal front. Wayne's actual western garb was used in the modeling. Robert Summers of Glen Rose, Texas, designed the statue. The 9-foot-high bronze statue cost $300,000 and sets on a 2-foot pedestal. The seven Wayne children and Pilar attended the dedication.

272. The "John Wayne—American, The Guardian Of The West" doll was made available in 1982. The doll is clothed in cavalry officer uniform. The cost for this collector's doll is $69.99 and is 17" tall. From Effanbee Doll Corporation. A second doll from Effanbee Doll Corporation was released showing Wayne in western garb holding a rifle in hand; it is 17" tall.

273. In March, 1983, Pat Stacy earned $40,000 from *Woman's Day* for first serial rights on her book, *Duke: A Love Story?*

274. "Entertainment This Week" on April 23, 1983, had a segment on celebrity dolls and their popularity? The cavalry officer Wayne doll and another Wayne doll were shown.

275. On Sunday, April 24, 1983, Tony Bennett, the singer, was honored at "The Eddie Cantor Charitable Foundation Dinner"? About $100,000 was raised. A sizeable portion of this went to The John Wayne Cancer Clinic.

276. Towards the end of April, 1983, *Duke: A Love Story* became available in book stores?

277. A seven-ton, 21-foot-high sculpture of Wayne on horseback in cowboy gear is being created by sculptor Harry Jackson? This project was started in 1982. On Tuesday August 30, 1983, the sculpture was unveiled in Camaiore, Italy. The statue was to be cast in bronze in conjunction with the July 1984 Olympics in Los Angeles. This was commissioned by Anthony C. La Scala, executive vice president of Great Western Finance Corporation of Beverly Hills, California. The Wayne family and Great Western Finance Corporation is paying for the statue. In attendance at the unveiling was Michael Wayne, Wayne's eldest son, U.S. Ambassador to Italy Maxwell Rabb, and Mayor of Camaiore, Fabio Pezzini. Michael Wayne said of the unveiling; "It's a wonderful tribute to my father. He would have been proud to be placed on this horse." The statue will be displayed in front of the Great Western Savings and Loan, the bank Wayne did television advertising for in California.

278. In the December 27, 1983, copy of *The National Enquirer*, Wayne was voted one of "Hollywood's 10 Best Actors Of All Time"?

279. Movie Galleria features a catalogue with various Wayne items for sale, including a Wayne commemorative print, a birthday card-a-gram, stationery and envelopes, memo pads, note cards, porcelain mugs, bar glasses, a brass bookmark, jumbo 2' × 5' prints, sepia art prints, nostalgia prints, greeting cards, 11 × 14 photo prints and a full color poster reproduction of *Sands of Iwo Jima!* Information on these items can be obtained from: Movie Galleria, 7352 West Atlantic Blvd., Margate, Florida 33063.

280. In *The National Enquirer* issue of January 3, 1984, a John Wayne Commemorative 16 × 20 poster is featured? The poster is free. The cost for the postage and handling of the poster is $1.49. Each additional poster cost $1.00 for postage and handling. A designed framed poster can be ordered for $6.98 plus $1.50 postage. Information can be obtained from: National Enquirer, Free Wayne Poster, 1 Eversley Avenue, Norwalk, Connecticut 06851.

281. On July 4, 1984, the John Wayne Birthplace Society and Winterset Chamber of Commerce co-sponsored a John Wayne Day Celebration? This was held at the Madison County Fairgrounds in Winterset. Highlights included the showing of John Wayne movies and a free afternoon country-western and bluegrass music fest. Rex Allen, Jr., entertained with a gala stage show. A fireworks display followed. Featured was a craft show and sale, an antique show and sale, kid games, a kiddie rodeo, barbecued pork and other concessions. Tours were held at the birthplace. An art contest featuring the birthplace was also held.

JOHN WAYNE QUOTES

1. "I figured I needed a gimmick, so I went to work on this Wayne character. I dreamed up the drawl, the squint and a way of moving. I even had to practice saying 'ain't.'"

2. Wayne was questioned about writing his autobiography. His reply was: "Those who like me already know me, and those who don't like me wouldn't want to read about me anyway."

3. "When you come slam bang up against trouble, it never looks half as bad if you face up to it."

4. "In my day they used to say to a scriptwriter: If you have a message, don't bother—send a telegram instead."

5. "Nobody should come to the movies unless he believes in heroes."

6. "If it hadn't been for football and the fact I got my leg broke and had to go into the movies to eat, why, who knows, I mighta turned out to be a liberal democrat."

7. "All I do is sell sincerity and I've been selling the hell out of that since I started."

8. "I think 45 was my best age physically, mentally and in my attitude toward life in general."

9. "I always look for a story with basic emotions: a dog, a kid, a woman's love, a man's love."

10. Once on a movie location, Wayne's double, Chuck Roberson, received a visit from his three-year-old grandson. While there, the boy asked Wayne what he did. Wayne replied: "I just stand in for your grandad on closeups."

11. "I've been in more bad pictures than just about anyone in the business."

12. "When the road looks rough ahead, remember the 'Man Upstairs' and the word H-O-P-E. Hang onto both and 'tough it out.'"

13. A heckler once asked Wayne if he could speak Spanish. He replied that he couldn't too well. The heckler said Wayne had three wives who spoke Spanish. Wayne said: "Wa-al, I guess I just never listened to 'em."

14. "I couldn't go to sleep at night if the director didn't call 'cut.'"

15. "We soften violence with humor in my films. Nobody ever goes out of the theatre bent on hurting anybody else after seeing one of my pictures."

16. Wayne had a comment on screen fighting in his films. "I really enjoy the look on a guy's face when he gets hit and uses the "Why me?" expression. I use it when I'm in a fight."

17. Wayne's opinion of a good story: "Get it out of doors, let some fresh air and sunlight into the story. Give the cameraman a chance to photograph something besides walls and doors and tea tables. Don't let your story expire for lack of air."

18. Asked how he prepared for a role, Wayne said: "I just ask the director which hat to put on and which door I come in."

19. "If it hadn't been for the personal interest and encouragement of director John Ford, I might still be shifting furniture for other actors."

20. "Nobody ever saw a cowboy on the psychiatrist's couch."

21. One of Wayne's disappointments was being rejected by Annapolis. Wayne reflected: "I'd probably be a retired admiral by now."

22. "I'm an investment. I got to protect that investment."

23. "In my movies, I try to remember that people are dropping those bills at the box-office so they can relax and enjoy. That's why I like to keep it simple and what used to be called decent."

24. "When you're in the public eye, you're on the spot."

25. "If everything isn't black and white, I say why the hell not."

26. "I changed the saintly boy scout of the original cowboy hero into a more normal kind of fella."

27. "When people you work with do their job to make things right and still have time to smile and get along with others, I want them around."

28. When Wayne got his start he said: "For $75.00 a week you could be a star. I jumped."

29. "I stopped getting the girl about 10 years ago. Which is just as well 'cause I'd forgotten what I wanted her for."

30. Of *The Conqueror*, Wayne said: "Hell, it's just another western with different costumes."

31. During the filming of *The Conqueror*, director Dick Powell was pleased with the stunt work. He asked Wayne if he thought it was because the stunt men were getting better. Wayne replied: "No, the horses are smarter."

32. During the filming of *The Barbarian and the Geisha*, Wayne kept bumping his head on the low rafters. He eventually started walking like a caveman with his arms dangling around his knees. Wayne said: "If this keeps up, I'll be ready for a re-make of '1,000,000 B.C.'"

33. Wayne said of his 1964 cancer surgery: "I don't care if I never sell another ticket at the boxoffice if it helps some other guy get a check-up and be as lucky as I was."

34. Of his Vietnam trip in 1966, Wayne said: "I can't sing or dance but I can go to the hospitals and give them something to write home about."

35. Of *The Green Berets*, Wayne said: "The left wingers are shredding my flesh, but like Liberace, we're bawling all the way to the bank."

36. During the filming of *Hellfighters*, Wayne exited a fire area of 202 degrees with steaming clothes. Wayne said: "I'll never steam another clam. Now I know how the clam feels. It hurts."

37. At the 1968 Republican convention, Wayne commented on his political ambitions: "About as political as a Bengal tiger."

38. Wayne commented on his casting of Rooster Cogburn in *True Grit*: "Rooster was a mean old bastard, a one-eyed, whiskey-soaked, sloppy old son-of-a-bitch, just like me."

39. After the 1970 Academy Award ceremonies, when Wayne won his Academy Award, he said: "I didn't think I was going to get all excited about this thing. You get all gooey."

40. After Wayne did the episode of "Laugh-In" in which he was dressed as a large bunny rabbit, Wayne said: "It could've been worse. They could've dressed me up as a liberal."

41. Of *The Cowboys*, Wayne said: "This has been the most refreshing location I've been on in more than 40 years of moviemaking. Usually you end up with the same old bunch of actors, the same old pack of tall tales and lies. But this one is different."

42. During the filming of *Cahill: U.S. Marshal,* a London journalist asked Wayne why he was so thankful for his nickname "Duke." Wayne replied: "My real name is Marion Michael Morrison. And if you were my size, wore cowboy boots and a big hat, outrode, outfought and outshot all the badmen in the west, how would you like to climb down off of a horse, throw your saddle over the corral rail and then walk off-camera and sit in a chair labelled 'Marion'?"

43. When Harvard University dared Wayne to visit them, Wayne answered their invitation: "Sorry to note in your challenge that there is a weakness in your breeding, but there is a ray of hope in the fact that you are conscious of it."

44. On January 16, 1974, Wayne visited Harvard. One of the questions he was asked was: "Has President Nixon ever given you any suggestions for your movies?" Wayne's answer was: "No, they've all been successful."

45. Emperor Hirohito visited the U.S. and had a desire to meet Wayne. After they had talked, a reporter asked Wayne about what was discussed. Wayne replied: "How the hell do I know? My Japanese ain't all that great."

46. On Sunday December 11, 1977, Wayne and actress Jane Fonda attended the Hollywood Women's Press Club. Wayne presented her with an award saying: "I'm surprised to find you at the right of me."

47. After Wayne had open heart surgery in 1978, he said: "Now with that damn pig valve in me, I not only have my voice back, but I go around saying 'Oink, oink.'"

48. At the Academy Awards in 1979, Wayne said: "That's just about the only medicine a fellow'd ever really need. Believe me when I tell you that I'm mighty pleased that I can amble down here tonight. Oscar and I have something in common. Oscar first came to the Hollywood scene in 1928. So did I. We're both a little weatherbeaten, but we're still here and plan to be around for a whole lot longer."

JOHN WAYNE FAMILY HISTORY

Wayne was born to parents Clyde and Mary Morrison on May 26, 1907. Wayne was named Marion Robert Morrison. Wayne's brother Robert was born on December 8, 1912. He died in 1970. Wayne's name was then changed to Marion Michael Morrison.

Wayne married Josephine Saenz 1933-1944. They had four children:

Michael, born November 23, 1934
*Toni, born February 25, 1936
Patrick, born July 15, 1938
Melinda, born December 3, 1940

Wayne's second wife was Esperanza "Chata" Bauer 1946-1954.

Wayne's third wife was Pilar Palette 1954-1973, separated.

They had three children:

Aissa, born March 31, 1956
Ethan, born February 22, 1962
Marisa, born February 22, 1966

Wayne had homes that were located in Encino and Newport Beach, California.

There are 23 grandchildren as of December 1983.

*Toni La Cava has a brief scene in *The Alamo.* Actor Guinn Williams kisses her hand as the women are being evacuated from the Alamo.

WHICH FILM STUDIOS RELEASED THE MOST WAYNE FILMS?

Republic (33)
Westward Ho
The New Frontier
The Lawless Range
The Oregon Trail
The Lawless Nineties
King of the Pecos
The Lonely Trail
Winds of the Wasteland
Pals of the Saddle
Overland Stage Riders
Santa Fe Stampede
Red River Range
The Night Riders
Three Texas Steers
Wyoming Outlaw
New Frontier
The Dark Command
Three Faces West
A Man Betrayed
Lady from Louisiana
Lady for a Night
In Old California
Flying Tigers
In Old Oklahoma
The Fighting Seabees
Flame of Barbary Coast
Dakota
Angel and the Badman
Wake of the Red Witch
The Fighting Kentuckian
Sands of Iwo Jima
Rio Grande
The Quiet Man

Warner Brothers (27)
The Drop Kick
Ride Him Cowboy
The Big Stampede
Haunted Gold
The Telegraph Trail
Central Airport
Somewhere in Sonora
The Life of Jimmy Dolan
Baby Face

The Man from Monterey
College Coach
Operation Pacific
Big Jim McLain
Trouble Along the Way
Island in the Sky
Hondo
The High and the Mighty
The Sea Chase
Blood Alley
The Searchers
Rio Bravo
The Green Berets
Chisum
The Cowboys
Cancel My Reservation
The Train Robbers
Cahill: U.S. Marshal
McQ

20th Century-Fox (16)
Mother Machree
Four Sons
Hangman's House
Words and Music
Salute
Men Without Women
Rough Romance
Cheer Up and Smile
The Big Trail
Girls Demand Excitement
Three Girls Lost
The Barbarian and the Geisha
North to Alaska
The Comancheros
The Longest Day
The Undefeated

Monogram (16)
The Dawn Rider
The Desert Trail
Riders of Destiny
Sagebrush Trail
The Lucky Texan
West of the Divide

Blue Steel
The Man from Utah
Randy Rides Alone
The Star Packer
The Trail Beyond
'Neath Arizona Skies
The Lawless Frontier
Texas Terror
Rainbow Valley
Paradise Canyon

Paramount (13)
Lady and the Gent
Born to the West
The Shepherd of the Hills
Reap the Wild Wind
The Man Who Shot Liberty
  Valance
Hatari
Donovan's Reef
Circus World
In Harm's Way
The Sons of Katie Elder
El Dorado
True Grit
The Shootist

RKO Radio (11)
Allegheny Uprising
A Lady Takes a Chance
Tall in the Saddle
Back to Bataan
Without Reservations
Tycoon
Fort Apache
She Wore a Yellow Ribbon
Flying Leathernecks
The Conqueror
I Married a Woman

United Artists (10)
Stagecoach
The Long Voyage Home

Red River
Legend of the Lost
The Horse Soldiers
The Alamo
McLintock
The Greatest Story Ever Told
Cast a Giant Shadow
Brannigan

Columbia (7)
Men Are Like That
The Deceiver
Range Feud
Maker of Men
The Voice of Hollywood
Texas Cyclone
Two Fisted Law

MGM (6)
Brown of Harvard
Reunion in France
They Were Expendable
Three Godfathers
The Wings of Eagles
How the West Was Won

WHICH ACTORS DID WAYNE WORK WITH MOST?

Yakima Canutt (30)
Shadow of the Eagle
The Telegraph Trail
The Three Musketeers
Riders of Destiny
Sagebrush Trail
The Lucky Texan
West of the Divide
Blue Steel
The Man from Utah
Randy Rides Alone
The Star Packer
The Lawless Frontier
'Neath Arizona Skies
Texas Terror
The Dawn Rider
Paradise Canyon
Westward Ho
The Lawless Range
The Oregon Trail
King of the Pecos
The Lonely Trail
Winds of the Wasteland
Pals of the Saddle
Overland Stage Raiders
Santa Fe Stampede
The Night Riders
Stagecoach

Wyoming Outlaw
The Dark Command
War of the Wildcats (stuntman)

Chuck Roberson (27)
Wake of the Red Witch
The Fighting Kentuckian
Rio Grande
The Conqueror (stuntman)
The Searchers
The Wings of Eagles
The Barbarian and the Geisha (stuntman)
The Alamo
Donovan's Reef
The Comancheros
The Man Who Shot Liberty Valance
McLintock
The Sons of Katie Elder
The War Wagon
The Green Berets
Hellfighters
The Undefeated
Chisum
Rio Lobo
Big Jake
The Cowboys
The Train Robbers
Cahill: U.S. Marshal

Rooster Cogburn
The Shootist
The Colter Craven Story (television)
McQ
Hondo (not included—briefly seen
    as an Indian and a trooper)

Paul Fix (25)
Three Girls Lost
Somewhere in Sonora
The Desert Trail
Pittsburgh
In Old Oklahoma
The Fighting Seabees
Tall in the Saddle
Flame of Barbary Coast
Back to Bataan
Dakota
Tycoon
Red River
Wake of the Red Witch
The Fighting Kentuckian
She Wore a Yellow Ribbon
Island in the Sky
Hondo
The High and the Mighty
The Sea Chase
Blood Alley
Jet Pilot
The Sons of Katie Elder

El Dorado
The Undefeated
Cahill: U.S. Marshal

Ward Bond (19)
Words and Music
Salute
The Big Trail
College Coach
Conflict
The Long Voyage Home
A Man Betrayed
The Shepherd of the Hills
Tall in the Saddle
They Were Expendable
Dakota
Fort Apache
Three Godfathers
Operation Pacific
The Quiet Man
Hondo
The Searchers
The Wings of Eagles
Rio Bravo

Jack Pennick (16)
Hangman's House
Stagecoach
The Long Voyage Home
Lady from Louisiana
They Were Expendable
Fort Apache
Three Godfathers
The Fighting Kentuckian
She Wore a Yellow Ribbon
Rio Grande
Operation Pacific
The Searchers
The Wings of Eagles
The Horse Soldiers
The Alamo

The Man Who Shot Liberty
  Valance

Gabby Hayes (15)
Riders of Destiny
The Lucky Texan
West of the Divide
Blue Steel
The Man from Utah
Randy Rides Alone
The Star Packer
The Lawless Frontier
'Neath Arizona Skies
Texas Terror
Rainbow Valley
The Lawless Nineties
The Dark Command
In Old Oklahoma
Tall in the Saddle

Hank Worden (15)
The Night Riders
Angel and the Badman
Fort Apache
Red River
Three Godfathers
The Fighting Kentuckian
The Searchers
The Horse Soldiers
The Alamo
McLintock
True Grit
Chisum
Rio Lobo
Big Jake
Cahill: U.S. Marshal

Bruce Cabot (11)
Angel and the Badman
The Comancheros
Hatari
McLintock

In Harm's Way
The War Wagon
The Green Berets
Hellfighters
The Undefeated
Chisum
Big Jake

Harry Carey, Jr. (10)
Red River
Three Godfathers
She Wore a Yellow Ribbon
Rio Grande
Island in the Sky
The Searchers
Rio Bravo
The Undefeated
Big Jake
Cahill: U.S. Marshal

Grant Withers (9)
A Lady Takes a Chance
In Old Oklahoma
The Fighting Seabees
Dakota
Tycoon
Fort Apache
Wake of the Red Witch
The Fighting Kentuckian
Rio Grande

Patrick Wayne (9)
Rio Grande
The Quiet Man
The Searchers
The Alamo
The Comancheros
Donovan's Reef
McLintock
The Green Berets
Big Jake

WHAT ACTRESSES DID WAYNE WORK WITH THE MOST?

Mae Marsh (6)
Fort Apache
Three Godfathers
The Fighting Kentuckian
The Quiet Man
The Wings of Eagles
Donovan's Reef

Maureen O'Hara (5)
Rio Grande
The Quiet Man
The Wings of Eagles
McLintock
Big Jake

Anna Lee (5)
Seven Sinners
Flying Tigers
Fort Apache
The Horse Soldiers
The Man Who Shot Liberty
    Valance

Vera Miles (4)
The Searchers
The Man Who Shot Liberty
    Valance
The Green Berets
Hellfighters

Mildred Natwick (4)
The Long Voyage Home
Three Godfathers
She Wore a Yellow Ribbon
The Quiet Man

Adele Mara (4)
The Fighting Seabees
Flame of Barbary Coast
Wake of the Red Witch
Sands of Iwo Jima

Claire Trevor (4)
Stagecoach
Allegheny Uprising
The Dark Command
The High and the Mighty

Ann Rutherford (3)
The Oregon Trail
The Lawless Nineties
The Lonely Trail

Marlene Dietrich (3)
Seven Sinners
Pittsburgh
The Spoilers

Susan Hayward (3)
Reap the Wild Wind
The Fighting Seabees
The Conqueror

Marie Windsor (3)
The Fighting Kentuckian
Trouble Along the Way
Cahill: U.S. Marshal

Olive Carey (3)
The Searchers
The Wings of Eagles
The Alamo

Angie Dickinson (3)
I Married a Woman
Rio Bravo
Cast a Giant Shadow

Aissa Wayne (3)
The Alamo
The Comancheros
McLintock

WHICH FILM DIRECTOR DID WAYNE WORK WITH MOST?

John Ford (31 Times)

1. Four Sons
2. Mother Machree
3. Hangman's House
4. Salute
5. Men Without Women
6. Stagecoach
7. The Long Voyage Home

8. They Were Expendable
9. Fort Apache
10. Three Godfathers
11. She Wore a Yellow Ribbon
12. What Price Glory (Stage Play)
13. Rio Grande
14. Bullfighter and the Lady (Editor)
15. The Quiet Man
16. Hondo (Second Unit Director-Uncredited)
17. The Searchers

18. Rookie of the Year (Television)
19. The Wings of Eagles
20. The Horse Soldiers
21. The Western (Television)
22. The Alamo (Second Unit Director-Uncredited)
23. Wagon Train (Television)
24. The Man Who Shot Liberty Valance
25. Flashing Spikes (Television)
26. How the West Was Won
27. Donovan's Reef
28. Chesty (Documentary)
29. Directed by John Ford (Documentary)
30. The American West of John Ford (Television)
31. American Film Institute Award (Television)

WHICH OTHER FILM DIRECTORS DID WAYNE WORK WITH MOST?

R. N. Bradbury (13)
1. Riders of Destiny
2. The Lucky Texan
3. West of the Divide
4. Blue Steel
5. The Man From Utah
6. The Star Packer
7. The Trail Beyond
8. The Lawless Frontier
9. Texas Terror
10. Rainbow Valley
11. The Dawn Rider
12. Westward Ho
13. The Lawless Range

George Sherman (9)
1. Pals of the Saddle
2. Overland Stage Riders
3. Santa Fe Stampede
4. Red River Range
5. The Night Riders
6. Three Texas Steers
7. Wyoming Outlaw

8. New Frontier
9. Big Jake

Henry Hathaway (6)*
1. The Shepherd of the Hills
2. Legend of the Lost
3. North to Alaska
4. Circus World
5. The Sons of Katie Elder
6. True Grit

Joseph Kane (5)
1. The Lawless Nineties
2. King of the Pecos
3. The Lonely Trail
4. Flame of the Barbary Coast
5. Dakota

William Wellman (5)
1. Central Airport
2. College Coach
3. Island in the Sky
4. The High and the Mighty
5. Blood Alley

Howard Hawks (5)
1. Red River
2. Rio Bravo
3. Hatari
4. El Dorado
5. Rio Lobo

Andrew McLaglen (5)
1. McLintock
2. Hellfighters
3. The Undefeated
4. Chisum
5. Cahill: U.S. Marshal

Mack V. Wright (4)
1. Haunted Gold
2. Somewhere in Sonora
3. The Man from Montery
4. Winds of the Wasteland

Arthur Lubin (4)
1. California Straight Ahead
2. I Cover the War
3. Idol of the Crowds
4. Adventure's End

*Faberge in 1973 spent approximately $10,000 to honor director Henry Hathaway. Over 200 film stars paid tribute, one of whom was Wayne.

WHAT IS THE NAME OF THE CHARACTER WAYNE PLAYED IN 8 FILMS? NAME THOSE FILMS.

Stony Brooke

1. Pals of the Saddle
2. Overland Stage Riders
3. Santa Fe Stampede
4. Red River Range
5 The Night Riders
6. Three Texas Steers
7. Wyoming Outlaw
8. New Frontier

JOHN WAYNE AND ACADEMY AWARD NOMINATIONS AND WINNERS

1939
Stagecoach
Best Picture
*Supporting Actor—Thomas Mitchell
Director—John Ford
Cinematography
Interior Decoration
Editing
*Best Score

1940
The Long Voyage Home
Best Picture
Screenplay
Cinematography
Editing
Original Score
Special Effects

1940
The Dark Command
Interior Decoration
Original Score

1942
Reap the Wild Wind
Cinematography
Interior Decoation
*Special Effects

1942
The Spoilers
Interior Decoration

1942
Flying Tigers
Sound
Scoring Of A Dramatic Picture
Special Effects

1943
In Old Oklahoma
Scoring Of A Dramatic Picture
Sound Recording

1944
The Fighting Seabees
Scoring Of A Dramatic Picture

1945
Flame of the Barbary Coast
Sound
Scoring Of A Dramatic Picture

1945
They Were Expendable
Sound
Special Effects

1948
Red River
Motion Picture Story
Editing

1949
She Wore A Yellow Ribbon
*Cinematography

1949
Sands of Iwo Jima
*Actor—John Wayne
Motion Picture Story
Editing
Sound

1952
The Quiet Man
Best Picture
Supporting Actor—Victor McLaglen
*Director—John Ford
Screenplay
*Cinematography
Art Direction
Sound

1953
Hondo
Supporting Actress—Geraldine Page

1954
The High and the Mighty
Supporting Actress—Claire Trevor
Supporting Actress—Jan Sterling
Director—William Wellman
Editing
*Scoring Of A Dramatic Picture
Song

1960
The Alamo
Best Picture
Supporting Actor—Chill Wills
Cinematography
*Sound
Editing
Scoring Of A Dramatic Picture
Song

1962
The Man Who Shot Liberty Valance
Costume Design

1962
Hatari
Cinematography

1962
The Longest Day
Best Picture
*Cinematography
Art Direction
Editing
*Special Effects

1963
How The West Was Won
Best Picture
*Best Story and Screenplay
Cinematography
Art Direction
*Sound
*Editing
Music Score
Costume Design

1965
The Greatest Story Ever Told
Cinematography
Art Direction
Music Score
Costume Design
Special Effects

1965
In Harm's Way
Cinematography

1969
True Grit
*Best Actor—John Wayne
Best Song

1976
The Shootist
Art Direction

---

*Won an Academy Award
25 of Wayne's films were nominated for Academy Awards
81 nominations were received
14 of these nominations became winners

**Wayne lost the Academy Award nomination for best actor to Broderick Crawford. Crawford won for *All the King's Men*.

WHAT MOVIE LOCATIONS DID WAYNE USE MOST?

Mexico (8)
Hondo (Carmargo)
The Sons of Katie Elder (Durango)
The War Wagon (Durango)
The Undefeated (Durango)
Chisum (Durango)
Big Jake (Durango)
The Train Robbers (Durango)

Cahill: U.S. Marshal (Durango)

Monument Valley (6)
Stagecoach
Fort Apache
Three Godfathers
She Wore A Yellow Ribbon
Rio Grande

The Searchers

Old Tucson, Arizona (4)
Rio Bravo
McLintock
El Dorado
Rio Lobo

WHO WAS WAYNE'S FAVORITE SCREENWRITER?

James Edward Grant (10)
1. Angel and the Badman
2. Sands of Iwo Jima
3. Flying Leathernecks

4. Big Jim McLain
5. Hondo
6. The Alamo
7. The Comancheros

8. Donovan's Reef
9. McLintock
10. Circus World

WHICH FILM COMPOSERS DID THE MOST WAYNE SCORES?

Victor Young (8)
The Dark Command
Three Faces West
Reap the Wild Wind
Flying Tigers
Sands of Iwo Jima
Rio Grande
The Quiet Man
The Conqueror

Roy Webb (7)
A Lady Takes a Chance
Tall in the Saddle
Back to Bataan
Without Reservations
Flying Leathernecks
The Sea Chase
Blood Alley

Richard Hageman (6)
Stagecoach
The Long Voyage Home

Angel and the Badman
Fort Apache
Three Godfathers
She Wore a Yellow Ribbon

Cy Feuer (3)
Pals of the Saddle
A Man Betrayed
Lady from Louisiana

Walter Scharf (3)
In Old Oklahoma
The Fighting Seabees
Dakota

Max Steiner (3)
Operation Pacific
Trouble Along the Way
The Searchers

Elmer Bernstein (8)

The Comancheros
The Sons of Katie Elder
Cast a Giant Shadow
True Grit
Big Jake
Cahill: U.S. Marshal
McQ
The Shootist

William Lava (6)
Santa Fe Stampede
Red River Range
The Night Riders
Three Texas Steers
Wyoming Outlaw
New Frontier

Dimitri Tiomkin (6)
Red River
The High and the Mighty

Rio Bravo
The Alamo
Circus World
The War Wagon

David Buttolph (3)
Lady For A Night

In Old California
The Horse Soldiers

Emil Newman (3)
Big Jim McLain
Island in the Sky
Hondo

Cyril Mockridge (3)
I Married A Woman
The Man Who Shot Liberty
    Valance
Donovan's Reef

FILM SCORE ALBUMS DONE ON WAYNE FILMS

1. The Alamo
2. The Barbarian and the Geisha
3. Cast a Giant Shadow
4. Circus World
5. The Cowboys
6. El Dorado
7. The Greatest Story Ever Told
8. Hatari
9. The Horse Soldiers
10. How the West Was Won
11. In Harm's Way
12. Island in the Sky
13. The Longest Day
14. McLintock
15. The Quiet Man
16. Rio Grande
17. Sands of Iwo Jima
18. The Searchers
19. The Sons of Katie Elder
20. Stagecoach
21. True Grit
22. The Undefeated

And "America, Why I Love Her"

In 1973, Warner Brothers released a record entitled "Fifty Years of Film" which had selections from two of Wayne's films: *Hondo* and *The Green Berets.* Also released was "Fifty Years of Film Music," which had a selection from *The High and the Mighty.*

Stagecoach is available as a radio program on a record. The 1949 broadcast was Wayne in the part of Ringo.

"Stars on Radio" is a record set of Radio Broadcasts. Wayne appears with Marlene Dietrich and Randolph Scott doing *Pittsburgh.*

"The Western Film World of Dimitri Tiomkin" features selections from *Red River* and *Rio Bravo.*

HOW MANY OF WAYNE'S FILMS WERE PROCESSED IN TECHNICOLOR?

Technicolor is the best color process which insures a truer color and sharper quality. Films with technicolor preserve better over the years, as contrasted to color by Deluxe, for example.

1. The Shepherd of the Hills
2. Reap the Wild Wind
3. Tycoon
4. Three Godfathers
5. She Wore a Yellow Ribbon
6. Flying Leathernecks
7. The Quiet Man
8. The Conqueror

9. The Searchers
10. Jet Pilot
11. Legend of the Lost
12. I Married a Woman (technicolor sequence)
13. Rio Bravo
14. The Alamo
15. Hatari
16. Donovan's Reef
17. McLintock
18. Circus World
19. The Greatest Story Ever Told
20. The Sons of Katie Elder
21. El Dorado
22. The War Wagon
23. The Green Berets
24. Hellfighters
25. True Grit
26. Chisum
27. Rio Lobo
28. Big Jake
29. The Cowboys
30. Cancel My Reservation
31. The Train Robbers
32. Cahill: U.S. Marshal
33. McQ
34. Rooster Cogburn
35. The Shootist

WHICH CINEMATOGRAPHERS WORKED WITH WAYNE MOST?

William Clothier (25)
Jet Pilot (aerial)
Island in the Sky (aerial)
The High and the Mighty
   (aerial)
The Sea Chase
Blood Alley
The Horse Soldiers
The Alamo
The Comancheros
The Man Who Shot Liberty
   Valance
Donovan's Reef
McLintock
The War Wagon
Hellfighters
The Undefeated
Chisum
Rio Lobo
Big Jake
The Train Robbers

Archie Stout (25)
Sagebrush Trail
The Lucky Texan
West of the Divide
Blue Steel
The Man from Utah

Randy Rides Alone
The Star Packer
The Trail Beyond
The Lawless Frontier
'Neath Arizona Skies
Texas Terror
The Desert Trail
The Dawn Rider
Paradise Canyon
Westward Ho
The Lawless Range
The Sea Spoilers
Conflict
Angel and the Badman
Fort Apache
Big Jim McLain
Trouble Along the Way
Island in the Sky
Hondo
The High and the Mighty

Jack Marta (10)
King of the Pecos
Red River Range
The Night Riders
The Dark Command
A Man Betrayed
Lady from Louisiana

In Old California
Flying Tigers
In Old Oklahoma
Dakota

Reggie Lanning (6)
Pals of the Saddle
Santa Fe Stampede
Wyoming Outlaw
New Frontier
Wake of the Red Witch
Sands of Iwo Jima

Winton Hoch (6)
Three Godfathers
She Wore a Yellow Ribbon
The Quiet Man
The Searchers
Jet Pilot
The Green Berets

HOW MANY WAYNE FILMS WERE FILMED IN A SCOPE PROCESS?

A scope process is designed for a wide screen. Films until 1953 had a squarish shape. With the advent of Cinemascope, the motion picture film could be transposed into a rectangular shape. Film directors can now use the old style or new style screen process, whichever better suits the content of the motion picture.

1. The High and the Mighty
2. The Sea Chase
3. Blood Alley
4. The Conqueror
5. Jet Pilot
6. Legend of the Lost
7. I Married a Woman
8. The Barbarian and the Geisha
9. The Alamo
10. North to Alaska
11. The Comancheros
12. The Longest Day
13. How the West Was Won
14. McLintock
15. Circus World
16. The Greatest Story Ever Told
17. In Harm's Way
18. The Sons of Katie Elder
19. Cast a Giant Shadow
20. The War Wagon
21. The Green Berets
22. Hellfighters
23. The Undefeated
24. Chisum
25. Big Jake
26. The Cowboys
27. The Train Robbers
28. Cahill: U.S. Marshal
29. McQ
30. Brannigan
31. Rooster Cogburn

16MM FEATURETTES ON WAYNE FILMS

These 16mm featurettes show what goes on behind the scenes. What appears to be complex on the movie screen is shown in a different light, with simplicity being the tool for achieving various screen effects. The *War Wagon* featurette, for example, shows how a fight scene is staged and how a bridge is exploded.

1. Brannigan
2. Cahill: U.S. Marshal
3. Chisum
4. The Cowboys
5. The Green Berets
6. Hatari
7. Legend of the Lost
8. McLintock
9. McQ
10. The Train Robbers
11. The Undefeated
12. The War Wagon

CAREER STATISTICS

Wayne appeared in 153 films in which he is visibly seen. Excluded from this number are those in which he merely was moving props or standing in for the body in *The Deceiver* as an example. Wayne was in seventy-six westerns amounting to 49.6 percent of his screen career. Films in a modern setting such as *Hellfighters* and *The High and the Mighty*, total thirty-two or 21.6 percent of his career. Wayne appeared in fourteen World War II related films totaling 9.1 percent of his career. Sports related movie settings such as *Brown of Harvard* and *Trouble Along the Way*, compile ten films or 6.5 percent of his career. Historical films such as *The Conqueror, The Alamo*, and *How the West Was Won* total nine or 5.8 percent of his career. Films with a nineteenth century setting such as *The Shepherd of the Hills*, and *Reap the Wild Wind* total five or 3.2 percent of his career. Wayne appeared in three Cold War related films, *Big Jim McLain, Blood Alley*, and *Jet Pilot*, compiling 1.9 percent of his career. *McQ* and *Brannigan* were the only two in which Wayne played a cop. This category compiles 1.3 percent of his career. He appeared in a modern day war film *The Green Berets* which is .6 percent of Wayne's career.

WAYNE'S TRUE-TO-LIFE CHARACTERS

During the course of Wayne's film career, he portrayed seven real-life figures, in addition to appearing as himself in *I Married a Woman*.
1. Temujin (Genghis Khan) in *The Conqueror*
2. Cmdr. Frank W. ''Spig'' Wead in *The Wings of Eagles*
3. Consul General Townsend Harris in *The Barbarian and the Geisha*
4. Col. David Crockett in *The Alamo*
5. Col. Benjamin Vandervoort, 82nd Airborne Division, in *The Longest Day*
6. Gen. William Tecumseh Sherman in *How the West Was Won*
7. John Simpson Chisum in *Chisum*

WAYNE'S ACADEMY AWARD HISTORY THROUGH THE EYES OF OSCAR

Lady and Gent (1932) was the first Academy Award-nominated film in which Wayne appeared. Following is the history of the nominations from 1932 to 1976.

Lady and Gent was nominated for Original Story but lost to *The Champ*.

Stagecoach (1939) was nominated for seven Academy Awards. *Gone With the Wind* was selected as Best Picture, defeating *Dark Victory, Goodbye, Mr. Chips, Love Affair, Mr. Smith Goes to Washington, Ninotchka, Of Mice and Men, Stagecoach, The Wizard of Oz*, and *Wuthering Heights*. Director John Ford was nominated for Best Director but lost to Victor Fleming (who directed *Gone With the Wind*). Thomas Mitchell won for Supporting Actor. Bert Glennon's cinematography (Black and White) was nominated but lost to Gregg Toland's (*Wuthering Heights*). Both Interior Decoration and Editing were nominated, both lost to *Gone With the Wind*. *Stagecoach*'s music score did win. It was by Richard Hageman, Frank Harling, John Leipold, and Leo Shuken.

The Long Voyage Home (1940) was nominated for six Academy Awards. Best Picture nominees included *All This, and Heaven Too, Foreign Correspondent, The Grapes of Wrath, The Great Dictator, Kitty Foyle, The Letter, The Long Voyage Home, Our Town, The Philadelphia Story*, and *Rebecca* (the winner). The screenplay by Dudley Nichols lost to *The Philadelphia Story* and the cinematography by Gregg Toland lost to *Rebecca*. Sherman Todd's editing was nominated but lost to *Northwest Mounted Police*. Richard Hageman's music score lost to *Pinocchio* and the Special Effects lost to *The Thief of Bagdad*.

The Dark Command (1940) was nominated for two Academy Awards: for Interior Decoration, losing to *Pride and Prejudice*, and for Original Score (Victor Young), losing to *Pinocchio*. (*The Long Voyage Home* and *The Dark Command* were in competition with each other in the latter category.)

Reap the Wild Wind (1942) was nominated for three Academy Awards: for the Cinematography (Color), losing to *The Black Swan*, and for Interior Decoration (Color), losing to *My Gal Sal*. The film was also nominated for Special Effects and won.

The Spoilers (1942) was nominated for Interior Decoration (Black and White) but lost to *This Above All*.

Flying Tigers (1942) was nominated for three Academy Awards. Music (Scoring of a Dramatic Picture) lost to *Now, Voyager*, and sound lost to *Yankee Doodle Dandy*. The Special Effects nomination lost to *Reap the Wild Wind*.

In Old Oklahoma (1943) was nominated for two Academy Awards. Music (Scoring of a Dramatic Picture) lost to *The Song of Bernadette*; sound lost to *This Land is Mine*.

The Fighting Seabees (1944) was nominated for Music (Scoring of a Dramatic Picture) by Walter Scharf but lost to *Since You Went Away*.

Flame of Barbary Coast (1945) was nominated for two Academy Awards. Music (Scoring of a Dramatic Picture) lost to *Spellbound* and Sound lost to *The Bells of St. Mary's*.

They Were Expendable (1945) was nominated for two Academy Awards. Sound lost to *The Bells of St. Mary's* and the Special Effects nomination lost to *Wonder Man*.

Red River (1948) was nominated for two Academy Awards. Writing (Motion Picture Story) by Borden Chase and Charles Schnee lost to *The Search* and Editing by Christian Nyby lost to *The Naked City*.

1949 was the first year in which Wayne was nominated for Best Actor for *Sands of Iwo Jima*. His competition in that category: Broderick Crawford (the winner) for *All the King's Men*, Kirk Douglas for *Champion*, Gregory Peck for *Twelve O'Clock High*, and Richard Todd for *The Hasty Heart*. *Sands of Iwo Jima* was nominated for three other Academy Awards. Writing (Motion Picture Story) lost to *The Stratton Story*, Sound to *Twelve O'Clock High*, and Editing to *Champion*.

She Wore a Yellow Ribbon (1949) also received a nomination for Winton C. Hoch's Cinematography (Color) and won.

The 1949 Oscar ceremony was held March 23, 1950, at the RKO Pantages Theatre in Hollywood. *All the King's Men* was nominated for seven Academy Awards and won three including Best Picture and Supporting Actress for Mercedes McCambridge. *Battleground* was nominated six times and won for Story and Screenplay and Cinematography (black and white). *Champion* also received six nominations and won for Editing. *A Letter to Three Wives* was nominated for three Oscars and won two for Direction and Screenplay, both by Joseph L. Mankiewicz. *Twelve O'Clock High* was nominated for four Academy Awards and won for Supporting Actor Dean Jagger as well as Sound. That year, forty films were nominated for Oscars in various categories.

The Quiet Man (1952) was nominated for seven Academy Awards, including Best Picture, along with *The Greatest Show on Earth* (the winner), *High Noon*, *Ivanhoe*, and *Moulin Rouge*. John Ford won the Academy Award for Director, beating out Cecil B. DeMille for *The Greatest Show on Earth*, John Huston for *Moulin Rouge*, Joseph L. Mankiewicz for *Five Fingers*, and Fred Zinnemann for *High Noon*. Supporting Actor nominee Victor McLaglen (for *The Quiet Man*) lost to Anthony Quinn for *Viva Zapata!* The

Frank Nugent Screenplay lost to *The Bad and the Beautiful* but the Cinematography (Color) by Winton C. Hoch won. The Art Decoration-Set Decoration (Color) lost to *Moulin Rouge* and Sound lost to *Breaking the Sound Barrier*.

Hondo (1953) received a nomination for Supporting Actress Geraldine Page, who lost to Donna Reed for *From Here to Eternity*.

The High and the Mighty (1954) was nominated for six Academy Awards. Director William Wellman was cited along with Alfred Hitchcock for *Rear Window*, Elia Kazan (the winner) for *On the Waterfront*, George Seaton for *The Country Girl* and Billy Wilder for *Sabrina*. Both Jan Sterling and Claire Trevor were nominated for Supporting Actress; but lost to Eva Marie Saint for *On the Waterfront*. Editing lost to *On the Waterfront* and the title song from *The High and the Mighty* lost to *Three Coins in the Fountain*. The Music (Scoring of a Dramatic Picture) by Dimitri Tiomkin won.

The Alamo (1960) was nominated for seven Academy Awards. Its competition for Best Picture included *The Apartment* (the winner), *Elmer Gantry*, *Sons and Lovers*, *The Sundowners*. Peter Ustinov won the Supporting Actor award for *Spartacus* over Peter Falk for *Murder, Inc.*, Jack Kruschen for *The Apartment*, Sal Mineo for *Exodus*, and Chill Wills for *The Alamo*. Cinematography (Color) by William H. Clothier lost to *Spartacus*. *The Alamo* won the Academy Award for Sound but lost for Editing to *The Apartment* and Music (Scoring of a Dramatic Picture) to *Exodus*. Dimitri Tiomkin's song "The Green Leaves of Summer" lost to the title song from *Never on Sunday*.

The Longest Day (1962) was nominated for five Academy Awards, including Best Picture. Other nominees were *Lawrence of Arabia* (the winner), *The Music Man*, *Mutiny on the Bounty*, and *To Kill a Mockingbird*. *The Longest Day* won for Cinematography (Black and White), as well as Special Effects. Art Decoration-Set Decoration (Black and White) lost to *To Kill a Mockingbird*; Editing to *Lawrence of Arabia*.

Hatari! (1962) was nominated for Cinematography (Color) by Russell Harlan and Joseph Brun but lost to *Lawrence of Arabia*.

The Man Who Shot Liberty Valance (1962) was nominated for Costume Design (Black and White) but lost to *What Ever Happened to Baby Jane?*

How the West Was Won (1963) received eight Academy Award nominations including Best Picture. Other nominees in that category were *America America*, *Cleopatra*, *Lilies of the Field*, and *Tom Jones*, the winner. Best Story and Screenplay won, as did Sound and Editing, but Cinematography (Color), Costume Design (Color), and Art Decoration-Set Decoration (Color) nominations lost to *Cleopatra*, and Original Music Score to *Tom Jones*.

In Harm's Way (1965) was nominated for Cinematography (Black and White) by Philip Lathrop, but lost to *Ship of Fools*.

The Greatest Story Ever Told (1965) was nominated for five Academy Awards. Four of the five award nominations—Cinematography (Color), Art Decoration-Set Decoration (Color), Original Music Score, and Costume Design (Color)—*all lost to Doctor Zhivago*, while the Special Visual Effects lost to *Thunderball*.

The 1969 Academy Award nominations had the following contenders. *Anne of the Thousand Days* (10 nominations), *Butch Cassidy and the Sundance Kid* (7), *Hello, Dolly* (7), *Midnight Cowboy* (7), *They Shoot Horses, Don't They?* (9), *Z* (4), and *Bob & Carol & Ted & Alice* (4). Those in the running for Best Picture were *Anne of the Thousand Days*, *Butch Cassidy and the Sundance Kid*, *Hello, Dolly!*, *Z*, and *Midnight Cowboy* (the winner). Although *True Grit* was overlooked in that category, it came as no surprise that Wayne was nominated for Best Actor for his portrayal of Rooster Cogburn. His competition: Richard Burton (*Anne of the Thousand Days*), Dustin Hoffman (*Midnight Cowboy*), Peter O'Toole (*Goodbye, Mr. Chips*), and Jon Voight (*Midnight Cowboy*). On April 7, 1970, Wayne was announced as the winner as Best Actor. Barbra Streisand presented him with his well deserved and long overdue Oscar. Though some critics thought he received the award for his body of work, Wayne justly earned the Academy Award for the cantankerous characterization that he created under Henry Hathaway's energetic direction. The film also received an Oscar nomination for Elmer Bernstein and Don Black's title song, but it lost to the popular "Raindrops Keep Fallin' on My Head" from *Butch Cassidy and the Sundance Kid*. In 1969, twenty-six films received nominations in assorted categories.

The Shootist was the last Wayne film nominated for an Academy Award. Art Decoration-Set Decoration was nominated but lost to *All the President's Men*.

Over the years, Wayne films were nominated in seventeen Academy Award categories:
Music Score 11
Sound 8
Editing 8
Cinematography (Color) 7
Writing 6
Best Picture 6
Special Effects 6
Art Decoration–Set Decoration (Color) 5
Cinematography (Black and White) 4
Art Decoration–Set Decoration (Black and White) 4
Director 3
Supporting Actor 3
Supporting Actress 3
Song 3
Actor 2
Costume Design (Color) 2
Costume Design (Black and White) 1

THE LAST DAYS OF *THE SHOOTIST*

The seventies would be the decade in which the western would slowly begin to fade from the screen. By the 1980s only a handful would be released. During the 1970s Wayne made eleven films of which nine were westerns. During the same period, Clint Eastwood would develop his reputation as a cowboy star, enhanced by his success in the Spaghetti Western. During 1970–76, Eastwood made thirteen films of which four were westerns. The times they were a changing for the movie cowboy. The anachronism theme—meaning something has outlived its purpose—was beginning to prevail in the later 1960s westerns. *Will Penny* (1968), starring Charlton Heston; *The Wild Bunch* (1969), Sam Peckinpah's master film; and *Butch Cassidy and the Sundance Kid* (1969), with Paul Newman and Robert Redford, dealt with the changing west and the encroachment of civilization in the "modern" era. Sometimes death would approach from within instead of a blazing gun.

As the movie house doors would close on Wayne's career, two 1976 westerns would emerge as best of the decade; Eastwood's *The Outlaw Josey Wales* and Wayne's *The Shootist*. Josey Wales survives the Civil War but is a wanted man by the Union army. His resourcefulness is put to use as he leads a ragtag group of outcasts to a new destiny. Eventually he faces his past, escaping his fate, and is given a new lease on life.

On the other hand, John Bernard Books, a well known gunfighter, a "Shootist," is literally running out of time. Arriving in Carson City, Nevada, on January 22, 1901, Books has his earlier diagnosis of cancer confirmed. Reluctantly he accepts his fate and hopes merely to die in peace. His notorious reputation precedes him resulting in twists and turns that will see his image "tarnished" in some cases and placated in others.

When the film is analyzed, Wayne doesn't have his character apologize for his actions. Surviving a gunfight is simply living through another day. The film takes the approach of a study in which the viewer fully understands the character and his actions. This study is conveyed by those around

Books who build upon the character from past actions in his life. Young Gillom Rogers, played by Ron Howard, knows who Books is but doesn't recognize him on first meeting. The dime novels built legends but missed the real essence of the character. Richard Boone as Mike Sweeney remembers Books from the past as the man who killed his (Sweeney's) brother. These characters portray the past, while the present is shown through Bond Rogers, played by Lauren Bacall, the operator of the boarding house at which Books stays. Through them Books is seen as a man facing his maker but not apologizing for his past. The two argue during the film but a mutual trust begins to form. The past and the present converge in a climactic gunfight.

Director Don Siegel uses a familiar theme that runs through his films: the time factor. Richard Widmark as Det. Dan Madigan in *Madigan* (1968) has seventy-two hours to bring in the killer. *Two Mules for Sister Sara* (1970) has Clint Eastwood trying to reach his destination by a certain date with uncertain factors deterring him from this deadline. *The Shootist*'s John Books will have only one week remaining in which to live. Siegel's characters accept their fate in stoic fashion. Steve McQueen's character in *Hell Is for Heroes* (1962) pays the price for his individuality as will Dan Madigan. Books will also face such a demise by setting up a gunfight with three shady characters. Hoping to meet his fate, Books survives but destiny is still close at hand.

If an actor has to film a final scene, *The Shootist* was the perfect vehicle for Wayne. A nostalgic journey is relived through the film clips that are seen before the opening credits. Four Wayne films—*Red River, Hondo, Rio Bravo,* and *El Dorado*—show scenes of the star in action, but for *The Shootist* they are moments in Books's life.

The film has three action sequences: one at the start, another when two gunmen enter Books's room, and the climactic showdown in the Metropole Saloon. All three sequences total less than ten minutes of screen time, keeping the focus on Books's character, which is the heart of the film. Books had a code of laws that stated:

> I won't be wronged. I won't be
> insulted and I won't be laid a
> hand on. I don't do these things
> to other people and I require
> the same from them.

The Shootist is not only a testament to John Bernard Books but also to John Wayne who in this film would finish his fiftieth year in motion pictures.

Films, in 1985, would see the western return in Clint Eastwood's *Pale Rider* and director Lawrence Kasdan's *Silverado*, both of which performed well at the box office. 1990 would find Kevin Costner's *Dances With Wolves* the second western to take the Oscar (after *Cimarron* nearly six decades earlier) and Clint Eastwood's *Unforgiven* (1992) would be the third to win the Academy Award for Best Picture. Eastwood won as Best Director as well.

The Eastwood film painted a portrait of no good guys or bad guys, but characters true to their own beliefs. The western image had changed by 1992 but many fans still appreciated the simplicity by which Wayne would resolve his problems in them. His image still survives; after all, one only has to turn on the television set or the VCR to see one of his films. A legacy was compiled into fifty years and was highlighted by the final days of the man they rightly called *The Shootist*.

Wayne in his final film appearance in *The Shootist*.

DUKE'S DREAM

John Wayne made a dream come true: The story of the Alamo was brought to the motion picture screen. Planning this production and bringing it to completion were to take years and money. The cost was to exceed $12,000,000. This was to be the most expensive film made in the U.S. at that time.

The film's genesis was to have its first stage in 1946. Wayne was not to enter the producing aspect of the epic until later. The pre-production work was to be in excess of $4,000,000.

The first major problem was the construction of the Alamo fortress and the town of San Antonio as it appeared in 1836. The reproduction of both was to cost $1,500,000. To catch the actual proportions of 1836, a half-mile distance between the fort and the town had to be planned.

The next problem was to find the proper location site. Beginning in 1947, Wayne and others had been looking for the proper setting. In 1949, Wayne hired Al Ybarra as art director on the film. Ybarra's job was to find the precise location. During the next eight years, Wayne and Ybarra were to travel thousands of miles with various locations in mind, but all proved unsatisfactory.

In 1951, Batjac, Wayne's production company, couldn't raise enough money, so Wayne and writer James Edward Grant did *Big Jim McLain.* Grant, a miser with words who created many of Wayne's better characters, and Wayne had a distribution deal that made them $3,000,000 richer.

In October, 1957, James T. "Happy" Shahan invited the Batjac staff to his Brackettville, Texas, cattle ranch. The 22,000 acre spread had more room than was needed. Shortly after a profitable meeting, ground was broken.

Originally at this time, Wayne wanted only to play Sam Houston and devote his energies to production. United Artists said they would help budget the film with the condition that Wayne would insure a good gross by playing Davy Crockett. Wayne agreed.

The construction time was to last from December, 1957, through September, 1959. Ybarra took photographs and made drawings from them so Wayne could view them. The sets were built from architect plans found in Mexico at the Mexico City Museum. The two sets were to cover over 400 acres. Minute detail was applied as the location turned into reality, an inch at a time. Over 1,000,000 adobe bricks were used for the entire construction. A rainstorm destroyed about 50,000 bricks and, as a result, drainage ditches had to be built.

Other details, such as ten miles of underground electric and phone wires, were added. Fourteen miles of heavy duty gravel and tar roads were built. Six deep wells were dug to produce 25,000 gallons of artesian water daily. One million square feet of lumber and forty miles of reinforced construction steel were needed; 125,000 square feet of concrete flooring and twelve miles of water pipe were built. Over 30,000 square feet of imported Spanish roof tile was installed.

Two months before location shooting, some $75,000 worth of portable air-conditioning was installed. A 4,000-foot landing strip was surfaced for visitors and for taking film to San Antonio. Two helicopters were chartered to transfer any seriously injured performers.

Stock corrals covering 500 acres were made for 1600 saddle horses, work horses and mules. A herd of 375 rare Texas longhorns were to be used in the stampede sequence. With the special care taken throughout the production, not one animal was injured.

Hiring the many extras needed for the massive battle scenes were handled through the Texas Employment Commission and Eagle Pass Employment Office.

Frank Beetson, the head customer of Batjac, saved $5,000 on the budget by using draw strings instead of zippers on the various costumes. Santa Anna's armies had 12 different uniform types, all of which were authentically recreated.

Artillery was the next obstacle. Ybarra made sketches of the various cannon types, as none no longer existed. All had to be built from scratch. All of these were cast in iron at Brackettville. Wheelrights made authentic wheels for the cannons and caissons.

A crew of 15 expert gunsmiths kept all of the rifles and various firearms working. Three times as much gunpowder was used in the film as was used in the original historical battle; 25,000 pounds of black nitrate powder was stored and was more than enough to blow up the entire set.

The stunts were planned months in advance. A group horse fall of 14 riders and horses was to be used in one of the battle scenes. The stunt was practiced for months and was eventually executed in one take. Eighteen top stuntmen were on the set continuously. The stuntmen trained their own horses for hours. There were no injuries worse than skinned knees or sprained wrists. Working with powder charges and falling horses is difficult under any circumstances. The stunts on the screen add to the realism, making a great action sequence during the final battle.

The company spent in excess of $4,000,000 on wages, supplies, lodgings, transportation, etc. in Brakettville. The food cost over $300,000 for the location period; 192,509 meals were catered, making this the most expensive undertaking in the history of catering. Servings were issued of 510,000 cups of coffee, 342,000 quarts of milk, 53,000 steaks, 24,000 pounds of roast beef and 18,000 pounds of ham.

Filming started on September 2, 1959. This was to last for 83 days. The only time lost while filming was due to inclement weather—a day and a half. Two additional days were lost during the filming of the ABC television special "The Spirit of the Alamo."

More than 560,000 exposed feet of technicolor film were used at a cost of $30,000 per hour. Todd-AO cameras were used to film the action.

Wayne said of the film: "This is real American history, the kind of movie we need today more than ever. It'll make money for years to come. This is going to shake hell out of people all over the world."

The Alamo filming was completed when the last crew member left on December 15, 1959.

The next battle after the post-production work (such as editing, adding the film score, sound, etc.) was the organization of promotional and publicity activities. Wayne hired the Russell Birdwell Organization to spearhead the media blitz Wayne needed. Birdwell, a master of promotion and highly sought after for top dollar results, organized a 185 page publicity release entitled "A News Release—John Wayne's *The Alamo.*" This was distributed to newspapers throughout the country.

Life Magazine was utilized twice. A three-page spread in the July 4, 1960, issue cost $150,000. On September 19, 1960, a four-page spread of color photographs was used. Four color shots from the film were shown. Used were a scene of the Mexicans entering the fort, Colonel Travis commanding a rifle squad, Santa Anna's armies crossing the plains of Texas, and Davy Crockett carrying a torch as the Mexicans persue him.

A comic book promotion used full-page ads with a popsicle tie-in for free tickets to the film if so many popsicle wrappers were sent in to the company.

"The Spirit of The Alamo" was shown on Monday, November 14, 1960, on the ABC Network. The special, shown at 8:30, had a full-page ad and a half-page summary in *TV Guide* Magazine of November 12-18, 1960. Pontiac sponsored the special. The special showed parts of the party held after filming, Wayne reading a letter written by Davy Crockett, the actors discussing their film roles, and, of course, clips from the feature.

Movie Digest Magazine of November 1960 had a three-page spread with color photographs on the making of the film.

The November issue of *Screen Stories* ran a seven-page spread with dialogue, photographs, and a plot summary.

The Alamo pressbook (used for advertising and promotion of the film) mentioned that there wasn't a film, including *Gone With the Wind*, that captured the epic sweep and imagery of the battle scenes used in *The Alamo.*

The Alamo was defeated by many movie reviewers who said that the plot was weak and the direction slow. However, Wayne received noteworthy compliments on the staging of the battle scenes, which swept the viewer into the action.

Time Magazine reviewed the film on November 7, 1960. The review stated the film's running time at three hours and 38 minutes.

Newsweek Magazine reviewed the film on October 31, 1960.

Boxoffice Magazine, a theatre owners publication, printed a laudatory review on October 24, 1960.

On the plus side, The National Board of Review named *The Alamo* the best film of 1960.

Good Housekeeping gave its seal of approval on the film. This was the first film to receive this award in their publication.

The World Premiere of *The Alamo* was held in San Antonio, Texas, on October 24, 1960. Wayne made a personal appearance for the three-day activities, including slicing a 30-foot cake which recreated the attack on the Alamo.

Wayne personally did other hyping by going on city promotional tours. In Chicago, one of Wayne's favorite cities, Wayne gave members of the press a Bowie Knife with a wooden handle and a protective guard. The single-edged blade was eight and a half inches long. The knife came with a polished board on which the knife could be mounted. When Wayne went on tour, everything was always first-class.

American Cinematographer, a technical magazine on photographic techniques, ran a five-page article entitled; "Filming *The Alamo.*" The lighting set-ups were the basis of the article.

In spite of *The Alamo*'s being shown in 70mm, the widest motion picture presentation process, promotional activities, and a reserved seat policy in the major cities, the film didn't generate the business Wayne sought. With the Academy Award Nominations around the corner and a spring market for business ahead, it was decided the film should be cut. The running time was shortened to 161 minutes.

When the Academy Award Nominations were announced, *The Alamo* received seven including: Best Picture, Best Supporting Actor (Chill Wills), Cinematography, Sound, Editing, Music Scoring and Best Song.

A battle ensued with a massive indulgence in politics and name calling. Chill Wills stepped on a few toes while campaigning for his award. Wayne was miffed by his approach.

Another controversy centered around the attitude that if one didn't see the film, one wasn't a good American. This enfuriated Wayne and he retaliated with ads in other publications denouncing the means by which his film was being touted.

When the fateful night of April 17, 1961, concluded at the Academy Awards, Wayne's film garnered only one award, for Best Sound. This was the first award given that night and Wayne thought the film would become a winner. But *The Alamo* once again met its fate.

In the spring release, the dollars weren't coming into the box-office. By late summer, the film had run its course.

The $12,000,000 budget wasn't achieved and the film lost investor dollars. Wayne was almost wiped out financially and he was mortgaged to the hilt. A new contract with 20th Century-Fox helped Wayne regroup some of his personal losses.

In 1967, United Artists re-issued the film. A moderate ad campaign was used and the film disappeared from most theatres after one week's run.

Wayne sold his interest to United Artists and the company now controlled the film. The U.S. and Canada gross was now at $7,910,000.

The television premiere of *The Alamo* was shown in two parts on the NBC Network. The first part was shown on Saturday, September 18, 1971, and the second half was shown on Monday September 20, 1971. The ratings were fair. United Artists recouped their losses and made a profit on the film.

Wayne should have shared in the profits, but his dream had almost turned into a nightmare. As with having children, you dream of their growth and future accomplishments when they arrive. They may disappoint you, but they are your children and you will love them just the same. "Duke's Dream" will remain in that light.

THE ALAMO: RESTORED EPIC

The end of July 1992 brought to a conclusion the search of the missing footage from *The Alamo*. A complete, original, uncut 70mm print was located in Toronto, Canada. This print, stored in thirteen film cases, was in a warehouse since being withdrawn from the 70mm Toronto engagement in early January 1961. *The Alamo* didn't perform that well north of the border, a fact that may have saved it from destruction. United Artists, which released *The Alamo*, issued a letter to all theaters exhibiting the 70mm prints throughout the U.S. market in December 1960 indicating that subsequent prints would be edited from 192 minutes of actual footage to 161.

Also missing, after a while, would be the overture, the entr'acte, and walk-out music. The Toronto print wasn't recut because the grosses indicated a shorter run, so the expense was spared and the film was removed from the market. The 70mm print remained in storage until November 1990. A showing on Thanksgiving weekend of 1990 confirmed the original running time of 202 minutes. The print was returned to the warehouse in Toronto until MGM/UA in Los Angeles was contacted two days after the showing. The print was shipped to L.A. where a careful transfer to videotape would eventually transpire. The color was faded in various parts but the sound track was in proper order. Meticulous care was utilized as the print was refurbished.

The Alamo was available by late July 1992 on videotape and laserdisc. The search for the complete *Alamo* was over. Both technologies feature the film in letterbox format. As it was photographed in Panavision, bars appear at the top and the bottom of the television screen. This process preserves more of the actual image as originally seen theatrically.

The continuity of *The Alamo* is highly enhanced, and despite a longer running time, the film's pacing is improved. After Jim Bowie (Richard Widmark) has decided to stop drinking, he is informed that Major Travis (Laurence Harvey) is now Colonel Travis, a decision not to his liking. Travis later talks with Captain Dickinson (Ken Curtis) about Jeffersonian Democracy. Travis with his aristocratic background seems to collide with Dickinson's beliefs.

A key sequence occurs in the San Antonio church cellar where weapons and powder are

AUTHOR'S NOTE: Brackettville, Texas, was used as a setting in John Ford's *Two Rode Together* and a James Stewart western, *Bandolero*. Recently, Brackettville was seen in the Willie Nelson film *Barbarosa*. The Alamo courtyard was seen in *Bandolero* and *Barbarosa*. A less than colorful comment was made on *The Alamo* in the film *An American Werewolf in London*. The film was referred to as "bloody awful."

stored. Davy Crockett (John Wayne), Bowie, Beekeeper (Chill Wills), the Parson (Hank Worden), and Smitty (Frankie Avalon) enter the cellar at night to view the cache. Beekeeper inadvertingly rings the church bell, alerting the merchant Emil Sand (Wesley Lau) and his men there are visitors in the cellar. The weapons and powder are being stored for Santa Anna's forces. As the heroes seem doomed, a fight occurs resulting in the death of Sand. Crockett, who has previously encountered Linda Cristal, tells her that he killed Sand. While relating this incident, Crockett discovers that Cristal's character name is Flaca. In Spanish, this means "skinny." This scene explains why Crockett later refers to her as Flaca.

As Crockett, Bowie, the Parson, and Smitty are taking the weapons and the powder to the Alamo, Mrs. Guy (Olive Carey) has a wagon mishap in town as Flaca offers to assist. Mrs. Guy is chastising her husband for joining Houston's army. Inside the fort, a reference is made to the fight in the church cellar. After the officer's meeting in Travis's quarters, Crockett and Bowie later discuss the meaning of pyrotechnics. This sequence furthers the conflict between Bowie and Travis.

During the scene where Crockett and Flaca talk beside a tree, Flaca tells Crockett she loves him as he philosophizes about life.

Inside the fort, Beekeeper and Thimblerig (Denver Pyle) discuss why the Tennesseans are in Texas. Bowie and Travis have a heated argument about the command with Crockett interrupting them as Jim Bonham (Patrick Wayne) arrives with news concerning Fannin's army. Travis is shown as being more of a manipulative character causing Dickinson and Bonham to have doubts about his commanding abilities. Dickinson later leads a patrol outside the fort which is attacked by a patrol of dragoons and lancers. Two losses occur and Travis orders no further patrols. Volunteers from Gonzales arrive and a birthday party for Dickinson's daughter is celebrated. After the first assault, Crockett is informed that the Parson has been wounded. Inside the chapel, the Parson dies after speaking with Crockett who later prays for his fallen friend.

A religious discussion between some of the volunteers occurs the night before the final battle. An original battle scene is edited differently in the shorter version as the dragoons enter the compound and Beekeeper dies. Crockett's death scene is longer as he contorts himself backwards to give him more momentum after he is stabbed. He then throws the torch into the magazine.

Restoration has added footage to such films as *Lawrence of Arabia* (twenty minutes) and *Spartacus* (six minutes). Thus far, *The Alamo* is the film with the most missing footage restored: thirty-one minutes. At one time, an early cut had the film running five hours; the first half was three hours long and the second half was two. That footage has now been lost but the restored version enhances the characters and gives a better understanding of the Alamo siege. This is as close to director John Wayne's original vision as one can achieve. He would be proud.

PLANNING STAGES

At one time, Wayne was set to costar with Clark Gable in MGM's *Lone Star*, a film dealing with Texas. Unable to play the part because of other commitments, Wayne left the project and his role was given to Broderick Crawford. The idea was to place Wayne and Gable, or Gable and Wayne in the same western for a box-office hit. The 1952 film ended up doing fair business. In November 1959, after completing *The Alamo*, Wayne announced he was going to film *Sam Houston*. The project was set to roll at the end of 1960. Perhaps the less-than-anticipated box-office receipts of *The Alamo* caused him to change his mind.

In March 1961, *The Bengal Tiger* was to have been filmed on location in India by Wayne and Director Howard Hawks. The background was set against the Sepoy Rebellion of 1857–58. This was based on a novel by Edison Marshall that was published under the pseudonym Hall Hunter. A tiger hunter becomes involved in a rebellion and has affairs with a British woman and a native girl. The story ends with the hunter searching for religious inspiration among Buddhist shrines.

UNSOLD TV PILOTS

Batjac Productions filmed a pilot for *Calamity Jane* that was to have appeared in the 1957–58 television season. *Flight* was a science-fiction pilot that was to have been an anthology about space travel that was to have appeared in the 1958–59 season. *The Wildcatters* was to have starred Claude Akins and L. Q. Jones as oilmen. Batjac Productions produced the pilot, and had it sold, Wayne was going to do narration and son Patrick would occasionally guest star in the series.

WAYNE ON THE CUTTING ROOM FLOOR

Wayne has given us many memories on the movie screen. There are some moments that were never used. These moments ended up on the cutting room floor. Included is a series of stills and a description of the stills. The scenes pictured are from *The Alamo, El Dorado, The Undefeated, The Cowboys* and *McQ*.

The Alamo: Wayne, Chill Wills, Hank Worden and RIchard Widmark look to see the merchant Emil and his men enter the church. Emil's plan is to kill all of the above because they have discovered his secret of stored powder and guns.

The Green Berets: This scene with Vera Miles was also dropped. Miles portrays Wayne's wife. During the course of the film they met in this brief sequence.

The Undefeated: Wayne and John Agar part ways in this scene. Agar seemed to appear when the script needed him but his disappearance was a mystery. Wayne refers to two comrades that won't live by Christmas. Perhaps Agar's character was one of them. John Agar's autograph was signed here when he confirmed my thoughts.

El Dorado: Charlene Holt, Wayne, Robert Mitchum and Paul Fix appear to be having a good time. This sequence occurs before Wayne leaves *El Dorado* after being shot by Michele Carey.

El Dorado: This scene with Wayne and Michele Carey is also missing. She is holding the rifle she shot Wayne with.

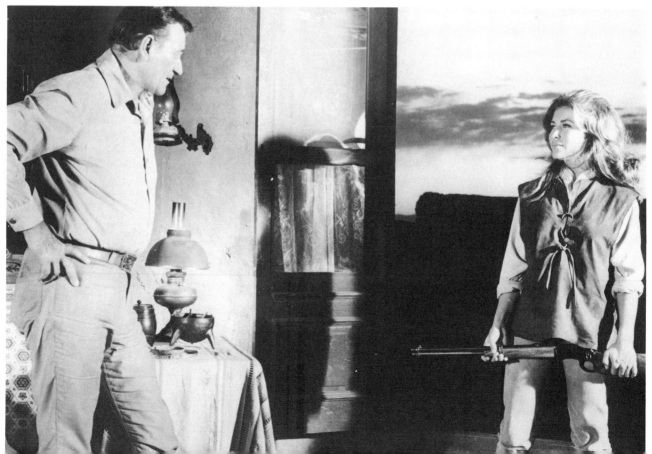

The Cowboys: Wayne takes a fall, perhaps from "Crazy Alice."

The Cowboys: Wayne and A. Martinez encounter a bear while checking the trail ahead. The bear had disappeared from the final print.

*McQ:*Wayne encounters a woman at the reception desk at the hospital. Diana Muldaur looms over the woman's shoulder. I suspect Wayne is trying to find where his partner is after being shot. Muldaur plays the wife of the wounded detective. In the final version, Wayne and Muldaur are in the hospital room.

During the course of Wayne's long career, his films were subject to occasional bloopers that can be easily seen or heard. Here is a list of those "goofs."

Red River

1. Wayne's wagon is struck by a flaming arrow, causing a large burn hole in the left front part of the wagon. At the Red River, the hole is visible. In the next shot, the hole isn't seen. The next shot shows the hole once again. Upon Wayne's arrival at his future ranch site, there is no longer a hole.

2. During the climactic fight between Wayne and Montgomery Clift, Wayne's hat is knocked off of his head. The scene cuts to Walter Brennan for his reaction to the punch. The next scene features Wayne's hat getting knocked off once again.

The Searchers

1. Martin Pawley (Jeffrey Hunter) refers to himself as one-eighth Cherokee. Later in the film, Wayne refers to Pawley as being one-quarter Cherokee.

2. Wayne and company encounter a dead Indian buried under a rock. As the rock is being lifted, the supposedly dead Indian takes a deep breath.

The Barbarian and The Geisha

1. Wayne fights a gigantic Japanese trickster. As Wayne punches him the last time, an audible click is heard of a 35mm camera snapping pictures on the set.

The Alamo

1. While Wayne and Colonel Travis (Laurence Harvey) talk in the cantina, a Tennessean punches another Tennessean. This causes the second Tennessean to fall down by a fireplace. In the next scene, the Tennessean has disappeared from the fireplace area as Wayne starts speaking.

2. After the women and children are evacuated from the Alamo, the first attack begins. Jim Bowie (Richard Widmark) fires his seven-barreled rifle. Widmark raises his arms too high and the wire going to the rifle stock causing the simulated gunfire is seen as the rifle is fired.

3. When the final attack begins, an explosion causes some men to jump off a wall onto mattresses to break their fall. The mattresses can be seen in the background of the shot.

4. When Colonel Travis is killed, he falls to the ground. As the Mexican soldiers pass his body, Harvey moves his arm so the Mexicans won't step on his hand.

5. As the battle draws to its conclusion, Mexican cavalry jump over a palisade to enter the Alamo compound. The next scene shows the cavalry still approaching the palisade before the jump.

6. Before Wayne is stabbed by a Mexican lance, a dried blood stain appears on his shirt. This stain was from a prior take.

7. Wayne throws a torch into the powder magazine, landing in front of some powder kegs. The explosion occurs from the back of the kegs.

North to Alaska

1. A climactic fight occurs in which Wayne is punched. As Wayne's head snaps back, his toupée falls off.

The Comancheros

1. During the Comanchero attack at the weigh station, a wagon is dragged onto its side. Wayne runs to the wagon for a better position. As he approaches the wagon, the wheel by his vantage point has stopped spinning. In the next scene, as Wayne fires his rifle, the wheel is still spinning.

2. Wayne and company flee the Comanchero camp at the film's conclusion. As the wagon leaves, Wayne fires his rifle into the camp, using his right hand. As a sentry is shot by Wayne, a film reversal shows Wayne firing the rifle left handed. In the next scene, Wayne is right handed again.

The Man Who Shot Liberty Valance

1. This film is in black and white. Wayne's westerns in the late 1950's and early 1960's featured him usually wearing a blue or a red double breasted shirt. In this film, Wayne is shown in a bar in a dark shirt. When Wayne arrives at his ranch, he has on a lighter shaded shirt. Inside his home, Wayne has on a darker shirt. When Wayne is carried out of his home by Woody Strode to his wagon, Wayne has on the lighter shirt. After Wayne has been in the wagon, the next shot shows Wayne wearing the darker shirt again.

Wayne adjusts his costume on the set of *The Alamo.*

The Sons of Katie Elder

1. Wayne pursues the villain into a gunshop in the film's conclusion. As Wayne peers over a counter, a shadowed form is seen on top of the counter. When the villain fires at Wayne, the same form lights up simulating a gunshot.

The War Wagon

1. Wayne is seen in the master shot of the saloon fight. Wayne's hat is not seen on his head. The next scene shows Wayne's hat on his head. The next scene shows Wayne hatless.

True Grit

Wayne is on horseback in the climactic gunfight with Lucky Ned Pepper and his three men. Wayne has a rifle in his right hand plus a revolver in his left hand as he charges into the four men. When Wayne charges a second time, a film reversal features Wayne firing the rifle with his left hand and the pistol is now in the right hand. The next scene shows Wayne preparing to fire again with the rifle in the right hand and the pistol in the left hand.

Rio Lobo

Wayne and two companions escort the villain from his home to nearby horses. Wayne's double, Chuck Roberson, is supposed to be Wayne walking towards the horses. Wayne looped a line of dialogue making it seem to be Wayne, but it is actually Roberson who is actually seen while Wayne says the line of dialogue.

Big Jake

1. Wayne has saved a sheep herder from hanging. In the next scene, a rider approaches Wayne with a message. The scene shows the rider approaching Wayne and practically handing Wayne the message. In the next scene, the rider hasn't approached Wayne yet. The matched action from one scene to another wasn't edited properly.

2. Patrick Wayne's shirttail is outside his pants after his fistfight with Wayne. Before Chris Mitchum arrives, the shirttail is out. As actor John Doucette approaches Wayne after Wayne falls in the mud, Patrick Wayne's shirttail is now tucked in. Patrick Wayne's next scene shows the shirttail out again.

3. Wayne encounters Chris Mitchum after Mitchum's motorcycle mishap. As Wayne punches Mitchum, the shutter of a camera is heard clicking at least four times.

Rooster Cogburn

1. Wayne and Katharine Kepburn are resting when the Indian Wolf informs them the bad guys are near. They mount their horses. Wayne is wearing a coat. As they near the hills, Wayne still has his coat on. In the next scene, the coat is not on Wayne. When the bad guys are spotted, Wayne's coat is back on again.

Wayne appears to be a man of action in *The Comancheros*.

This was a special publicity photo that I received at
the Chicago press activities for *The Cowboys* on
January 16, 1972.

PART FOUR

THE
COMMEMORATIVES

THE BIRTHPLACE OF JOHN WAYNE

"The Birthplace of John Wayne" is located at 224 South Second Street in Winterset, Iowa. Wayne had spent an early part of his life in this home and also at Earlham, Iowa, located 15 miles northwest of Winterset. Wayne, who was of Irish and Scottish ancestry, lived in Iowa until 1914 when his family moved to Palmdale, California, because of his father's poor health. Wayne never returned to Iowa. About 4100 people reside in Winterset.

In October, 1979, a yard sign commemorating the birthplace of Wayne was donated to Winterset by John and Sally Dwyer of Rockport, Massachusetts. The hand-carved sign measures 15 inches by 43 inches. The birthplace was acquired by the Chamber of Commerce in 1981, and was restored to the original 1907 appearance. The birthplace features a kitchen, a parlor and a third room exhibiting Wayne memorabilia. The Chamber of Commerce office is also located in the birthplace. A bed that Wayne used is located in the kitchen, as this was the warmest room in the house during the winter months.

Persons pledging a $20.00–$99.00 contribution to the birthplace will receive a John Wayne Congressional Medal, a 1982 Covered Bridge Coin featuring the birthplace, an 8×10 Wayne print, a birthplace brochure and a certificate of membership in the John Wayne Birthplace Society.

Persons pledging or donating $100.00 or more will receive all of the above plus a 12×16 limited edition print, numbered and signed, of Wayne in front of the birthplace.

Contributions should be sent to the John Wayne Birthplace Fund, P.O. Box 55, Winterset, Iowa, 50273.

The birthplace, located 35 miles southwest of Des Moines, is open Monday through Sunday and holidays 10:00 A.M. to 5:00 P.M., from April 1 through October 31. These are the correct hours as of July 1984.

The dedication of the birthplace was held on Sunday, October 10, 1982, in conjunction with the Covered Bridge Festival, a yearly local occurrence. About 50,000 people attended the festival held on Saturday, October 9th, and Sunday, October 10, 1982. Michael Wayne, John Wayne's eldest son, attended the two-day festival, riding in the parade and attending various related functions. He visited the birthplace for the first time on Saturday. He attended the dedication, which started shortly after 1:00 P.M. About 2500 people attended the ceremony.

Ken Weldon, a consultant of the birthplace committee, escorted Michael Wayne to the ceremony. Weldon worked for a year and a half setting up Wayne's visit. Wayne announced a $5,000 bronze bust of his father was to be sent and placed in the home. The 60-pound bust is currently on display. Five special Congressional Gold Medal bronze replicas were presented as gifts from the Wayne family.

Bill Judd represented Colt Industries, a supplier of a $3,000 Colt revolver in commemoration of John Wayne. A revolver was presented to the birthplace. Pat Corkrean, the chairman of the Covered Bridge committee, accepted the revolver for the birthplace.

After the revolver presentation, Michael Wayne was given a framed print of his father in wood taken from the front porch of the birthplace. Congressman Tom Harkin presented Wayne with the special print of John Wayne and the birthplace. The print was number 3 of 300 prints made by Tom Williams of Des Moines, Iowa. The Chamber of Commerce sells these prints at a cost of $100.00 each.

U.S. Senator Roger Jepsen presented an American flag which had flown over the Capitol in Washington, D.C., to the birthplace. Michael Wayne received the flag and presented it to a home guard.

Before his departure, Wayne told Weldon: "This was one of the highlights of my life." He stated of his father: "The impact he made on the country can't be denied and couldn't be changed."

On Monday, May 2, 1983, Michael Wayne returned to Winterset accompanied by his brothers Patrick and John Ethan. The occasion was Colt Industries' introduction of a new Colt revolver called "The Duke," which was presented to the birthplace. The cost of the revolver is $475.00.

Ken Weldon accepted the revolver that was presented to the birthplace. The three Wayne sons spoke to the audience, as did representatives of Colt Industries and birthplace committee members. Also presented to the birthplace was an eyepatch that Wayne used in *True Grit*.

Approximately 400 people attended the ceremony. The three Wayne sons signed autographs throughout their stay. A reception was held that evening at the Gold Buffet. About 300 people attended that function. A bowling tournament was held between the three Wayne sons and the Colt representatives.

The birthplace features a John Wayne Commemorative Rifle that was presented by the U.S.

Repeating Arms Company in 1981. Also on display are movie stills, two suitcases used in John Ford's *Stagecoach*, letters from film stars, a letter from President Reagan and other memorabilia.

The bronze bust of Wayne is on display with the following words: "Tomorrow is the most perfect thing in life, comes into us at midnight very clean. It's perfect when it arrives and puts itself in our hands. It hopes we've learned something from yesterday."

JOHN WAYNE CANCER CLINIC

The UCLA Division of Surgical Oncology and the John Wayne Cancer Clinic is located on the ninth floor of the Louis Factor Building in Los Angeles.

Progress against cancer is constantly taking place. Tumors are studied (Oncology) and treatments are undertaken. Research and discoveries can be applied to patient care at the clinic.

The professor and chief of UCLA's Division of Surgical Oncology is David L. Morton, M.D. Morton is known for his work in Immunotherapy, a program used to stimulate patient's immune responses that fight cancer cells. Morton is also head of the John Wayne Cancer Clinic.

In April, 1971, The Division of Surgical Oncology joined the UCLA School of Medicine.

The John Wayne Cancer Clinic has benefited from various social activities. *Rocky III* premiered at the Academy of Motion Picture Arts and Sciences on May 26, 1982, for the benefit of the clinic. The clinic received $60,000 from the premiere. A John Wayne Commemorative rifle was auctioned, as were the gloves and robe worn by Sylvester Stallone in the film.

Another $20,000 was raised on August 4, 1982, through the Ringling Bros. and Barnum and Bailey Circus.

On April 24, 1983, the Eddie Cantor Charitable Foundation honored Tony Bennett. This benefited the clinic $50,000.

Another $10,000 was received from a wine testing at the San Marcos home of Barbara and Vince Marchetta.

The clinic was redecorated in 1983. Wayne memorabilia now takes away from the standard waiting room look. Posters of Wayne's films appear throughout the clinic. An eyepatch from *True Grit*, a kerchief, film stills, an autographed card signed by Wayne, and two souvenir coffee cups are on display. A small Bowie knife that was a gift to Wayne is also on display, as is a color picture of Wayne's boat, *Wild Goose*. Two busts of Wayne and a small statue of Wayne on horseback is displayed. A bronze statue by David Emmanuel also appears.

Any information or contributions should be sent to:

The Committee to Cure Cancer Through Immunization
John Wayne Cancer Clinic
P.O. Box 24177
Village Station
Los Angeles, Calif. 90024

A first limited edition print issued by the Greenwich Workshop was released by Wayne Enterprises in the fall of 1980. The prints total 1000 and are all signed and numbered by artist Bob McGinnis. Entitled "Ethan," the size is 24" by 28½". The representation of Wayne is from the film *The Searchers*, showing Wayne looking down at the doll Topsy by gravestones. The cost is $90.00 and the net proceeds went to the John Wayne Cancer Clinic.

"Under Attack," by Frank McCarthy, is a limited edition print of a scene from *Hondo*. It is 35" by 18¼" and sells for $125. All prints are personally signed by McCarthy, with a portion of the sales going to the Clinic. It may be obtained through The Greenwich Workshop, Inc., 30 Lindeman Drive, Trumbull, CT 06611.

THE OFFICIAL U.S. MINT JOHN WAYNE COMMEMORATIVE MEDAL

The John Wayne Commemorative Medal was authorized by the United States Congress, and was struck by the U.S. Mint. Each medal is inscribed with a permanent edition number and is individually electroplated with 24 Karat Gold. This is the first time an American film actor has been so honored. Wayne was the 32nd person to be awarded such a special congressional tribute.

Frank Gasparro of the U.S. Mint designed the medal. Photographs from Michael Wayne were supplied to Gasparro on June 1, 1979, to capture the Wayne likeness. On June 8th, the drawings were sent to Michael Wayne for approval. Work started on the medal the following Monday.

The bronze coin is available in two sizes: 1⅝ inches and three inches in diameter. At the time the announcement was made concerning the medals, 10,000 orders were received for the three-inch medal.

The obverse side has a head shot of Wayne from *The Alamo* with the words: "John Wayne American" inscribed at the top. The reverse has an engraving of Wayne on horseback with a Monument Valley-type background. The scene is from *Hondo*.

The coin is inset into an 8 × 10-inch piece of cardboard with reproductions of three paintings of Wayne. (See "The John Wayne Lithograph.") The coin can be removed from the inset. On the back of the board is a list of Wayne's film credits.

The date of Wayne's death (June 12, 1979) is incorrect, as Wayne died on June 11th. Wayne made more than the 151 films listed with the coin.

The actual gold medal was presented to the Wayne family at the U.S. Capitol on March 6, 1980.

The 1⅝-inch medal costs $1.15 and the three-inch medal costs $8.30. These are sold through the mail. As of March 1984, over 50,000 orders were received on the larger medal and over 550,000 orders were received on the smaller medal.

Information on the medals can be obtained from: The Historic Providence Mint, 222 Harrison Street, Providence, Rhode Island 02901.

The Wayne medal is available in "The National Historical Series." It is the most popular of all the issued medals.

THE JOHN WAYNE LITHOGRAPH

The Historical Providence Mint commissioned Artist Douglas Charlesworth Hart to do an original portrait of Wayne. Five hundred prints of the portrait lithograph were made available.

The lithograph comprises three portraits of Wayne. The first pose on the left is a scene from *True Grit*. Wayne is astride his horse as he prepares for the gunfight with Lucky Ned Pepper. The central figure has a head-to-waist shot of Wayne in a red shirt. This is a publicity pose from *Circus World.* The third portrait on the right is a head-to-toe shot of Wayne resting his rifle on his right shoulder. This is a publicity shot from *The*

Man Who Shot Liberty Valance.

The Wayne persona is shown in the craggy, strong features that have made him an institution. The facial features compare with Wayne's film image.

However, the portrait from *The Man Who Shot Liberty Valance* (1962) has Wayne with the yellow-handled pistol. *The Sons of Katie Elder* (1965) was the first film in which that pistol was used by Wayne.

Each lithograph is accompanied by a certificate of authenticity, as is the coin.

The cost of the lithograph is $145.00.

THE JOHN WAYNE PLATE

A third item offered by The Historic Providence Mint is "John Wayne—The Man of the Golden West Plate." This Historic First Edition Collec-

tor's Plate was designed by Endre Szabo. The plate has a 10¼-inch diameter, and is produced in fine porcelain. This was mae by The Lynell Studio

Collection. The picture of Wayne on the plate is a scene from *Big Jake,* showing Wayne with a partial smile and squinting eyes. Szabo's portrait of Wayne so pleased Wayne that he permitted the painting to be reproduced. The issue price is $45.00.

Any information concerning the medal, lithograph and plate can be made to:

The Historic Providence Mint
222 Harrison Street
Providence, Rhode Island
02901

JOHN WAYNE COMMEMORATIVE CARBINE

In 1981, The John Wayne Winchester Model 94 Commemorative Carbine was issued. When director John Ford cast Wayne in the film *Stagecoach,* the vehicle that made Wayne a star, he decided that Wayne would look more like a western hero with a carbine than a Colt Six Shooter. Wayne and stunt coordinator Yakima Canutt devised a large loop on the lever so Wayne could cock the rifle while twirling it. The barrel had to be shortened two inches so Wayne wouldn't injure himself during the twirling motion.

The carbine is a Model 94, not the Model 92 Wayne used. The Commemorative has an 18½-inch barrel and a full-length magazine for five .32-40 cartridges. Extra features are: the rear of the carbine is made of semi-buckhorn, has the blade post-type front sight, pewter plating on the receiver, barrel bands, bow lever and lower tang. A saddle ring and stud are included. The buttplate is carved blue steel and the buttstock is made of cut-checkered American walnut. The stock is in the "Frontier Style" square comb. On one receiver side is a cattle drive scene with 12 Wayne western film titles outlining the receiver. The other receiver side is a stagecoach scene with eight Wayne western film titles. A nickel-silver medallion of Wayne is inlaid into the buttstock with Monument Valley in the background. The words "John Wayne Commemorative" appear under the sight. The suggested retail price is $600.00.

For the sum of $2250.00 the perfectionist collector can purchase a limited edition made of fancy grained walnut, with gold plating triple-level etching on the receiver and lever. "The Duke One Of A Thousand" is supplied in a fitted wooden display case with red velvet lining and brass hardware. The 1,000 run has deluxe casing and plating. The rifle comes in full-color packaging sleeve with the prevalent themes of western decoration and Wayne himself.

If either carbine is out of one's means, the sum of $15.50 will purchase a box of 20 limited issue .32-40 cartridges with the name "Duke" incorporated into the headstamp.

As the years pass, both the carbine and the bullets will become more valuable. A major selling point is the fact that Wayne is known internationally and many collectors would like to share a part of the legacy by purchasing the carbine. A scabbard is also available.

Some of the proceeds will be donated to the John Wayne Memorial Fund and the John Wayne Cancer Clinic.

THE JOHN WAYNE COMMEMORATIVE COLTS
THE JOHN WAYNE COMMEMORATIVE HOLSTER AND GUNBELT SET
"JOHN WAYNE AMERICAN"

THE COLT JOHN WAYNE PRESENTATION EDITION

The presentation grade version is a .45 Colt Single Action Army revolver with a 4¾-inch barrel length. Each gun has a custom presentation case.

The presentation edition is hand engraved and has embellishments including a 24K gold eagle and banner inlaid in relief on the left side of the barrel. The banner is inscribed "John Wayne." A 24K gold sunburst appears on the front sight. Inlaid in relief on the left recoil shield of the frame is a 24K gold portrait of Wayne. The loading gate has a 24K gold border. A star is inlaid in relief. On the left side of the cylinder appears a 24K gold flush inlay of a Wayne "silhouette." This representation of Wayne is a scene from his film *The Searchers.* The cylinder is non-fluted. A design entitled "The Rampant Colt" appears on the right cylinder in 24K gold flush inlay. Engraved on the backstrap is Wayne's signature. Cylinder bands and frame borders are in 24K gold. Approximately 50 percent of the gun is engraved in an American style scroll. A gold-plated backstrap, trigger guard, hammer, trigger, base pin and ejector rod head are handsomely represented. The handle is a genuine two-piece checkered ivory stock.

The finish is in royal blue and gold plated, with 24K gold inlaid motifs.

One hundred presentation editions were issued. With each edition, a screwdriver, brush and oiler is included. This model was offered to the first 100 reserved serial number holders of record. The suggested retail value is $20,000. The John Wayne Cancer Clinic will receive a donation from each sale.

THE JOHN WAYNE DELUXE EDITION

The Deluxe Grade version is a .45 Colt Single Action Army revolver with a 4¾-inch barrel length. Each gun has a custom presentation case.

This version is hand engraved and has embellishments including an 18K gold eagle and banner inlaid in relief on the left side of the barrel. The banner is inscribed "John Wayne." An 18K gold John Wayne holster and gun is inlaid in relief on the left recoil shield of the frame. On the loading gate appears 18K gold Wayne spurs inlaid in relief. On the top of the backstrap appears an 18K gold Red River "D" brand flush inlaid. This brand is represented in the Wayne film Red River. Engraved on the backstrap is Wayne's signature. Over approximately 50 percent of the gun has Helfrich style scroll engraving. Etched on the left side of the cylinder is a gold-plated portrait of Wayne. This representation from The Alamo was taken from one of Wayne's favorite photographs of himself. Etched on the right side of the cylinder is a gold-plated image of Wayne on horseback. This scene is from Chisum. Two custom piece ebony stocks comprise the handle. A one-inch diameter scrimshawed ivory disk is inlaid in the left stock. "Colt" appears on the disk. The finish is silver-plated with 18K gold inlaid motifs. The cylinder is non-fluted.

Five hundred deluxe editions were issued. These 500 editions were first offered to the 500 reserved serial numbers of record. With each edition, a screwdriver, brush and oiler is included. The suggested retail price is $10,000. The John Wayne Cancer Clinic will receive a donation from each sale.

THE STANDARD MODEL

The Standard edition is a Model P1840 .45

Single Action Army Colt. The barrel length is 4¾ inches. This model is custom etched and gold-plated and has a blue finish.

The left side of the barrel has a gold-etched American eagle motif. American scroll also appears on that side. A banner entitled "John Wayne" appears under the eagle. American scroll appears on the right side of the barrel as well.

The cylinder is etched with selective gold-plated motifs of Wayne. A gold-etched face of Wayne appears on the left side of the cylinder framed in American scroll. The scene is from The Alamo. Wayne on horseback appears on the right cylinder side. This scene is from Chisum.

The handle is made of genuine ivory grips. Wayne's signature is etched on the backstrap. The Red River "D" appears on the top of the backstrap. This representation was used in Wayne's film Red River.

The presentation case is in a deluxe hand-finished oak. The inside of the case is french-fitted with genuine burgundy suede lining. Wayne's signature is branded into the lid. An etched and selectively gold-plated plaque is included, commemorating Wayne.

This model series had a run of 3100. The first 1500 serial numbers were reserved for commemorative collectors. The price is $2995.00. A portion of each sale will be donated to the John Wayne Cancer Clinic.

"THE DUKE"

Colt Firearms and the Wayne family have introduced "The Duke," a limited edition .22 Single Action Frontier revolver. This .22 New Frontier is a working firearm.

The blued barrel is 4⅖ inches long and is etched with a sterling silver plated inscription, "John Wayne, The Duke."

Included is an adjustable rear sight and a blade front sight. These sights are in keeping with the style of the Frontier Peacemaker.

The one-piece backstrap and triggerguard unit are made of an aluminum alloy with a flat black coating.

The two-piece stock is traditional black in a composite "eagle" style.

Other features include a nickel-plated hammer, trigger, cylinder base pin and base pin lock assembly. Also appearing is a nickeled ejector rod, rod head and ejector spring.

The barrel ejector housing and the cylinder are in a blued finish.

"The Duke" is presented in a red-velvet-lined

wood case. Included in the case is a sterling silver-plated plaque etched with a portrait of Wayne and his birthplace in Winterset, Iowa, along with the date May 26, 1907.

The suggested retail price is $475. A portion of the proceeds from each sale will be donated to the John Wayne Cancer Clinic.

Information on the four Wayne editions can be obtained from:

Colt Firearms
P.O. Box 1868
Dept. JW
Hartford, Connecticut 06102

THE JOHN WAYNE COMMEMORATIVE HOLSTER AND GUN SET

A John Wayne Commemorative holster and gunbelt set is issued by John Bianchi of Bianchi Gunleather in Temecula, California.

The Colt John Wayne Commemorative revolver should fit perfectly in the holster. Each belt has a metal plate properly numbered in the Bianchi archives.

The holster is right-handed only and the belt is for waist sizes 30"-44".

Each set is packaged in a box bearing Wayne's likeness, and contains a signed certificate of registration. A 10-page color booklet is enclosed.

There are 3,000 sets of this limited edition.

The gunbelt, holster and trouser belt cost $250.00. Some of the proceedings will also go to the John Wayne Cancer Clinic.

This set can be ordered from:

Frontier Museum Historical Center
100 Calle Cortez
Department GW7
Temecula, California 92390

"JOHN WAYNE AMERICAN"

John Bianchi has commissioned a limited edition of 250 bronze sculptures entitled "John Wayne American."

The statue is 30 inches high and is fashioned by Artist Dave Manuel. The cost is $485.

This can be ordered from:

Frontier Museum Historical Center
100 Calle Cortez
Department GW7
Temecula, California 92390

THE JOHN WAYNE LIMITED EDITION COMMEMORATIVE DECANTERS

Four John Wayne commemorative decanters filled with Kentucky straight bourbon whiskey, 80 proof, were released as limited editions.

The first commemorative is framed in a decanter that is finished in 23K gold. The limited edition ceramic commemorative painting framed by the decanter was created by portrait artist Everett Raymond Kinstler. The picture bottle is 10 inches tall and costs approximately $49.95. This commemorative is on display at the John Wayne Birthplace.

"John Wayne American" is the title of the second decanter. This bust of Wayne is 11 inches tall and costs approximately $59.95.

"John Wayne" is the third decanter title. Wayne is represented as a standing bronze figural measuring 18 inches in height. The approximate cost is $75.00.

The fourth decanter titled "John Wayne" is the last of the series of the limited edition decanters. This standing gold figural is glazed in genuine 23 karat gold and measures 18 inches in height. The approximate cost is $80.00. This decanter was sold empty in Iowa.

These four limited editions are no longer available, but information can be obtained from:

Roman Distilled Products Company
4849 Golf Road
Skokie, Ill. 60077

JOHN WAYNE COLLECTOR PLATES

A "John Wayne Collectors Plate" has been issued in a two plate series. These plates were reproduced from an original painting, "John Wayne" by Cassidy J. Alexander.

Both plates had a 10,000 edition and engraved numbers on the plate back. The plate circumference is 8¾ inches.

The first plate has representations of Wayne from *True Grit*, *The Longest Day* and *Tall in the Saddle*. The price is $39.50 per plate.

The second plate, "John Wayne—Military," has Wayne shown in a white naval uniform and representations of Wayne from *The Wings of Eagles* and *The Green Berets*. The price is $42.50 per plate.

A mini-plate of Wayne is being planned.

Information concerning the plates can be obtained from:

Hackett American Collectors Company
5122 Bolsa Avenue
Unit 107
Huntington Beach, California 92649

219

Wayne appears on "The Dean Martin Roast of Dean Martin."

PART FIVE

JOHN WAYNE FILMS AND TELEVISION APPEARANCES AND OTHER MEDIA USES

How Many Films Did John Wayne Make?

1926
1. Brown of Harvard

1927
2. The Drop Kick

1928
3. Mother Machree
4. Hangman's House
   Wayne is uncredited
5. Four Sons

1929
6. Salute
   Wayne billed as Duke Morrison
7. Words and Music
   Wayne billed as Duke Morrison

1930
8. Men Without Women
   Wayne billed as Duke Morrison
9. Rough Romance
   Wayne billed as Duke Morrison
10. Born Reckless
11. Cheer Up and Smile
    Wayne billed as Duke Morrison
12. The Big Trail

1931
13. Girls Demand Excitement
14. Three Girls Lost
15. Men Are Like That
16. Range Feud
17. Maker of Men
18. The Deceiver

1932
19. Haunted Gold
20. Texas Cyclone
21. Lady and Gent
22. Two Fisted Law

23. Ride Him Cowboy
24. The Big Stampede
25. The Hollywood Handicap
26. The Voice of Hollywood
    Second Series #13

1933
27. The Telegraph Trail
28. His Private Secretary
29. Central Airport
30. Somewhere in Sonora
31. The Life of Jimmy Dolan
32. Baby Face
33. The Man from Monterey
34. Riders of Destiny
35. Sagebrush Trail
36. College Coach
37. The Lucky Texan

1934
38. West of the Divide
39. Blue Steel
40. The Man from Utah
41. Randy Rides Alone
42. The Star Packer
43. The Trail Beyond
44. 'Neath Arizona Skies
45. The Lawless Frontier

1935
46. Texas Terror
47. Rainbow Valley
48. Paradise Canyon
49. The Dawn Rider
50. The Desert Trail
51. Westward Ho
52. The New Frontier
53. The Lawless Range

1936
54. The Lawless Nineties

55. King of the Pecos
56. The Oregon Trail
57. Winds of the Wasteland
58. The Sea Spoilers
59. The Lonely Trail
60. Conflict

1937
61. California Straight Ahead
62. I Cover the War
63. Idol of the Crowds
64. Adventure's End
65. Born to the West

1938
66. Pals of the Saddle
67. Overland Stage Riders
68. Santa Fe Stampede
69. Red River Range

1939
70. Stagecoach
71. The Night Riders
72. Three Texas Steers
73. Wyoming Outlaw
74. New Frontier
75. Allegheny Uprising

1940
76. The Dark Command
77. Three Faces West
78. Melody Ranch
79. The Long Voyage Home
80. Seven Sinners

1941
81. A Man Betrayed
82. Lady from Louisiana
83. The Shepherd of
    the Hills
84. Lady for a Night

1942
85. Reap the Wild Wind
86. The Spoilers
87. In Old California
88. Flying Tigers
89. Reunion in France
90. Pittsburgh

1943
91. A Lady Takes a Chance

1944
92. In Old Oklahoma
93. The Fighting Seabees
94. Tall in the Saddle
95. Memo for Joe (National War Fund 8 minutes)

1945
96. Flame of the Barbary Coast
97. Back to Bataan
98. They Were Expendable
99. Dakota

1946
100. Without Reservations

1947
101. Angel and the Badman
102. Tycoon

1948
103. Red River
104. Fort Apache
105. Wake of the Red Witch
106. Three Godfathers

1949
107. Hollywood Rodeo (Western Film Star Review)
108. She Wore a Yellow Ribbon
109. The Fighting Kentuckian

1950
110. Sands of Iwo Jima
111. Rio Grande

1951
112. Operation Pacific

113. Flying Leathernecks

1952
114. The Quiet Man

1953
115. Big Jim McLain
116. Trouble Along the Way
117. Island in the Sky

1954
118. Hondo
119. The High and the Mighty
120. Hollywood Cowboy Stars (Short Film of Cinema Western Heroes)

1955
121. The Sea Chase
122. Blood Alley
123. The Challenge of Ideas (U.S. Information Agency Film on Anti-Communism)

1956
124. The Conqueror
125. The Searchers

1957
126. The Wings of Eagles
127. Jet Pilot
128. Legend of the Lost
129. I Married a Woman

1958
130. The Barbarian and the Geisha

1959
131. Rio Bravo
132. The Horse Soldiers

1960
133. The Alamo
134. North to Alaska

1961
135. The Comancheros

1962
136. The Man Who Shot Liberty Valance
137. Hatari
138. The Longest Day
139. How the West Was Won

1963
140. Donovan's Reef
141. McLintock

1964
142. Circus World

1965
143. The Greatest Story Ever Told
144. In Harm's Way
145. The Sons of Katie Elder

1966
146. Cast a Giant Shadow
147. The Artist and the American West (Western Paintings)

1967
148. El Dorado
149. The War Wagon

1968
150. The Green Berets
151. Hellfighters

1969
152. True Grit
153. The Undefeated

1970
154. Chisum
155. U.S. Information Agency Film—Wayne narrated a 15 minute film on Spiro Agnew's Asian trip on July 6, 1970
156. Chesty: Tribute to a Legend—one-half hour documentary on Chester Fuller

1971
157. Rio Lobo
158. The Best of 1971—A
     Budweiser Industrial Film
     (27 Minutes)
159. No Substitute for Victory
160. Big Jake
161. Directed by John Ford
     September 14, 1971

1972
162. The Cowboys
163. Cancel My Reservation

1973
164. The Train Robbers
165. Cahill U.S. Marshal

1974
166. McQ

1975
167. Brannigan
168. Rooster Cogburn

1976
169. The Shootist

1978
170. A Hell of a Life—Howard
     Hawks documentary released
     on March 3rd

WAYNE'S TELEVISION APPEARANCES

 1. 1953 "Milton Berle Show"
 2. Sept. 10, 1955 "Gunsmoke" Prologue
 3. Sept. 27, 1955 "Milton Berle Show"
 4. Oct. 10, 1955 "I Love Lucy"
 5. Dec. 7, 1955 "Screen Director's Playhouse" ("Rookie of the Year")
 6. March 26, 1958 "Academy Awards"
 7. June 8, 1958 "Wide, Wide World" ("The Western")
 8. April 6, 1959 "Academy Awards"
 9. April 4, 1960 "Academy Awards"
10. Nov. 14, 1960 "The Spirit of the Alamo"
11. Nov. 23, 1960 "Wagon Train" ("Colter Craven Story," Wayne billed as Michael Morris)
12. April 17, 1961 "Academy Awards"
13. Oct. 4, 1962 "Alcoa Premiere" ("Flashing Spikes")
14. March 26, 1963 "Dick Powell Theatre" ("Host The Third Side")
15. Oct. 21, 1963 "Hollywood and the Stars" ("They Went Thataway")
16. Jan. 27, 1964 "Hollywood and the Stars" ("Hollywood Goes to War")
17. March 20, 1964 "Inside the Movie Kingdom"
18. April 6, 1964 "Hollywood and the Stars" ("The Oscars: Moments of Greatness")
19. July 6, 1964 "Hollywood and the Stars" ("They Went Thataway")
20. March 2, 1965 "Merv Griffin"
21. Sept. 23, 1965 "Dean Martin Show"
22. Feb. 21, 1966 "Golden Globe Awards'
23. March 1, 1966 "Red Skelton Show"
24. March 2, 1966 "Merv Griffin"
25. 1966 "Merv Griffin" (on the set of *The War Wagon*)
26. Oct. 27, 1966 "Dean Martin Show"
27. Nov. 21, 1966 "The Lucy Show"
28. May 15, 1967 "Dateline Hollywood"
29. May 16, 1967 "Dateline Hollywood"
30. May 17, 1967 "Dateline Hollywood"
31. May 18, 1967 "Dateline Hollywood"
32. May 19, 1967 "Dateline Hollywood"

33. June 20, 1967 "Red Skelton Show"
34. July 19, 1967 "Beverly Hillbillies"
35. March 1968 "Merv Griffin" (on the set of *The Green Berets*)
36. March 4, 1968 "Rowan and Martin's Laugh-In"
37. March 11, 1968 "Rowan and Martin's Laugh-In"
38. April 8, 1968 "Rowan and Martin's Laugh-In"
39. April 15, 1968 "Rowan and Martin's Laugh-In"
40. April 22, 1968 "Rowan and Martin's Laugh-In"
41. April 29, 1968 "Rowan and Martin's Laugh-In"
42. July 2, 1968 "Joey Bishop Show" (Wayne promoted *The Green Berets*)
43. Sept. 5, 1968 "College Talent"
44. Sept. 16, 1968 "Rowan and Martin's Laugh-In"
45. Sept. 23, 1968 "Rowan and Martin's Laugh-In"
46. Oct. 27 1968 "Rowan and Martin's Laugh-In"
47. Nov. 27, 1968 "Bob Hope Special"
48. Feb. 19, 1969 "Glen Campbell"
49. June 1, 1969 "D-Day Revisited"
50. Aug. 6, 1969 "Joey Bishop Show"
51. Oct. 1, 1969 "Glen Campbell"
52. Oct. 28, 1969 "Red Skelton Show"
53. April 7, 1970 "Academy Awards"
54. April 26, 1970 "Raquel"
55. Nov. 28, 1970 "Merv Griffin"
56. Nov. 29, 1970 "Swing Out, Sweet Land"
57. Dec. 9, 1970 "Shootout at Rio Lobo"
58. Feb. 8, 1971 "Johnny Carson"
59. Feb. 11, 1971 "Merv Griffin"
60. March 10, 1971 "Jack Benny Special"
61. March 16, 1971 "Grammy Awards"
62. April 8, 1971 "Swing Out, Sweet Land"
63. April 26, 1971 "Shootout at Rio Lobo"
64. Sept. 14, 1971 "Glen Campbell"
65. Nov. 1, 1971 "Rowan and Martin's Laugh-In"
66. Nov. 4, 1971 "Rowan and Martin's 100th Laugh-In"
67. Nov. 7, 1971 "Bob Hope Special"
68. Dec. 5, 1971 "The American West of John Ford"
69. Jan. 10, 1972 "Super Comedy Bowl"
70. Jan. 14, 1972 "Johnny Carson"
71. Jan. 28, 1972 "Young Reporters"
72. Jan. 31, 1972 "Rowan and Martin's Laugh-In"
73. March 13, 1972 "Rowan and Martin's Laugh-In"
74. June 7, 1972 "Johnny Carson"
75. Sept. 10, 1972 "Salute to Television's 25th Anniversary"
76. Sept. 11, 1972 "Rowan and Martin's Laugh-In"
77. Jan. 1, 1973 "Tournament of Roses Parade"
78. Feb. 12, 1973 "Rowan and Martin's Laugh-In"
79. March 23, 1973 "Merv Griffin"
80. April 2, 1973 "American Film Institute Salute to John Ford"

81. April 3, 1973 "Academy Awards"
82. Sept. 13, 1973 "Rowan and Martin Special"
83. Nov. 4, 1973 "Men Who Made the Movies"
84. Dec. 19, 1973 "Warner Brothers Movies—A 50-Year Salute"
85. Jan. 15, 1974 "Wayne at Harvard"
86. March 8, 1974 "Glen Campbell—The Musical West"
87. March 18, 1974 "American Film Institute Salute to James Cagney"
88. March 27, 1974 "Paramount Presents"
89. March 31, 1974 "The Movies"
90. April 1, 1974 "The Movies"
91. Sept. 9, 1974 "Maude"
92. Oct. 31, 1974 "Dean Martin Roast of Bob Hope"
93. Jan. 19, 1975 "Don Rickles Special"
94. Feb. 27, 1975 "Dean Martin Roast of Dean Martin"
95. March 12, 1975 "People's Choice Awards"
96. April 8, 1975 "Academy Awards"
97. April 17, 1975 "Bob Hope Special"
98. July 5, 1975 "Violent Men of the Movies"
99. Sept. 27, 1975 "Saturday Night Live with Howard Cosell"
100. Oct. 15, 1975 "Johnny Carson"
101. Oct. 24, 1975 "A Quarter Century of Bob Hope on Television"
102. Jan. 8, 1976 "Johnny Carson"
103. Feb. 19, 1976 "People's Choice Awards"
104. April 5, 1976 "Dick Cavett's Hollywood"
105. Aug. 20, 1976 "Mike Douglas Show"
106. Sept. 26, 1976 "Big Party"
107. Sept. 27, 1976 "Merv Griffin"
108. Sept. 28, 1976 "Merv Griffin"
109. Sept. 29, 1976 "Merv Griffin"
110. Oct. 29, 1976 "Hope's World of Comedy"
111. Oct. 31, 1976 "Life Goes to the Movies"
112. Nov. 26, 1976 "All-Star Tribute to John Wayne"
113. Nov. 28, 1976 "Lucy: The First 25 Years"
114. Dec. 9, 1976 "America Salutes Richard Rodgers"
115. Dec. 12, 1976 "Bob's Traditional Christmas Show"
116. Jan. 8, 1977 "Super Night at the Super Bowl"
117. Jan. 19, 1977 "Inaugural Eve Gala Performance"
118. Jan. 30, 1977 "American Sportsman"
119. Feb. 10, 1977 "People's Choice Awards"
120. April 21, 1977 "Sinatra and Friends"
121. June 21, 1977 "Photoplay Gold Medal Awards"
122. Nov. 27, 1977 "Oscar Presents the War Movies and John Wayne"
123. Dec. 1, 1977 "All-Star Tribute to Elizabeth Taylor"
124. Jan. 29, 1978 "Golden Globe Awards"
125. Feb. 5, 1978 "ABC Silver Anniversary Special"
126. Feb. 20, 1978 "People's Choice Awards"
127. March 15, 1978 "American Film Institute Achievement Award to Henry Fonda"
128. April 1, 1978 "CBS: On the Air"
129. May 29, 1978 "Happy Birthday, Bob"

130. June 3, 1978 "America Salutes Richard Rodgers" (rerun)
131. May 23, 1978 "Oscar's Best Actors"
132. June 18, 1978 *Photoplay* Awards"
133. Sept. 29, 1978 "General Electric All-Star Anniversary"
134. Nov. 28, 1978 *Photoplay* Gold Medal Awards"
135. Dec. 7, 1978 "All-Star Tribute to James Stewart"
136. Dec. 13, 1978 "Perry Como Special"
137. March 13, 1979 "Barbara Walters Special"
138. April 9, 1979 "Academy Awards"
139. July 31, 1979 "The Barbara Walters Summer Special"
140. Sept. 5, 1979 "John Wayne—An American Legend"
141. Feb. 9, 1980 "The Duke Lives On" (Home Box Office)
142. Feb. 26, 1980 "Highlights of the Dean Martin Roasts"
143. Nov. 17, 1980 "Merv Griffin" (one-hour special devoted to Wayne)
144. Feb. 5, 1981 "A Love Letter to Jack Benny"
145. March 7, 1981 "Great Mysteries of Hollywood: Did America Kill John Wayne"
146. Aug. 5, 1981 "The Wonderful World of Those Cuckoo, Crazy Animals" ("It's Showtime")
147. Aug. 18, 1981 "That's Hollywood—Best Actors" (clips from *The Big Trail, The Longest Day* and *True Grit*)
148. May 26, 1982 "Entertainment Tonight" (small section devoted to 3rd anniversary of Wayne's death—this date was his birthday)
149. Nov. 7, 1982 "Television's Greatest Commercials—II" ("Great Western Savings" commercial was shown)
150. Dec. 20, 1982 "Bob Hope Christmas Special" (a special Christmas memory of Wayne)
151. April 11, 1983 "Academy Awards" (film clip of 1953 ceremonies with Wayne was shown)
152. May 19, 1983 "I Love Television Test" ("Gunsmoke" introduction with Wayne was shown)
153. June 13, 1983 "Good Morning America" (Pat Stacy plugging her book about Wayne)
154. Sept. 1, 1983 "Screen Legend: James Stewart" (Wayne clips with Stewart shown)
155. Sept. 8, 1983 "Sneak Previews" *The Searchers* and *Star Wars*
156. Sept. 29, 1983 "Entertainment Tonight" (Wayne featured in western film clips)
157. Nov. 8, 1983 "Dean Martin in London" (clips were shown of Wayne on Martin's show)
158. Nov. 17, 1983 "World's Funniest Commercial Goofs!" (Wayne bloopers were shown)
159. Nov. 24, 1983 "Hollywood's Private Home Movies—II" (Patrick Wayne showed movies of *The Alamo*)
160. Jan. 16, 1984 "PM Magazine" (Wayne's yacht supposedly "haunted")
161. Feb. 22, 1984 "Woman to Woman" (two of Wayne's daughters discussed having a famous parent)
162. March 15, 1984 "People's Choice Awards" (Wayne was shown at awards show of 1976 accepting his award)
163. March 18, 1984 "10 Years of People Magazine" (Wayne featured in tribute section)
164. May 29, 1984 "A Golden Jubilee Celebration"
165. August 15, 1984 "World's Funniest Commercial Goofs"
166. September 10, 1984 "Barbara Walters Special Celebration"
167. September 28, 1984 "Bob Hope—No Thanks for These Memories"
168. November 27, 1984 "Heroes and Sidekicks"

Addenda:
169. December 7, 1954 "This Is Your Life—William Wellman"
170. March 27, 1966 "Ed Sullivan Show" (Kirk Douglas showed bloopers from *Cast a Giant Shadow*)

Notes:

On Oct. 3, 1955, "I Love Lucy" featured Lucille Ball stealing John Wayne's footprints. Wayne was not featured in this episode.

Wayne appeared on "Hollywood Squares" as a guest star for a week. I don't have an exact date of the year but this did appear in the mid 1960s.

Supposedly in March, 1956, Wayne appeared with Susan Hayward on "Climax!" I could not confirm this.

Wayne appeared in episodes of "That's Hollywood," including "Hollywood's War Heroes," "Stars Early in Their Careers" and "The Fondas."

In late 1985 Wayne appeared on a Bloopers special in a scene in which he attempted to film a shoe commercial.

HOW MANY TIMES DID WAYNE MEET A SCREEN DEATH?

The following film titles are the films that show Wayne meeting a screen death.

1. *Central Airport*
2. *Reap the Wild Wind*
3. *The Fighting Seabees*
4. *Wake of the Red Witch*
5. *Sands of Iwo Jima*
6. *The Alamo*
7. *The Cowboys*
8. *The Shootist*

Wayne does not have a screen death in *The Man Who Shot Liberty Valance*. His coffin is shown with a small glimpse of his boots. Therefore I do not count this as a screen death.

HOW MANY SERIALS DID JOHN WAYNE MAKE?

1. *Shadow of the Eagle* 1932 12 Chapters
2. *The Hurricane Express* 1932 12 Chapters
3. *The Three Musketeers* 1933 12 Chapters

DID WAYNE EVER APPEAR IN A STAGE PLAY?

1. *Red Sky at Evening*, 1936.
2. *What Price Glory*, 1949; John Ford directed this and Wayne had a cameo role in the production.

JOHN WAYNE ON RADIO

1. NBC Radio, 1940, "Three Sheets to the Wind" 26 episodes.
2. CBS Radio, April 12, 1943: Lady Esther Presents "The Screen Guild Players." *Pittsburgh*, with Marlene Dietrich and Randolph Scott. (On the air, Wayne blows some of his lines and Dietrich berates him.)
3. NBC Radio, January 9, 1949: "NBC Theatre." *Stagecoach*, with Ward Bond and Claire Trevor. (Show introduced by John Ford.)
4. CBS Radio, March 12, 1951: "Lux Radio Theatre." *She Wore a Yellow Ribbon*, with Mala Powers and Mel Ferrer.
5. NBC Radio, August 5, 1949: "Screen Director's Playhouse." *Fort Apache*, with Ward Bond.
6. *What Price Glory*, circa 1950.
7. CBS Radio, March 7,1949: "Lux Radio Theatre." *Red River*, with Joanne Dru and Walter Brennan.

JOHN WAYNE AND THE CANCER CRUSADE

Wayne was cancer spokesperson in 1971 and 1977.

1. John Wayne Cancer Crusade 1971:
   60-second spot.
   30-second spot.
   The theme of the promotion was Wayne and his screen fights. This tied in with his fight with cancer. Film clips from *North to Alaska*, *The Sons of Katie Elder*, *True Grit* and *Chisum* were shown, among others.

2. John Wayne Cancer Crusade 1977:
   60-second spot.
   30-second spot.
   10-second spot.
   10-second spot.
   The theme of the 60- and 30-second spot was tying in Wayne's character from *The Shootist* receiving the news he has cancer. Wayne was pushing the check-up angle.

PART SIX

WAYNE AND THE WRITTEN WORD

HARDCOVER BOOKS ON WAYNE

The Complete Films of John Wayne, Mark Ricci, Boris and Steve Zmijewsky. Citadel Press, Secaucus, New Jersey, 1983. (Also softcover)

Duke: The Life and Times of John Wayne, Donald Shepherd, David Grayson. Doubleday, New York, 1985.

Duke: A Love Story. Pat Stacy with Beverly Linet. Atheneum, New York, 1983.

Duke: The Story of John Wayne, Mike Tomkies, Henry Regnery Company, Chicago, 1971.

John Wayne (Memorial Edition), Allen Eyles, A.S. Barnes and Company, Cranbury, New Jersey, 1979.

John Wayne: A Bibliography, Judith M. Riggin, Greenwood Press, Westport, Connecticut, 1992.

John Wayne: Actor, Artist, Hero, Richard McGhee. McFarland and Company, Jefferson, N.C., 1990.

John Wayne and the Movies, Allen Eyles, A.S. Barnes and Company, Cranbury, New Jersey, 1976. (Also softcover)

John Wayne in the Camera Eye, Sam Shaw, Exeter Books, New York, 1979.

John Wayne My Father, Aissa Wayne and Steve Delsohn. Random House, New York, 1991.

John Wayne: My Life With the Duke, Pilar Wayne and Alexandra Thorleifson. McGraw Hill, New York, 1987.

John Wayne's America, Why I Love Her, with Billy Liebert and John Mitchum. Simon and Schuster, New York, 1977.

The John Wayne Story, George Carpozi, Jr. Arlington House, New York, 1979.

John Wayne: The Actor, The Man, George Bishop. Caroline House Publishers, New York, 1979.

The Life and Times of John Wayne, David Hanna. Lorelei Publishing Company, New York, 1979.

On Board With the Duke, Bert Minshall with Clark Sharon. Seven Locks Press, Arlington, Virginia, 1992.

Shooting Star, Maurice Zolotow. Simon and Schuster, New York, 1974.

Starring John Wayne, Gene Fernett. Brevard Printing Company, Florida, 1969.

SOFTCOVER BOOKS ON WAYNE

Campfire Conversations: Big Trail Interviews with Some of John Wayne's Coworkers, Tim Lilley; softcover, 1992.

Duke: The John Wayne Album, John Boswell and Jay David. Ballantine Books, New York, 1979.

John Wayne, Alan G. Barbour. Pyramid Publications, New York, 1974.

John Wayne. Cinema Books by Post, Washington, 1975.

John Wayne: All-American Hero, Mario DeMarco. New York, 1988.

John Wayne: A Tribute. Norm Goldstein. The Associated Press, New York, 1979.

John Wayne Paper Dolls, Tom Tierney. Dover Publications, Inc., New York, 1981.

The John Wayne Scrapbook, Lee Pfeiffer. Citadel Press, Secaucus, New Jersey, 1989.

John Wayne: The All-American Legend. Dell Purse Books, New York, 1979.

PAPERBACK BOOKS ON WAYNE

Duke: Starring John Wayne, Gene Fernett. Neptune Books, Florida, 1976.

Duke: The Real Story of John Wayne, Jean Ramer, Grosset and Dunlap, New York.

Duke: The Story of John Wayne, Mike Tomkies. Avon Books, New York, 1972.

The John Wayne Story, George Carpozi, Jr. Dell Publishing, New York, 1979.

John Wayne's America Why I Love Her, with Billy Liebert and John Mitchum. Ballantine Books, New York, 1979.

Shooting Star, Maurice Zolotow. Pocket Books, New York, 1979.

AUDIO BOOK

John Wayne: The Duke in His Own Words, Len Brideau. Raymond Enterprises, two cassettes, 1992.

NEWSPAPER SPECIAL PUBLICATIONS ON WAYNE

Modern People Collector's Edition, 1978, Modern People Productions, Inc., Illinois, "John Wayne Last Of The Legends"

Modern People, July, 1979, Vol. 13, No. 26, Modern People Productions, Inc., Illinois, "John Wayne Last of the Legends"

Special Sellers Extra, 1979, Vol. 1, No. 1, N.P.D. Publishing Company, Illinois, "John Wayne America's No. 1 Hero Is Gone But Not Forgotten"

MAGAZINES ON WAYNE

John Wayne, edited by Ron Haydock, published by E-Go Enterprises, Inc., California, 1976.

John Wayne, text by David Hanna, published by Lorelei Publishing Company, New York, 1979.

John Wayne: An American Legend, edited by Robert Schwarzkopf, Ideal Publishing Corporation, New York, 1978.

John Wayne: An American Legend, edited by Nicholas Gaansvoort, Calny Communications, Inc., California, 1979.

John Wayne and the Great Cowboy Heroes, Norman Jacobs and Kerry O'Quinn, A Starlog Press Publication, New York, 1979.

John Wayne: Duke's Own Story, edited by Bessie Little, Reliance Publications, Inc., New York, 1979.

John Wayne Is Dead, published by Les Editions de l'ore'e Inc., Canada, 1979.

Rona Remembers John Wayne, editor-in-chief Bill Royce, published by Laufer Publishing Company, California, 1979.

A Tribute to John Wayne, edited by Rana Arons, A Platinum Publications, Inc., New York, 1979.

A Tribute to John Wayne: The Duke, edited by Peter R.A. Fryd, published by Bunch Books, England, 1979.

Wayne adds an eyepatch to his persona in *True Grit*.